EFFECTIVE
MATERIALS MANAGEMENT

Herbert H. Peckham

Manager of Industrial Engineering
Specialty Chemicals Division
Allied Chemical Corporation

EFFECTIVE
MATERIALS
MANAGEMENT

Prentice-Hall, Inc.
Englewood Cliffs, N. J.

Prentice–Hall International, Inc., *London*
Prentice–Hall of Australia, Pty. Ltd., *Sydney*
Prentice–Hall of Canada, Ltd., *Toronto*
Prentice–Hall of India Private Ltd., *New Delhi*
Prentice–Hall of Japan, Inc., *Tokyo*

Library of Congress
Catalog Card Number: 74-160540

Printed in the United States of America
ISBN 0-13-244293-0
B & P

This book is dedicated to the many persons who have contributed to my education over the years, but especially to Dorothy.

ABOUT THE AUTHOR

Herbert H. Peckham is the Manager of Industrial Engineering of the Specialty Chemicals Division of the Allied Chemical Corporation in Morristown, New Jersey. He received Bachelor of Chemistry and Chemical Engineer degrees from Cornell University at Ithaca, New York.

His business experience started with Allied Chemical as a production apprentice in 1934. He held various positions in manufacturing up to the level of superintendent before switching to industrial engineering in 1951. Mr. Peckham has held his present position since 1965.

The author's work has been involved with the development and implementation of maintenance management systems; training and development programs; sales forecasting, inventory management, and control systems; warehouse operations; and computerized materials management. He is an active member of the American Production and Inventory Control Society and the American Institute of Industrial Engineers.

How This Book Will Help You Direct a Profitable Materials Management System

A number of years ago I was given an assignment to "do something about the inventories" for a set of products consisting of over 7,000 stockkeeping units. The line was produced at a single location and shipped from that factory directly, or alternately through a number of field warehouses, to customers. This appeared to be an interesting problem capable of fairly rapid solution, but, in fact, it was like an iceberg; the visible portion was only a fraction of the whole.

I soon learned manufacturing wanted long runs to minimize changeovers and high stocks to minimize customer delays. Sales wanted orders to be shipped the day they were received. Customers wanted us to carry their inventory. Management wanted a low inventory investment. Purchasing wanted plenty of lead time in which to shop around for best buys. Traffic looked for the cheapest cost of transportation. Each area looked out for its own interest. Best for any area was often not very attractive to the overall business.

The problem thus became better defined as doing something about inventory, production planning, customer service, purchasing, traffic, warehousing, paperwork, and other integrated elements. I had to learn how these activities interfaced and interacted with one another; plus, I had to discover how to achieve trade-offs between these several areas of activity to reach the lowest overall cost of doing business. In time, I learned I was really putting together a materials management system.

Materials management is seen as a system for assuring the availability of products desired by customers at the best obtainable cost of manufacture and distribution. True enough, quality and cost of production are manufacturing responsibilities, but materials management must see to timely delivery of raw materials of proper quality and quantity at the factory. Pricing is a sales function, but materials management must be in a position to advise sales of laid-down costs at various destinations. Starting with customer demand, a flow of materials is initiated. Raw materials move from vendor to plant warehouses and thence to the manufacturing process. From the manufacturing process, finished goods move to plant warehouse, field warehouses, or to customers directly. The management of this whole flow of materials is, more often than not, called materials management.

In researching the field, I found many bits and pieces of information published in various business magazines and trade papers. There are a few texts on materials management and physical distribution. Some of these are more strongly oriented to a departmental point of view than to materials management or physical distribution. A rare few offered the materials management concept. I found no single source which covered all of the factors involved in materials management in a major industry, such as the chemical business. This book was written with this need in mind.

To be useful to the reader, a book such as this one must offer ideas on the means to resolve problems. In this book, I have discussed the factors involved in an effective materials management system and various means for arriving at solutions to problems. Chapter 1 covers EFFECTIVE SALES FORECASTING, starting with some rather simple methods which may be useful and progressing to quite sophisticated approaches which are useful in forecasting demands for thousands of items. In Chapter 2, I discuss MANAGING INVENTORY. There are sound manual systems, but when the inventory increases to thousands of items, a computerized system is required for the management and control of factory and warehouse stocks, using a logical, mathematical approach. Such methods are described.

The MATERIALS MANAGEMENT DEPARTMENT is covered in Chapter 3. A department holding down these responsibilities is relatively new in the business world. Many companies have not yet moved to consolidate the functions under unitary control, perhaps because they are only marginally aware of the extent of expenditures in this area. A method of establishing these costs is given as is an approach to drawing them to the attention of top management levels. The structuring of such a new department is discussed in the event a decision is made to proceed.

WAREHOUSE LOCATION AND DESIGN is the subject of the fourth chapter. A logical approach to locating a warehouse is offered, not only in the sense of a geographical site but also in terms of labor availability, transportation services, site factors, and other interdependent conditions. Means of determining space requirements are given, as well as the ways in which good space utilization may be achieved and adequate peripherals supplied. Inflatable buildings and automatic warehousing are covered also.

Chapter 5 is on WAREHOUSE OPERATION MANAGEMENT, starting with a cost control system and labor measurement methods. Specific means of measuring labor performance are given. A method for establishing the correct number of fork trucks needed is presented, as well as the procedure to follow to select the best buy. Since today we sometimes lease rather than buy, leasing practices and problems are covered. To help find stored materials, a stock-locater system is described. Other tools and equipment are described.

Chapter 6 looks at DISTRIBUTION COST ANALYSIS and shows the need to look at all interrelated costs in arriving at sound decisions in making changes. The cost factors in warehouse operations are evaluated.

Chapter 7 covers QUANTITATIVE METHODS most likely to be useful to those engaged in materials management. Starting with problem-solving techniques, this chapter also covers data handling, the normal and Poisson distributions, sampling techniques, models and simulations, systems analysis, linear programming, waiting-line problems, and Monte Carlo methods. This coverage is not comprehensive, but it does cover the principal tools needed.

Chapters 8 and 9 cover the advantages, disadvantages, and problems of PRIVATE MOTOR CARRIAGE and of RAIL AND OTHER MODES OF TRANSPORTATION. Insights are offered concerning these operations. Chapter 10 explores the INTERFACES AND INTERACTIONS BETWEEN MATERIALS MANAGEMENT AND PURCHASING, TRAFFIC, AND SYSTEMS AND DATA PROCESSING. Materials management will have continuing contact with these related functions.

Chapter 11 pulls all of the foregoing together in A COMPUTERIZED SYSTEM. In this chapter, the construction of a computerized system is described. The system is a composite of several such systems, and it contains the best features of each. The problems involved and the time requirement for implementation are emphasized.

The book is seen as providing the newcomer to the field with a comprehension of the ramifications and difficulties in the materials management field. For the experienced practitioner, the presentation offers a different point of view than so far seen in the literature and as such may stir a re-examination of his views. If the book does these two things, I will be satisfied that its writing was worth the time and effort.

H. H. PECKHAM

ACKNOWLEDGMENTS

My thanks are extended to Miss Irma Goerler, who accurately transcribed my longhand into a first-draft typescript, and to my wife, Dorothy, who worked long on the editing and did much of the typing of the final copy. It was also Dorothy who gave continued encouragement and exhibited patient tolerance with my many hours of involvement in putting this book together. For this she deserves, and has, my special gratitude.

LISTING OF TABLES

13

LISTING OF FIGURES

TABLE OF CONTENTS

Chapter 1

An old maxim advises we can judge the future by the past. Thus, in making short-range sales forecasts, we lean heavily upon our past sales experience, but historic forecasts should be modified on the basis of customer requirement information developed by sales, such as new or added business, lost business, and marketing promotion plans.

In making long-range forecasts, we also depend upon the historic sales record. We consider trends in the direction of sales. We question the sales department on their judgments concerning the direction in which the market is moving. Sometimes we are

EFFECTIVE SALES FORECASTING

able to develop leading indicators from government or trade association data and thus have some insight on possible changes in the overall level of our business. All of these factors are combined in making forecasts for 12 or more months ahead.

Month-to-Month Forecasts

The simplest forecast is one which assumes the business is steady, so we forecast the same sales for the next period as for the current period. This method is simplistic and has the disadvantage of not allowing time for any necessary forward planning. The new forecast cannot be made until the current period is completed, or at best with the last few days of the period extrapolated. Where sales change substantially, the month-to-month forecast is not helpful, but if changes are not too drastic, raw material and finished product inventory can buffer the changes that do occur. This forecast method is sometimes used as a simple planning tool in continuous and semicontinuous process industry.

Several other methods of forecasting will be discussed. To illustrate the effectiveness of any method, data in Table 1-1 will be used as the basis for the various methods demonstrated. Data for the first three years will be used to forecast the fourth-year

TABLE 1-1
Monthly Sales Data

Month	1st Year	2nd Year	3rd Year	4th Year
January	2,825	2,700	2,775	2,700
February	2,500	2,600	2,500	2,400
March	2,775	2,900	2,800	2,750
April	2,750	2,950	2,750	2,800
May	2,725	2,800	2,775	2,650
June	2,650	2,775	2,600	2,775
July	2,700	2,825	2,650	2,775
August	2,750	2,600	2,700	2,700
September	2,550	2,725	2,450	2,600
October	2,700	2,650	2,600	2,700
November	2,700	2,800	2,650	2,800
December	2,450	2,700	2,650	2,500

demand. Maximum deviation of the demand from that forecasted will be shown in the earlier examples. As an overall measure of the forecast error for the fourth year, the monthly deviations will be added without regard to sign and then divided by 12 to find the average annual absolute forecast error. This is called the "Mean Absolute Deviation" or MAD.

TABLE 1-2
Month-to-Month Forecast,
Fourth Year

Month	Forecast	Actual	Difference	Cumulative Difference
January	2,650	2,700	+50	+50
February	2,700	2,400	−300	−250
March	2,400	2,750	+350	+100
April	2,750	2,800	+50	+150
May	2,800	2,650	−150	0
June	2,650	2,775	+125	+125
July	2,775	2,775	0	+125
August	2,775	2,700	−75	+50
September	2,700	2,600	−100	−50
October	2,600	2,700	+100	+50
November	2,700	2,800	+100	+150
December	2,800	2,500	−300	−150
Totals		32,150	1,700	

Average monthly sales = 2,679
MAD = 141.6

Table 1-2 illustrates the use of the data in Table 1-1 for a month-to-month forecast. Using third-year December sales of 2,650 units as the forecast for January of the fourth year, we see that actual sales were 2,700 units, with a positive error of 50 units. The January actual then becomes the February forecast, and so on throughout the year. During the fourth year, maximum positive forecast error was 350 units, maximum negative was 300. MAD was 141.6 and the cumulative difference was 150 units.

Moving-Average Forecast

It can be seen that a month-to-month forecast will be subject to much fluctuation and a high level of nervous response, but perhaps if we use the average for two months to forecast the third month we will obtain a smaller margin of error. In Table 1-3 we have used a two-month moving average to forecast the third month. The January forecast is the average of November and December of the previous year. The February forecast is the average of December and January, and so on through the year.

TABLE 1-3
Two-Month Moving Average

Month	Forecast	Actual	Difference	Cumulative Difference
January	2,650	2,700	+50	+50
February	2,675	2,400	−225	−175
March	2,550	2,750	+200	+25
April	2,575	2,800	+225	+250
May	2,775	2,650	−125	+125
June	2,725	2,775	+50	+175
July	2,712	2,775	+63	+238
August	2,775	2,700	−75	+163
September	2,737	2,600	−137	+26
October	2,650	2,700	+50	−76
November	2,650	2,800	+150	+226
December	2,750	2,500	−250	−24

Maximum positive variation = 225
Maximum negative variation = 250
MAD   = 133

Table 1-4 shows results of calculations for moving averages of 2,3,4,5,6,8,10,12,24, and 36 months. It will be recalled that the month-to-month forecast showed a MAD of 141.6. This drops to 133 with a two-month average, to 107 with a three-month average, then holds relatively steady through a 12-month average, finally dropping to 94 at 24 months and 91 at 36 months. This is typical with products which have fairly stable sales patterns. To summarize, with essentially stable sales, the longer the history

TABLE 1-4
Summary of Moving Average
Calculations

Number of Months in Forecast	Maximum Positive Deviation	Maximum Negative Deviation	MAD	Cumulative Forecast Error
2	225	250	133	−24
3	183	267	107	−283
4	175	250	113	+49
5	170	215	112	+90
6	175	225	114	+137
8	187	225	109	+224
10	185	253	111	−270
12	160	252	105	+236
24	109	305	94	−73
36	113	291	91	−36

included in a moving-average forecast, the smaller the forecast error will be. For extended long-period moving averages, it is safe to update the average only once or twice a year.

Weighted-Average Forecast

Forecasters sometimes argue that the most recent data is more significant than data two, three, four, or more months old. Recognition is given to the worth of historical data, but this is discounted by giving it a smaller weight in the forecast. In the month-to-month forecast, the current month is weighted 100% and all older data is weighted 0. In the next case, using a two-month weighted average, we have prepared a forecast where the current month is given double weight and the previous month single weight to arrive at the new forecast. The January forecast in Table 1-5 is (2 x December sales + 1 x November sales) divided by 3 = (2 x 2,650 + 1 x 2,650)/3 = 2,650. The February forecast is (2 x 2,700 + 1 x 2,650)/3 = 2,683, and so on for the other months.

TABLE 1-5
Two-Month Weighted Average

Current month weighted 2, previous month 1

Month	Forecast	Actual	Difference	Cumulative Difference
January	2,650	2,700	+50	+50
February	2,683	2,400	−283	−233
March	2,500	2,750	+250	+17
April	2,633	2,800	+167	+184
May	2,744	2,650	−94	+90
June	2,700	2,775	+75	+165
July	2,733	2,775	+42	+207
August	2,775	2,700	−75	+132
September	2,725	2,600	−125	+7
October	2,633	2,700	+67	+74
November	2,667	2,800	+133	+207
December	2,767	2,500	−267	−60

MAD = 136

Using three months of history-weighted 3-2-1 and four months weighted 4-3-2-1, we find that the forecast responds more rapidly to changes in sales activity. This is of no great advantage with demand as stable as in Table 1-1, as shown by the comparative MAD's:

Months	MAD Moving Average	MAD Weighted Average
2	133	136
3	107	123
4	113	109

The method does have some advantage where the demand is erratic or in trying to follow trend or seasonality in a simple way.

Time-Weighted-Average Forecast

Examination of the data in Table 1-1 shows a pattern of low sales in February (short month) and in December (year-end inventory reduction by customers). Together with the variation in calendar months (30 and 31 days), there are also from eight to 12 regular holidays which serve to reduce the number of business days in some months. If we take monthly data for several years, say years 1-2-3 in our case, and calculate the average January sales, the average February sales, and so on through the year, and then add all of these averages together, we can determine the percentage of the average yearly sales contributed by each month. A forecast is made for the next year's total sales, which is then broken down into increments by multiplying the total by each month's percentage contribution.

TABLE 1-6
Time-Weighted-Average Forecast

Fourth-year total forecast = 32,000 units.

	1st Year Sales	2nd Year Sales	3rd Year Sales	Average	% of Avg. Year	4th Year F'cst	Actual	Diff.	Cum. Diff.
Jan.	2,825	2,700	2,775	2,767	8.55	2,736	2,700	−36	−36
Feb.	2,500	2,600	2,500	2,533	7.83	2,506	2,400	−106	−142
Mar.	2,775	2,900	2,800	2,825	8.73	2,794	2,750	−44	−186
Apr.	2,750	2,950	2,750	2,817	8.71	2,787	2,800	+13	−173
May	2,725	2,800	2,775	2,767	8.55	2,736	2,650	−86	−259
Jun.	2,650	2,775	2,600	2,675	8.27	2,646	2,775	+129	−130
Jul.	2,700	2,825	2,650	2,725	8.42	2,694	2,775	+81	−49
Aug.	2,750	2,600	2,700	2,683	8.29	2,653	2,700	+47	−2
Sept.	2,550	2,725	2,450	2,575	7.96	2,547	2,600	+53	+51
Oct.	2,700	2,650	2,600	2,650	8.19	2,621	2,700	+79	+130
Nov.	2,700	2,800	2,650	2,717	8.40	2,688	2,800	+112	+242
Dec.	2,450	2,700	2,650	2,600	8.04	2,572	2,500	−72	+170

MAD = 71.5

This is illustrated in Table 1-6 where the usual calculations have been made on deviations. We see that MAD has dropped to 71.5 units. The maximum positive deviation is down to 129, and though not the lowest, we have seen it is one of the lower ones. The maximum negative deviation is only 106, by far the lowest we have yet seen.

Exponential Smoothing

Use of any of the foregoing techniques is relatively easy in a manual system, although somewhat tedious. However, in this day of electronic data processing, the methods are cumbersome and heavy users of expensive computer time. A mathematical technique known as "exponential smoothing" has been developed that overcomes these difficulties. The method can be expressed:

$$\text{New forecast} = \text{old forecast} + \alpha\,(\text{new demand} - \text{old forecast})$$
$$= \text{old forecast} + \alpha \text{ new demand } \alpha \text{ old forecast}$$
$$= (1 - \alpha)\,\text{old forecast} + \alpha \text{ new demand},$$

where the Greek letter alpha (α) is used to indicate a smoothing constant with value between 0 and 1. To illustrate, the old forecast is 100, current demand is 120, and the smoothing constant to be used is $\alpha = 0.2$. Then:

$$\text{New forecast} = (1 - 0.2)\,100 + 0.2\,(120)$$
$$= 80 + 24$$
$$= 104.$$

Thus, all we need to prepare a new forecast is the old forecast, current demand, and a selected value of α. We select α to give enough historical data to meet our needs, just as we do with a weighted average. It can be seen that as data gets older, it is progressively discounted in value. Suppose we run the data immediately above again, but substitute $\alpha = 0.5$. Then we have:

$$\text{New forecast} = (1 - 0.5)\,100 + .5\,(120)$$
$$= 50 + 60$$
$$= 110.$$

Now let's further examine what happens to these two numbers on subsequent forecast updates:

```
Next update shows
new forecast    = (1 - .5) 50 + (1 - .5) 60 + .5 (new data)
                =     25         30
These become        12.5        15        the next time around
and become          6.25        7.5       the next time around, etc.
```

In this way, the historical data is automatically discounted in value; yet, with the kind of data we have been using, the forecast levels will be maintained through the continuous infusion of new actual values.

TABLE 1-7
Alpha Values vs.
Equivalent Moving Average

Alpha	Equivalent Months
0.500	3
0.400	4
0.333	5
0.250	7
0.200	9
0.100	19
0.050	39
0.010	199

Exponential forecasts have been made for the fourth year, using alpha values to correspond to weightings up to 36 months. These are tabulated in Table 1-8. Comparing this with Table 1-4, we see that the error of the forecast, as measured by MAD, is

TABLE 1-8
Summary of Forecasts
by Exponential Smoothing

α Factor	Equiv. Months	MAD	Max. + Dev'n.	Max. - Dev'n.	Cumulative Forecast Error
0.500	3	120.6	205	290	−118
0.400	4	115.2	180	283	−90
0.333	5	110.9	157	290	−103
0.286	6	107.8	151	292	−108
0.222	8	104.3	149	293	−83
0.154	12	98.5	132	297	−134
0.080	24	84.8	117	202	−83
0.054	36	91.0	110	302	−210

generally within 5% of the moving-average MAD. As was noted above, the best forecasts are made when the forecast has a base of 24 to 36 months of data.

Forecasting Trend

So far, all of our forecasts have been made using essentially stable data, although random ups and downs appear throughout the year, plus some probably nonrandom activity in February and December of each year. What happens if we recast our data so we have a definite trend? Table 1-9 is Table 1-1 with 10 units added to February of the first year, 20 units to March, 30 units to April, 40 to May, etc., across the entire record.

Then calculations were repeated using this data and the moving average, time-weighted

TABLE 1-9
Monthly Sales Data Modified to
Show a Ten-Unit-per-Month
Increasing Trend

	1st Year	2nd Year	3rd Year	4th Year
January	2,825	2,820	3,015	3,060
February	2,510	2,730	2,750	2,770
March	2,795	3,040	3,060	3,130
April	2,780	3,100	3,020	3,190
May	2,765	2,960	3,055	3,050
June	2,700	2,945	2,890	3,185
July	2,760	3,005	2,950	3,195
August	2,820	2,790	3,010	3,130
September	2,630	2,925	2,770	3,040
October	2,790	2,860	2,930	3,150
November	2,800	3,020	2,990	3,260
December	2,560	2,930	3,000	2,970

average, and exponential smoothing methods already described. Remember, we have used the same method of calculation described above and have ignored the trend we know was built into the new data. The results are tabulated in Table 1-10. Notice

TABLE 1-10
Summary of Trend Forecasts by
Various Methods

α	Months in Forecast	Max. + Deviation	Max. − Deviation	Cumulative Forecast Error	MAD	Weighting
Moving Average						
—	1	360	290	−50	145	—
—	2	240	260	+105	140	—
—	3	203	247	+283	109	—
—	4	200	225	+350	117	—
—	5	200	185	+450	115	—
—	6	210	190	+559	128	—
—	9	233	192	+853	139	—
—	12	225	187	+1053	140	—
—	24	248	180	+1428	158	—
—	36	297	106	+2081	192	—

TABLE 1-10 (Cont'd)
Summary of Trend Forecasts by
Various Methods

α	Months in Forecast	Max. + Deviation	Max. – Deviation	Cumulative Forecast Error	MAD	Weighting
Weighted Moving Average						
—	1	360	290	–50	145	1-0
—	2	263	270	+66	142	2-1
—	3	225	258	+158	124	3-2-1
—	4	205	245	+224	121	4-3-2-1
Time-Weighted Average						
—	36	333	0	+2732	228	—
Exponential Smoothing						
0.500	3	237	247	+211	122	—
0.400	4	235	208	+427	127	—
0.333	5	220	210	+480	122	—
0.286	6	214	204	+571	125	—
0.200	9	215	208	+700	128	—
0.154	12	221	199	+864	134	—
0.080	24	239	180	+1284	150	—
0.054	36	303	109	+2083	194	—

that cumulative forecast error gets larger and larger in all methods as we increase the amount of historical data used in the forecast. MAD's are similarly affected.

Graphic Methods

Examination of the data in Table 1-9 does reveal a trend to casual inspection. A plot of the data in Tables 1-1 and 1-9 shown in Figure 1-1 gives a better picture, the trend shows up clearly. How much of a trend is there? The simplest way to find out is graphical. The data for the series of months is plotted as in Figure 1-2. Then, a straightedge is laid over the data so that half of the points are visible and half are beneath the straightedge, and a line is drawn at the balance point. The equation for this straight line is $Y = a + bX$ where Y is the value on the vertical axis, a is the point where the line intercepts the left-hand vertical margin, b is the slope of the straight line, and X is the number of periods on the bottom margin. From Figure 1-2, in the upper plot, the intercept is about 2,720, and the slope b is $320/36 = +8.8^*$, a positive number indicating an upward trend. To prepare a forecast for the fourth year, we extend the trend line

---

*Slope is not 10 because the data in Table 1 actually has a slight downward trend, as shown in lower plot in Figure 2.

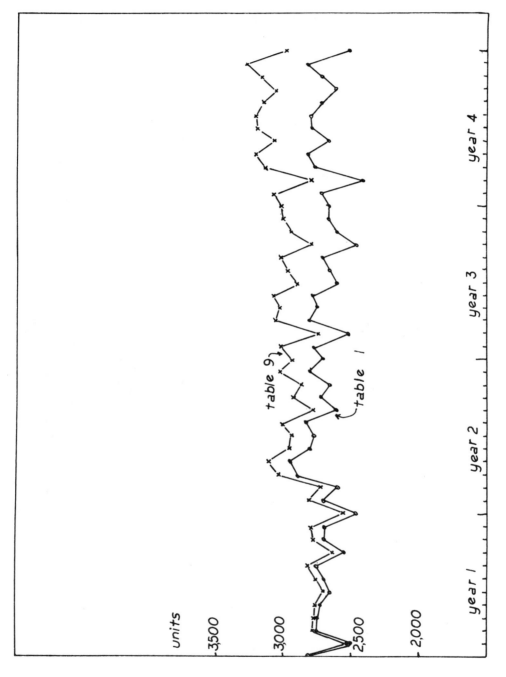

Figure 1-1. Month-to-month plot of data in Tables 1-1 and 1-9.

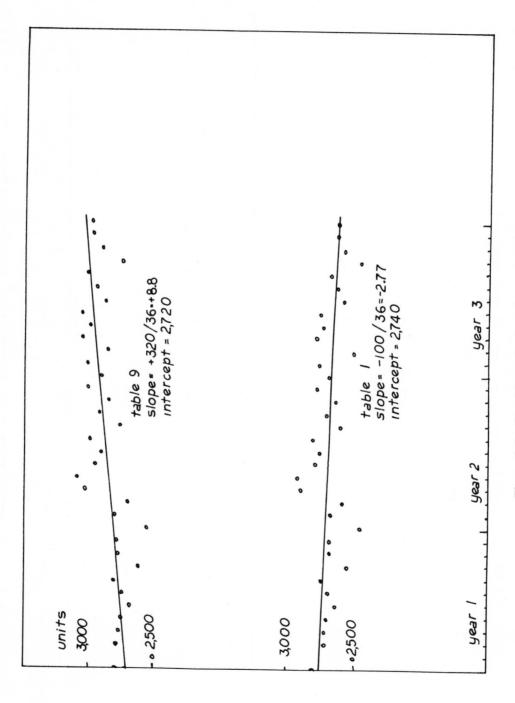

Figure 1-2. *Graphic method to determine slope.*

for 12 months, in effect taking the last reading on the trend line in Figure 1-2 (3,040) and adding 8.8 units per month for the January forecast = 3,049, adding another 8.8 units for February = 3,058, etc. Running through the usual calculations, we find maximum positive and negative deviations of 122 and 288. Cumulative error is -44 and MAD is 92.8. This compares favorably with the moving-average forecasts for 24 and 36 months, as shown in Table 1-4.

Use of Regression Analysis

The use of a graphical method is fine if we have only a few sets of data to chart and we are running a manual system. Where we have hundreds of items to chart, we will soon run out of patience with the method. A mathematical method for calculating trend is the "least-squares" or regression technique. With a least-squares solution, the sum of the positive and negative vertical distances of actual values from the trend line is equal to zero, and the sum of the squares of these distances is a minimum; i.e., smaller than about any other line.

The use of the method is illustrated in Table 1-11. The column headed Y is the tabulation of monthly sales for the years 1-2-3 as listed in Table 1-9. The column headed X is a measure of time in half-months. In column X, June 30 or July 1 in year 1 is considered to be the origin of the trend line. The sales for each period are considered to be centered in the period; to avoid calculations in fractions, each period is taken as two half-periods.

TABLE 1-11
Least-Squares Analysis of Trend Sales Data,
Years 1-2-3

	Y	X	XY	X^2	Y_t
Year 1					
Jan.	2,825	-35	-98,875	1,225	2,723
Feb.	2,510	-33	-82,830	1,089	2,731
Mar.	2,795	-31	-86,645	961	2,739
Apr.	2,780	-29	-80,620	841	2,748
May	2,765	-27	-74,655	729	2,756
June	2,700	-25	-67,500	625	2,764
July	2,760	-23	-63,480	529	2,773
Aug.	2,820	-21	-59,220	441	2,781
Sept.	2,630	-19	-49,970	361	2,789
Oct.	2,790	-17	-47,430	289	2,798
Nov.	2,800	-15	-42,000	225	2,806
Dec.	2,560	-13	-33,280	169	2,815

TABLE 1-11 (Cont'd)
Least-Squares Analysis of Trend Sales Data,
Years 1-2-3

	Y	X	XY	X^2	Y_t
Year 2					
Jan.	2,820	−11	−31,020	121	2,823
Feb.	2,730	−9	−24,570	81	2,831
Mar.	3,040	−7	−21,280	49	2,840
Apr.	3,100	−5	−15,500	25	2,848
May	2,960	−3	−8,880	9	2,856
June	2,945	−1	−2,945	1	2,865
July	3,005	+1	+3,005	1	2,873
Aug.	2,790	3	8,370	9	2,882
Sept.	2,925	5	14,625	25	2,890
Oct.	2,860	7	20,020	49	2,898
Nov.	3,020	9	27,180	81	2,907
Dec.	2,930	11	32,230	121	2,915
Year 3					
Jan.	3,015	13	39,195	169	2,923
Feb.	2,750	15	41,250	225	2,932
Mar.	3,060	17	52,020	289	2,940
Apr.	3,020	19	57,380	361	2,949
May	3,055	21	64,155	441	2,957
June	2,890	23	66,470	529	2,965
July	2,950	25	73,750	625	2,974
Aug.	3,010	27	81,270	729	2,982
Sept.	2,770	29	80,330	841	2,990
Oct.	2,930	31	90,830	961	2,999
Nov.	2,990	33	98,670	1,089	3,007
Dec.	3,000	35	105,000	1,225	3,015
Total:	103,300	0	65,050	15,542	

Equation of trend line: $Y = a + bX$.

a = Sum of all Y/number of periods
 = 103,300/36
 = 2,869.

b = Sum of XY/Sum of X^2
 = 65,050/15,542
 = 4.185.

Y_t = 2,869 + 4.185 X

and where X = ½ month, slope = $2b$ = + 8.37

In Table 1-12 a forecast is made for the fourth year, using the constants derived in Table 1-11. We have maximum positive and negative deviations of 152 and 262,

TABLE 1-12
Fourth-Year Forecast Using
Least-Squares Trend Calculated
in Table 1-11

	X	Forecast	Actual	Difference
January	37	3,024	3,060	+36
February	39	3,032	2,770	−262
March	41	3,041	3,130	+89
April	43	3,049	3,190	+141
May	45	3,057	3,050	−7
June	47	3,066	3,185	+119
July	49	3,074	3,195	+121
August	51	3,082	3,130	+48
September	53	3,091	3,040	−51
October	55	3,099	3,150	+51
November	57	3,108	3,260	+152
December	58	3,116	2,970	−146

MAD = 102

cumulative error is + 291, and MAD is 102. The slope of the calculated curve is 8.37 vs. the graphic estimate of 8.8, or a difference of about 5%. For a manual method, this is time-consuming also, requiring about an hour to complete the given example. This could probably be reduced if many such calculations were to be made, but the method is a time consumer. A computer handles the method without difficulty so that trend could be tracked monthly if desired.

Second-Order Exponential Smoothing

There is a simpler method of tracking trend than least squares, known as second-order exponential smoothing. The exponential method described above is termed first-order smoothing. Later in this chapter, a "third-order" method for seasonal forecasts will be described. In first-order smoothing, we stated: New forecast = $(1 - \alpha)$ old forecast + α new demand. Subsequently, we introduced a new set of sales data with an upward trend and found that first-order smoothing did not give very good results. Other methods of forecasting with this data were equally bad. Moving-average forecasts behave poorly in the presence of trend, because the average is centered in the time interval for the historic data used; i.e., with a perfect slope, the average is at the center of the ramp. Where there is a definite trend, the simple moving averages lag far behind the true movement we are trying to forecast, with lag proportionately greater where many time periods are used for history. We can correct any of these forecasts by adding a correction for trend to the basic forecast. With a moving-average type forecast, we would add trend multiplied by half the number of time periods to the basic average forecast.

With exponential smoothing, we do the same thing in a different way. First we make a basic forecast, using the first-order formula:

New forecast = $(1 - \alpha)$ old forecast + α current demand,

To correct for trend we are going to use exponential smoothing of the trend to add to the basic forecast. Brown* has shown a trend exists where the arithmetic average will be less than actual by $(i - \alpha)/\alpha$ trend. A new trend estimate is calculated as the difference between the current basic forecast and the previous basic forecast. Current trend estimate is calculated:

Current trend estimate = $(1 - \alpha)$ previous trend estimate + α new trend estimate.

Then if we combine our basic average forecast and our current estimate of trend, we will have a forecast for the next period which is corrected for trend: New trend-adjusted forecast = $(1 - \alpha)$ old average forecast + α current demand + $(1 - \alpha)/\alpha$ [α (new basic forecast - previous basic forecast) + $(1 - \alpha)$ previous trend estimate]. This looks more complicated than it really is. Table 1-13 shows a set of calculations which illustrate this concept.

TABLE 1-13
Fourth-Year Forecast, First- and Second-Order Smoothing

Alpha = 0.1

A Period	B Actual Sales	C Basic Avg. F'cst	D New Trend Est.	E $\alpha \times D$	F $(1 - \alpha) \times$ Col. G	G Cols. E + F	H Corrected Trend Est. $G \times (1 - \alpha)/\alpha$	I Trend Adj'd F'cst	J F'cst Error	K Smoothed MAD
Start, 3rd Year Dec.		3,024**				+8.37**				100
4th Year										
Jan.	3,060	3,028	+4	+0.4	+7.5	+7.9	71	3,099	-329	123
Feb.	2,770	3,002	-26	-2.6	+7.1	+4.5	41	3,043	+87	120
Mar.	3,130	3,015	+13	+1.3	+4.1	+5.4	49	3,064	+126	121
Apr.	3,190	3,032	+17	+1.7	+4.9	+6.6	59	3,091	-41	113
May	3,050	3,034	+2	+0.2	+5.9	+6.1	55	3,089	+96	112
June	3,185	3,050	+16	+1.6	+5.5	+7.1	64	3,114	+59	107
July	3,195	3,065	+15	+1.5	+6.4	+7.9	71	3,136	-10	97
Aug.	3,130	3,071	+6	+0.6	+7.1	+7.7	69	3,140	-87	96
Sept.	3,040	3,068	-3	-0.3	+6.9	+6.6	59	3,127	+23	88
Oct.	3,150	3,076	+8	+0.8	+5.9	+6.7	60	3,136	+96	89
Nov.	3,260	3,094	+18	+1.8	+6.0	+7.8	70	3,164	-194	99
Dec.	2,970	3,082	-12	-1.2	+7.0	+5.8	52	3,134		

*See Bibliography; reference #3.

**Calculated from least squares, Table 1-11

In Table 1-13: Column *A* = calendar period.

B = actual sales.

C = basic average forecast made in the calendar period for the next calendar period; e.g., 3,024 is a forecast made in January for February.

D = New trend estimate = new basic average forecast - previous basic forecast; e.g., Jan. = 4 = 3,028 - 3,024 in column *C*.

E = α x new trend estimate.

F = (1 - α) x corrected trend estimate for previous month.

G = Corrected trend estimate = Column *E* + *F*.

H = Trend correction = (1 - α)/α x *G*.

I = Adjusted forecast for next month = Column *C* + *H*.

J = Forecast error = Feb. actual, 2,770 - Feb. forecast, 3,099 = -329.

K = Smoothed MAD's using α = 0.1.

Calculations for the fourth year were made in about ten minutes, using a desk calculator. The method is thus much quicker than least squares. Comparing the least-squares forecast with the exponential forecast, we see least-squares MAD is 102 and exponential MAD is 104. It cannot be said the difference in MAD between the two methods is significant.

TABLE 1-14
Fourth-Year Forecast Using Graphic Starting
Point and First- and Second-Order Smoothing

A Period	B Actual Sales	C Basic Avg. F'cst	D New Trend Est.	E α x Col.D	F (1 - α)x Col. G	G Cor-rected Trend Est.	H Trend Cor-rection G(1 - α)/α	I Trend Adj'd F'cst	J F'cst Error	K Smoothed MAD
Start		3,020*				+8.8*				100
4th Year										
Jan.	3,060	3,024	+4	+0.4	+7.9	+8.3	75	3,099	-329	123
Feb.	2,770	2,999	-25	-2.5	+7.5	+5.0	45	3,044	+86	120
Mar.	3,130	3,012	+13	+1.3	+4.5	+5.8	52	3,064	+126	121
Apr.	3,190	3,030	+18	+1.8	+5.2	+7.0	63	3,093	-41	113
May	3,050	3,032	+2	+0.2	+6.3	+6.5	59	3,091	+94	111
June	3,185	3,048	+16	+1.6	+5.9	+7.5	68	3,116	+79	108
July	3,195	3,063	+15	+1.5	+6.8	+8.3	75	3,138	-8	98
Aug.	3,130	3,070	+7	+0.7	+7.5	+8.2	74	3,144	-104	98
Sept.	3,040	3,067	-3	-0.3	+7.4	+7.1	64	3,131	+19	90
Oct.	3,150	3,075	+8	+0.8	+6.4	+7.2	65	3,140	+90	90
Nov.	3,260	3,094	+19	+1.9	+6.5	+8.4	76	3,170	-200	101
Dec.	2,970	3,082	-12	-1.2	+7.6	+6.4	58	3,140		

*From trend curve, Figure 1-1

As a matter of interest to the reader, an exponential forecast was made using the graphed starting points, and trend from Figure 1-2 and this data is shown in Table 1-14 with 11 months' MAD = 107. This is a slightly poorer forecast than using least-squares data for the starting point. This is further illustrated in Table 1-15 by taking the same starting point but using an arbitrary trend of 20. Note that forecast is consistently overstated, as shown by the monthly negative error of forecast in Column J. (The arbitrary trend of 20 might have been a sales projection which did not materialize.) Note also that trend estimate dropped from 20 to 9 in the course of 12 months. If α had been 0.2 or 0.3, the drop would have been much more rapid. This indicates the wisdom of increasing α value when sales projections are locked into an exponential forecast, thus increasing the rate of correction if the projection is wrong.

TABLE 1-15
First- and Second-Order Smoothing Where
Trend Is 20 Instead of 10

A Period	B Actual Sales	C Basic Avg. F'cst	D New Trend Est.	E $\alpha \times D$	F $(1 - \alpha)x$ Col. G	G Corrected Trend Estimate	H Trend Corr'n. $(1 - \alpha)/$ $\alpha \times G$	I Trend Adj'd F'cst	J F'cst Error	K Smoothed MAD
Starting Point		3,024				+20				109
4th Year										
Jan.	3,060	3,028	+4	+0.4	+18.0	+18.4	166	3,194	−192	109
Feb.	2,770	3,002	−26	−2.6	+16.6	+14.0	126	3,128	−113	109
Mar.	3,130	3,015	+13	+1.3	+12.6	+13.9	125	3,140	−108	109
Apr.	3,190	3,032	+17	+1.7	+12.5	+14.2	128	3,160	−117	110
May	3,050	3,034	+2	+0.2	+12.8	+13.0	117	3,151	−120	111
June	3,185	3,050	+16	+1.6	+11.7	+13.3	120	3,170	−121	112
July	3,195	3,065	+15	+1.5	+12.0	+13.5	121	3,186	−114	112
Aug.	3,130	3,071	+6	+0.6	+12.1	+12.7	114	3,185	−104	111
Sept.	3,040	3,068	−3	−0.3	+11.4	+11.1	100	3,168	−92	109
Oct.	3,150	3,076	+8	+0.8	+10.0	+10.8	97	3,173	−79	106
Nov.	3,260	3,094	+18	+1.8	+9.7	+11.8	103	3,197	−115	106
Dec.	2,970	3,082	−12	−1.2	+10.3	+9.1	82	3,164		

MAD = 116

Forecasting Seasonal Demands

So far we have not discussed making forecasts of demands which fluctuate seasonally. In the section on weighted forecasts, we gave a method based on an annual forecast that takes care of sales variations which are attributable to variation in the number of selling days or for other reasons. Over a period of years, the pattern of this variation will show up quite plainly, but it should not be considered as seasonal demand. By definition, a product is considered to have seasonal demand only when three conditions are met:

(1) The peak demand should be substantially higher than the random fluctuations or "noise" in the demand.

(2) The peak demand must occur during the same time period each year.

(3) The reason for the peak must be known.

Examples of seasonal products are heating oils, air conditioners, refrigerant gases, and automobile antifreeze. These items meet the three criteria for seasonal products.

Where true seasonality exists, it is important to use a method of forecasting which will anticipate the ups and downs of movement. It should be noted that truly seasonal items are exceptions, as most products have generally stable movement or modest trends up or down.

The seasonal forecasting technique uses a series of demand factors, one for each period of the year (week or month) plus the average, or deseasonalized, demand for the year. Demand for a specific period in the year is forecast by multiplying the deseasonalized demand by the demand factor specific to that period. The activity is a dynamic one, so the forecast should be updated each period.

To illustrate the calculations, the sales statistics in Table 1-1 have been given seasonality by adding 100 units to February sales for each year, 300 to March, 600 units to April, 200 units to May, and 50 units to June. It is very unlikely that such smooth, regular peaks will occur in real life. The altered data is shown in Table 1-16. In

TABLE 1-16
Monthly Sales Shown in Table 1-1
with Built-In Seasonality

Month	1st Year	2nd Year	3rd Year	4th Year	Added Seasonal Weight
Jan.	2,825	2,700	2,775	2,700	—
Feb.	2,600	2,700	2,600	2,500	100
Mar.	3,075	3,200	3,100	3,050	300
Apr.	3,350	3,550	3,350	3,400	600
May	2,925	3,000	2,975	2,850	200
June	2,700	2,825	2,650	2,825	50
July	2,700	2,825	2,650	2,775	—
Aug.	2,750	2,600	2,700	2,700	—
Sept.	2,550	2,725	2,450	2,600	—
Oct.	2,700	2,650	2,600	2,700	—
Nov.	2,700	2,800	2,650	2,800	—
Dec.	2,450	2,700	2,650	2,500	—

the calculations, we are going to use the data for years 1-2-3 to establish the initial monthly factors and thereafter calculate the estimated new factors, the average sales, and MAD, using exponential smoothing on all three.

TABLE 1-17
Example of Calculations for
Seasonal Forecast

	Jan.	Feb.	Mar.	Apr.	May	June	July	Aug.	Sept.	Oct.	Nov.	Dec.	Total	Avg. Sales
1st-year sales	2,825	2,600	3,075	3,350	2,925	2,700	2,700	2,750	2,550	2,700	2,700	2,450	33,325	2,777
Monthly factor	1.017	0.936	1.107	1.206	1.054	0.972	0.972	0.990	0.919	0.972	0.972	0.883	12.000	1.000
2nd-year sales	2,700	2,700	3,200	3,550	3,000	2,825	2,825	2,600	2,725	2,650	2,800	2,700	34,275	2,856
Monthly factor	0.945	0.945	1.121	1.243	1.051	0.989	0.989	0.910	0.954	0.928	0.980	0.945	12.000	1.000
3rd-year sales	2,775	2,600	3,100	3,350	2,975	2,650	2,650	2,700	2,450	2,600	2,650	2,650	33,150	2,763
Monthly factor	1.004	0.941	1.123	1.213	1.077	0.959	0.959	0.977	0.888	0.941	0.959	0.959	12.000	1.000
Sum of factors	2.966	2.822	3.351	3.662	3.182	2.920	2.920	2.877	2.761	2.841	2.911	2.787		
Average	0.989	0.941	1.117	1.221	1.061	0.973	0.973	0.959	0.920	0.947	0.970	0.929		
4th-year forecast														
Jan. Estimated factor	0.992	0.941	1.117	1.220	1.063	0.971	0.971	0.967	0.915	0.946	0.968	0.934	12.000	
Forecast sales	2,741	2,600	3,086	3,371	2,937	2,683	2,683	2,658	2,528	2,614	2,675	2,575		
Actual sales	*2,700*													2,748
Actual factors*	0.983	0.946	1.128	1.219	1.083	0.964	0.964	0.983	0.892	0.946	0.964	0.964	12.036	
Corrected factors	0.980	0.943	1.125	1.215	1.081	0.961	0.961	0.980	0.889	0.943	0.961	0.961	12.000	
Feb. Estimated factor	0.989	0.940	1.117	1.219	1.066	0.970	0.970	0.964	0.913	0.946	0.968	0.934	12.000	
Forecast sales	2,718	2,853	3,070	3,350	2,929	2,665	2,665	2,649	2,509	2,600	2,660	2,578		
Actual sales		*2,500*												2,709
Actual factors	0.997	0.923	1.144	1.237	1.098	0.978	0.978	0.997	0.904	0.960	0.978	0.978	12.172	
Corrected factors	0.983	0.910	1.128	1.219	1.083	0.964	0.964	0.983	0.891	0.947	0.964	0.964	12.000	
Mar. Estimated factor	0.985	0.936	1.120	1.220	1.070	0.969	0.969	0.967	0.909	0.946	0.967	0.942	12.000	
Forecast sales	2,667	2,536	3,034	3,305	2,899	2,625	2,625	2,619	2,463	2,562	2,620	2,552		
Actual sales			*3,050*											2,762
Actual factors	0.978	0.905	1.104	1.213	1.077	0.959	0.959	0.978	0.887	0.941	0.959	0.959	11.919	
Corrected factors	0.985	0.910	1.111	1.220	1.085	0.966	0.966	0.985	0.892	0.948	0.966	0.966	12.000	
Apr. Estimated factor	0.985	0.932	1.119	1.220	1.071	0.969	0.969	0.970	0.906	0.946	0.967	0.946	12.000	
Forecast sales	2,720	2,574	3,090	3,370	2,958	2,675	2,675	2,679	2,504	2,614	2,671	2,612		
Actual sales				*3,400*										2,861
Actual factors	0.944	0.874	1.066	1.188	1.040	0.926	0.926	0.944	0.856	0.909	0.926	0.926	11.525	
Corrected factors	0.983	0.911	1.110	1.237	1.083	0.964	0.964	0.983	0.891	0.946	0.964	0.964	12.000	
May Estimated factor	0.985	0.929	1.118	1.222	1.072	0.968	0.968	0.972	0.904	0.946	0.967	0.949	12.000	
Sales forecast	2,817	2,657	3,197	3,496	3,067	2,770	2,770	2,781	2,585	2,707	2,765	2,715		
Actual sales					*2,850*									2,859
Actual factors	0.944	0.874	1.067	1.189	0.997	0.927	0.927	0.944	0.857	0.909	0.927	0.927	11.489	
Corrected factors	0.986	0.912	1.114	1.242	1.042	0.968	0.968	0.986	0.896	0.950	0.968	0.968		
June Estimated factor	0.985	0.926	1.117	1.225	1.067	0.968	0.968	0.974	0.903	0.947	0.967	0.952	12.000	
Forecast sales	2,816	2,648	3,196	3,503	3,052	2,768	2,768	2,785	2,581	2,706	2,765	2,721		
Actual sales						*2,825*								2,854
Actual factors	0.946	0.876	1.069	1.191	0.999	0.990	0.929	0.946	0.858	0.911	0.929	0.929	11.573	
Corrected factors	0.981	0.908	1.109	1.234	1.036	1.027	0.963	0.981	0.890	0.945	0.963	0.963	12.000	
July Estimated factor	0.984	0.923	1.117	1.227	1.062	0.977	0.967	0.975	0.901	0.947	0.966	0.954	12.000	
Forecast sales	2,810	2,635	3,158	3,502	3,031	2,788	2,760	2,783	2,572	2,702	2,758	2,722		
Actual sales							*2,775*							2,841
Actual factors	0.950	0.880	1.074	1.197	1.003	0.994	0.977	0.950	0.862	0.915	0.933	0.933	11.668	
Corrected factors	0.977	0.905	1.105	1.232	1.032	1.022	1.004	0.977	0.886	0.942	0.959	0.959	12.000	
Aug. Estimated factor	0.983	0.920	1.115	1.228	1.057	0.984	0.973	0.975	0.899	0.946	0.965	0.955	12.000	
Forecast sales	2,792	2,614	3,168	3,488	3,004	2,795	2,763	2,771	2,553	2,688	2,741	2,713		
Actual sales								*2,700*						2,819
Actual factors	0.958	0.887	1.082	1.206	1.011	1.002	0.984	0.958	0.869	0.922	0.908	0.908	11.695	
Corrected factors	0.983	0.910	1.110	1.237	1.037	1.028	1.010	0.983	0.892	0.946	0.932	0.932	12.000	
Sept. Estimated factor	0.983	0.918	1.114	1.229	1.054	0.991	0.979	0.976	0.898	0.946	0.960	0.952	12.000	
Forecast sales	2,771	2,859	3,141	3,466	2,971	2,793	2,759	2,752	2,531	2,667	2,706	2,683		
Actual sales									*2,600*					2,785
Actual factors	0.969	0.898	1.095	1.221	1.023	1.014	0.996	0.969	0.934	0.934	0.952	0.952	11.957	
Corrected factors	0.973	0.902	1.099	1.226	1.027	1.018	1.000	0.973	0.937	0.937	0.955	0.955	12.000	
Oct. Estimated factor	0.982	0.916	1.112	1.229	1.050	0.995	0.982	0.975	0.904	0.945	0.959	0.952	12.000	
Forecast sales	2,733	2,550	3,096	3,421	2,924	2,771	2,736	2,717	2,517	2,630	2,661	2,653		
Actual sales										*2,700*				2,772
Actual factors	0.974	0.902	1.100	1.227	1.028	1.019	1.001	0.974	0.938	0.974	0.956	0.956	12.049	
Corrected factors	0.970	0.898	1.096	1.222	1.024	1.015	0.997	0.970	0.934	0.970	0.952	0.952	12.000	
Nov. Estimated factor	0.980	0.913	1.110	1.228	1.045	0.998	0.984	0.974	0.909	0.949	0.958	0.952	12.000	
Forecast sales	2,722	2,531	3,076	3,404	2,900	2,767	2,728	2,701	2,519	2,630	2,655	2,639		
Actual sales											*2,800*			2,776
Actual factors	0.973	0.901	1.099	1.225	1.027	1.018	1.000	0.973	0.937	0.973	1.009	0.955	12.090	
Corrected factors	0.966	0.895	1.090	1.215	1.020	1.010	0.993	0.966	0.930	0.966	1.001	0.948	12.000	
Dec. Estimated factor	0.978	0.910	1.107	1.226	1.041	1.000	0.985	0.973	0.912	0.952	0.965	0.951	12.000	
Forecast sales	2,715	2,527	3,073	3,403	2,890	2,776	2,735	2,700	2,532	2,642	2,678	2,641		
Actual sales												*2,500*		

*Actual factors are for the period Feb., third year through Jan., fourth year, etc.

In Table 1-17, we have listed the monthly sales for years 1-2-3 as the first three rows of data. Sales for each year have been totalled and the average monthly sales for each year determined. Next the monthly sales were divided by the annual average monthly sales to establish the monthly factor. Note that monthly factors have been added across for each year and that the total is 12.000. This is done as an error check and to assure that final factors are not equal to more or less than 12 months' sales. For any given year, the error is apt to be a rounding error, but in the initialization stage, there may be substantial differences in the summation of history, even with correct arithmetic.

The next step is to add the monthly January factors for the three years and then divide by three to get the average January factor. When completed across the page, we should have the initial monthly factors. However, if the sum of the factors is not 12, they must be corrected by multiplying each factor by the ratio 12.000/actual sum of the factors.

The new monthly factors for January of the fourth year are now estimated thus:

New estimated monthly factor = α old monthly factors + (1 - α) x
average monthly factor.

TABLE 1-18
Calculation of Monthly Factors and Forecast
Demand for Fourth Year, Starting with January

Month	α x Old Monthly Factor	+ (1 - α) x Avg. Monthly Factor	= Est'd. Factor x	3rd Year Avg. Sale	= Forecast
Jan.	0.154	1.004	0.846	0.989	0.992	2,763	2,741
Feb.	0.154	0.941	0.846	0.941	0.941	2,763	2,600
Mar.	0.154	1.123	0.846	1.117	1.117	2,763	3,086
Apr.	0.154	1.213	0.846	1.221	1.220	2,763	3,371
May	0.154	1.077	0.846	1.061	1.063	2,763	2,937
June	0.154	0.959	0.846	0.973	0.971	2,763	2,683
July	0.154	0.959	0.846	0.973	0.971	2,763	2,683
Aug.	0.154	0.977	0.846	0.959	0.962	2,763	2,658
Sept.	0.154	0.888	0.846	0.920	0.915	2,763	2,528
Oct.	0.154	0.941	0.846	0.947	0.946	2,763	2,614
Nov.	0.154	0.959	0.846	0.970	0.968	2,763	2,675
Dec.	0.154	0.959	0.846	0.929	0.934	2,763	2,575

The calculation of estimated monthly factors is shown in Table 1-18, using α = 0.154. This data is listed in Table 1-17 as the 12-month forecast, beginning with January of the fourth year. Using the same alpha value, the sales for the period February of the third year through January of the fourth year are smoothed and equal 2,748 units. Next, the actual sales for each of the same 12 months are divided by 2,748 to establish the new monthly factors. Here we found the sum of the actual factors was 12.036 and correction was made as indicated above. The initialization data is used only in making the first forecast.

The February and all future forecasts are made in similar fashion except:

New estimated monthly factors = α (previous monthly factor) + $(1 - \alpha)$ previous month's estimate of new monthly factor.

For the reader's convenience, this data is shown in Table 1-19. Note, however, that the January forecast is now for January of the fifth year. Results of calculations made

TABLE 1-19
Calculation of Estimated Monthly Factors and
12-Month Demand Starting February of Fourth Year

$\alpha = 0.154$

Month	α x	Jan. Act. Factor	+	$(1 - \alpha)$ x	Jan. Est'd. Factor	=	New Est'd. Factor	x	Preceding 12 Mos. Avg. Sales	=	Sales Forecast
Jan.	0.154	0.980		0.846	0.992		0.989		2,748		2,718
Feb.	0.154	0.943		0.846	0.941		0.940		2,748		2,583
Mar.	0.154	1.125		0.846	1.117		1.117		2,748		3,070
Apr.	0.154	1.215		0.846	1.220		1.219		2,748		3,350
May	0.154	1.081		0.846	1.063		1.066		2,748		2,929
June	0.154	0.961		0.846	0.971		0.970		2,748		2,665
July	0.154	0.961		0.846	0.971		0.970		2,748		2,665
Aug.	0.154	0.980		0.846	0.962		0.964		2,748		2,649
Sept.	0.154	0.889		0.846	0.915		0.913		2,748		2,509
Oct.	0.154	0.943		0.846	0.946		0.946		2,748		2,600
Nov.	0.154	0.961		0.846	0.968		0.968		2,748		2,660
Dec.	0.154	0.961		0.846	0.934		0.934		2,748		2,578

N. B. January forecast is now for January of fifth year

during each month of the fourth year are shown in Table 1-17, so the reader may see how the forecasts vary each month with the change in average sales. The forecast for the current month is italicized.

The calculations involved in this example took between three and four hours to complete manually, and you may well ask, "Is the effort worthwhile?" The answer can only be "yes" if you have seasonal sales and you want to manage your inventory so as to provide good service to customers. MAD and cumulative differences are excellent with this method. If only simple averages were used to control the inventory, the forecast demand would have been between 2,709 and 2,861 vs. actual demands of 2,500 and 3,400. This would have resulted in severe stock-outs during the season. With the simple averages, the MAD and cumulative error were more than twice as large as with the exponential method. The calculations in the example were on data we would call "horizontal seasonal." Trend-seasonal forecasts would combine trend and seasonal smoothing techniques to arrive at a forecast.

How to Manage Forecasting

We have already touched on MAD as a measure of forecast error. A natural question is, "How big should MAD be in relation to the level of demand?" The answer is, "It all depends." Reviewing the demand data we have shown in Tables 1-1, 1-9, and 1-16, it is apparent that demand fluctuates from month to month around the average, trend, or cycle. This variability is to be expected, but the variability of demand is different for every product. At one end of the pattern we might have an absolutely uniform demand, such as occurs when a housewife buys 2 quarts of milk each day from her milkman. Of course she might run to the supermarket for fill-in supplies. At the other end of the pattern could be a very volatile product, where the demand shows no trend or seasonality yet demand varies from month to month over a wide range in a purely random way.

Cumulative sums of the error of a forecast is one method of determining whether the forecast model is good; i.e., whether the current activity has changed from the level of a stable or horizontal forecast, whether trends have changed, etc. Going back to Table 1-15, in which we assumed an arbitrary trend of 20, the difference between actual and forecast (forecast error) was found to be negative every month in the range -79 to -192, but the cumulative error started at -192 and climbed every month during the year to -1,275. In this case, we made a false assumption of trend and the MAD gave no strong indication of error, but the cumulative error did. Not all changes in the model are strongly signalled as in this instance.

TABLE 1-20
Summary of Forecasts in Table 1-17

Month	Forecast	Actual	Difference	Cumulative Difference	MAD*
Jan.	2,741	2,700	−41	−41	41.0
Feb.	2,583	2,500	−83	−124	47.5
Mar.	3,034	3,050	+16	−108	42.7
Apr.	3,370	3,400	+30	−78	40.2
May	3,067	2,850	−217	−295	67.4
June	2,768	2,825	+57	−238	65.8
July	2,760	2,775	+15	−223	58.0
Aug.	2,771	2,700	−71	−294	60.0
Sept.	2,531	2,600	+69	−225	61.4
Oct.	2,630	2,700	+70	−155	62.7
Nov.	2,655	2,800	+145	−10	75.3
Dec.	2,641	2,500	−141	−151	85.4

*By exponential smoothing, α = 0.154, starting with the January difference as the initial MAD

Another technique which will pick up changes and provide a positive indication is a "tracking signal." This is simply a ratio between the cumulative error and MAD and nicely gets around the fact that MAD can be a large or small number. There is one chance in 20 that your model is not functioning properly if the tracking signal lies between +4 and -4. As an example, if we go to Table 1-20, and if we calculate a tracking signal, we find:

	Cumulative Difference	MAD	Tracking Signal
January	−41	41	−1.0
February	−124	47.5	−2.6
March	−108	42.7	−2.5
April	−78	40.2	−1.9
May	−295	67.4	−4.4
June	−238	65.8	−3.6
July	−223	58.0	−3.8
August	−294	60.0	−4.9
September	−225	61.4	−3.7
October	−155	62.7	−2.5
November	−10	75.3	−0.1
December	−151	85.4	−1.8

In this example, the tracking signal was triggered in May and again in August. In both months, the actual demand was quite a bit below the forecast. Tracking signals may be triggered for several reasons:

a. While we expect variations in demand to balance on either side of the forecast, random variations do not always balance out this way. We know from experience in tossing a coin that it does not alternate heads and tails; we have all seen runs of heads (or tails) to the extent that we want to take a close look at the coin. The same persistence can exist in demand without existence of error in the forecast model.

b. An unusually high or low demand will produce a larger forecast error, which when added to an existing cumulative sum produces a tracking signal trigger.

c. The initial values for forecasting were based on too short an historical record and as a result the base is in error.

d. It may have been judged that demand pattern was horizontal when in fact it was trend or some other model.

e. A change in demand pattern is emerging.

In our example, it appears that persistent variation of actual demand on the low side of the forecast is the cause of the triggers and implies the model we are using is not exactly right; i.e., there may be an upward trend we have not yet recognized.

What action should be taken to investigate tracking signal triggers? As pointed out above, with tracking signal set at ±4, we would expect that 95% of the time the signal would lie within control limits, but this still indicates a probability of 5% of the items being triggered by the random variations in demand. If you have 56,000 items in your forecast, there is a possibility of having 250-300 triggered each period by random variation alone. This creates pretty much of a burden on the forecast manager, because he has to go back and check out the reason for every trigger. A single-triggered signal is usually no great cause for alarm, and in most cases no action is taken. In a computerized system, a counter in the computer will show, as a part of the signal, first time, second consecutive, third consecutive, etc., with the signals either all in the positive or negative direction. Thus, with the 250-300 items signalled for the first time any month, it will be found that most of these have fallen back into control the next month. The computer counter is set back to zero for these; the remainder will show up as second consecutive. Of these some will fall back into control by the third month, the remainder should be investigated.

Specific action taken during the investigation will depend upon the needs of the user. The first thing to do would be to consider items a-b-c-d-e above to determine if possible which might be the cause. If the cause can be ascertained, correct the model and the initial value as appropriate. This may involve the replotting of all available historical data together with necessary calculations, or it may be satisfactory to develop a new model from the most recent six to eight months of data. Cumulative sums of errors are calculated, consecutive trigger counts are set to zero, and the normal routines are continued. If it is not possible to assign a cause for the trigger, either because the cause could not be determined or because of failure to complete the examinations, let the cumulative sums of errors and consecutive trigger count continue. Should as many as six consecutive triggers occur, establishment of a new model should be almost automatic.

It is wise to concentrate attention on those triggered items which are most important to your business in terms of high dollar value or demand. However, if consecutive triggers reach six, it is highly possible something is seriously wrong with the forecast model for that item and a reinitialization should be mandatory.

Things to Watch for in Forecasting

It is common to make forecasts on the basis of goods shipped because the data is readily available from accounting as a part of the invoicing routine, but it should be recognized this does not represent true demand. For example, suppose a number of products compete for productive time on the same manufacturing equipment and inventory replenishment for several falls due at the same time. Management may establish a priority for these products which precludes production of one or more items, so that no goods are available for shipment. Demands have been made for the unscheduled products and orders accepted are, of necessity, delayed. Perhaps during the following month production for the delayed items is completed. We then have a situation in which shipments are zero during one month and much above normal in the following month. Where such conditions exist, we would expect to see a major change in MAD and a tracking signal in both months. For this reason, it is desirable to have forecasts based on accepted demands rather than on invoiced shipments. If only invoicing data is available, be alert for situations such as described. In designing a computerized forecasting system, it is possible to build in an automatic "unusual" activity signal. Since signals are not wanted for the random noise in the system, but are needed to flag unusual occurrences such as one-time large orders, clerical or key-punch errors, or the example cited above, it is good practice to check the difference between forecast and actual demand vs. a multiple of MAD. If the limits are based on four MAD's, we can be sure the variance is due to a significant factor which should be checked out. With the answers obtained, it may be desirable to add a manual correction to the forecast by rectifying the errors or automatically discarding the unusual occurrence. There is no rule for this; the forecast manager must exercise judgment and discretion based upon the current circumstances. In fact, while we have talked much about rules and formal procedures throughout, the manager should not accept a mechanized procedure completely. Forecasting always requires know-how about your own system and application of judgment in handling the exceptions.

The manager must also be aware of the addition of new customers for established products. It is true that forecasting techniques will track these demands, but as has been pointed out already, it may take months for the forecast to catch up with what is happening. In the meantime customer service will be suffering, and the sales department will in all likelihood be screaming about delayed orders. The unusual order signal and other controls will flag these changes, but it is up to the forecast manager to track down the reasons and to make appropriate changes through a manual forecast correction.

It is very helpful if the sales department advises the forecast manager of new business so that changes can be made as early as possible, but sometimes salesmen are not aware that a relatively small order may represent a big change in the demand for a low-volume product. A special case of erratic demand is often found among low-volume, slow-moving items. There is a particularly apt term for the product which shows many periods with zero demand, a low-average demand, and occasional demands which may be five or ten times the average. This kind of demand is called "lumpy." Lumpy products are almost always found at the low end of the distribution of demand and can usually be found by simple examination of the data. A problem arises in that it is often deemed necessary to forecast the activity of these products. If this is the case, the best solution is to assume the demand to be horizontal and track the movement with a very low value of alpha, say 0.02 to 0.05. The forecast may well turn out to be zero units per month with a MAD of 6 or more. Tracking signals are meaningless and should not be calculated because the demand is an abnormal distribution, and as a result the forecast error distribution is also abnormal. Safety stocks are handled in two ways. In the case of the first method, the attitude may be that business in these items is so small that no such stocks are warranted; if orders are received they will be made to order, and "while you are at it make a few more in case we get another order." The second policy may be to carry safety stocks on the basis of horizontal demand and MAD, adhering to the theory that since movement is so low, some degree of protection may not be too expensive an investment and will prevent stock-out harassment.

Forecasting Without Historic Data

This type of forecasting usually occurs with new products, but it can also be utilized when a computerized system is being initiated from a straight manual system. In the latter case, it may be felt that the clerical effort to develop the history is not worthwhile. With new products, take the best estimate of the sales group on sales volume and use this value in the initial forecast. The model will obviously depend upon what the sales group predicts will happen. The forecast manager will work from demand data as it develops, using an alpha of 0.3-0.5. This gives a high level of response to new data, perhaps even a nervous response. As the demand begins to develop and stabilize, the alpha can be dropped to appropriate levels.

When no data is available, the forecast manager can only start from where he is. All products will be assumed to represent horizontal models, and forecasts will be prepared using alpha = 0.2 or 0.3. During the first five to six months of operation, cumulative sums and MAD's can be collected and tentative forecasts made. After six months or so, the various sales patterns can be reviewed and models changed to suit immediate requirements. After 12-24 months, products which are horizontal or simple trend will have been solidly identified, but at least 36 months are required to be sure of weakly seasonal items. Management should know the strong seasonals. Other than seasonals, you should be able to make sound forecasts with 18-24 months of history. Fortunately, demand for most products is horizontal or mild trend, and fair forecasts can be made for these with less than a year's history; however, you won't be sure they are horizontal or mild trend until much later.

BIBLIOGRAPHY AND FURTHER READING

(1) Barish, N.N., *Economic Analysis*, New York, N.Y., McGraw-Hill Book Co., Inc., 1962. Beginner's mathematical methods.

(2) "Basic Principles of Wholesale IMPACT," White Plains, N.Y., Technical Publications Dept., International Business Machines Corp., publication #E20-8105-1. Covers the basic theories in the IBM proprietary forecasting and inventory control system.

(3) Brown, R.G., *Statistical Forecasting for Inventory Control*, New York, N.Y., McGraw-Hill Book Co., Inc., 1959. A lucid, mostly nonmathematical explanation of forecasting methods.

(4) DeSalvia, D.N., "Exponential Smoothing," *American Production and Inventory Control Society Journal*, Volume 9, #1, 1968.

(5) "Management Operating System; Forecasting, Materials Planning and Inventory Control-General," IBM, publication #E20-0031-0.

(6) "Statistical Forecasting," publication of Imperial Chemical Industries, London, England. Describes the exponential smoothing methods of Professor C.C. Hill of Carnegie Institute of Technology and their applications in the chemical business.

(7) "Wholesale IMPACT. Advanced Principles and Implementation," IBM, publication #E20-0174-0.

Chapter 2

No company has access to unlimited capital. With most, capital is definitely limited. New facilities, replacement facilities, raw materials, finished products, credit to customers, and other demands all compete for the available supply. Careful management of inventory is a necessity in order to have adequate stockpiles of raw materials, supplies, and finished goods to provide the desired level of customer service, and no more. Inventory demands on capital will then be held to the lowest practical value.

Inventory management is amenable to logical and mathematical control in handling

MANAGING INVENTORY
SUCCESSFULLY

routine replenishment problems. The judgment of knowledgeable persons will override the established routine in the face of an abnormal situation, such as a strike. It is the purpose of this chapter to deal only with the more common, routine practices concerning the replenishment of inventory and the setting of safety stocks.

ABC Analysis

The amount of attention given to specific items of inventory will vary. There must be more concern for the high-volume, high-value items than for the opposite extreme. Inventory is often classified by the use of ABC analysis, a principle first outlined in the 1800's by V. Pareto, an Italian engineer and mathematician. Simply stated, Pareto found where a great many items are involved, relatively few items will account for a major part of the activity.

When arranged in descending order of value on hand, an inventory of 15% of the high-volume, high-value items accounts for about 70% of the total value of the stockpile. Another 20% of the items will account for about 20% of the value at hand, while the remaining 65% of the items will account for the balance of the value. See Figure 2-1 for a typical ABC curve. In labelling the groups, the A group is always the group containing 15% of items and 70% of value, with B and C following in order. Parenthetically, the technique can be used for other analyses — customers vs. purchases,

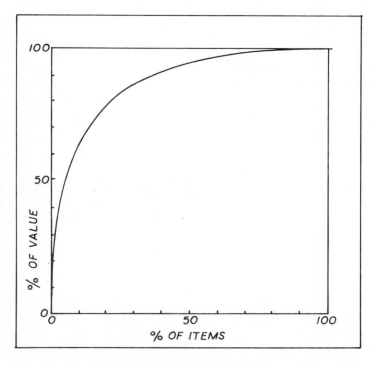

Figure 2-1. *ABC analysis*

population vs. income, etc. Once inventory is classified, we have a firm base for deciding where we will put our effort. Logically, we expect to maintain strong controls over the A items, taking whatever special actions needed to maintain availability of these items and hold stocks at the lowest possible levels consistent with meeting demands. At the other end of the scale, we cannot afford the expense of rigid controls, frequent ordering, expediting, etc., because of the low dollars in this area. Thus, with the C group, we may maintain somewhat higher safety stocks, order more months of supply, expect lower levels of customer service, or all three.

Manual Systems

Manual regulation of an inventory need not imply a lack of logical controls. When there are thousands of items in stock, it is common to find that items have been ranked in an order of importance and separated into three or more inventory groups. Safety stock may be at the lowest levels with A items but accompanied by continuous attention and expediting, or alternately at substantial levels to assure service in the face of random fluctuations in demand. With slow-moving items, service levels are apt to be very good, because it is economically sound to buy a supply equivalent to a year or more of demand, when this is only valued at a few dollars. Safety stocks are often expressed as "periods of demand," with the same number of periods used for all items in an inventory group. Nor is it unusual to find safety stock and reorder point combined. For example, replenishment may be from internal or external sources and the inventory manager has found that he doesn't run out of material very often if goods on hand, on order, and in transit do not fall below a certain level, say three or four months' demand. There can be surplus safety in such a procedure.

With a manual system, the overall procedures are simplified so they are easy to learn and simple to use. The manual systems observed by the writer have generally been well thought out, and they do function. However, there have often been strong indications of out-of-balance inventories, of playing too safe on reorder points and reorder quantities, and of excessive stocks on hand for many items.

Computerized Systems

Since this book is directed to the management of a system having thousands of stockkeeping units, as with a line of chemicals, the main emphasis of this chapter is aimed at a computerized inventory system. Figure 2-2 shows a schematic of a chemical manufacturing, packaging, and distribution operation. Raw materials are procured and brought together in the proper proportion for processing through reactors, purifiers, separators, dryers, and other equipment. The finished bulk product is either packaged directly into a stockkeeping unit (SKU) or into a transfer container for packaging at a later time. Finished goods are stored in the factory warehouse and shipped on demand to customers or to field warehouses to meet demands of remote customers.

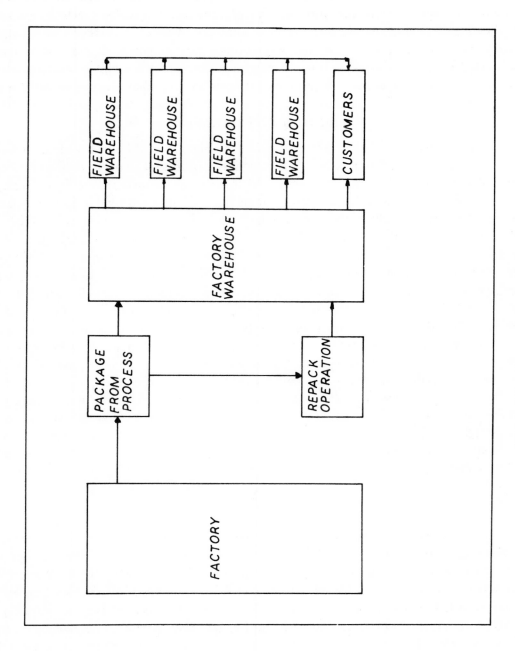

Figure 2-2. *Chemical operation schematic.*

There are three parts to managing inventory: First, there is the need of keeping track of goods on hand; second, there is the need to check the "book" inventory against the physical stock; and third, there is the need to replenish stocks. Figure 2-3 is a schematic diagram showing a system of factories and warehouses interlocked for communication flow through a central computer. Figure 2-4 shows a simplified information flow network for the system. There is affiliated with each sales office, one or more warehouses with product stocks appropriate to the area served. If the sales office is to accept an order for shipment from a local warehouse, it should know whether the goods are available or whether arrangements must be made to ship from the factory or another warehouse. In the typical manual system, the sales office will have access to a local record, but can learn of stocks at the factory or other stocking points only through a series of telephone calls. In the computerized system (Figure 2-4), a customer order is entered into the computer via a teleprocessing device and the local stock record, as kept by the computer, is checked for availability of the desired item. If available, the computer response is "accept order" and depletes the available inventory by the amount sold; on the other hand, reply may be "insufficient stock." The sales office may then key in an all-points inquiry and determine the availability of goods at all stocking points. If there is any stock elsewhere, the order may be placed against the point having inventory.

The number of transactions which can be carried in the computer is dependent upon the needs of your own system. For example, you could:

- Change the reorder point for field stocks.
- Change the replenishment quantity for field stocks.
- Transfer stock from warehouse to warehouse.
- Post receipt of goods from manufacturing to factory quality control.
- Transfer goods from committed to uncommitted inventory.
- Handle customer returns.
- Register a demand to the proper territory when a warehouse ships goods into another area.
- Post physical gain or loss in stocks.
- Register damage and breakage.

Periodically, the location stocks are reviewed by computer to determine the SKU's which have reached the reorder point. An automatic warehouse stock replenishment order is then issued to the appropriate factory. The frequency of this operation will depend upon the products handled, economic mode of transport, volume of business handled by the warehouse, sources of supply, etc.

Once the stockkeeping record is tied directly to the acceptance of customer orders, it is feasible to move away from manual preparation of the initial internal hard copy of the order, with all of the subsequent paper handling, and go directly to a fully

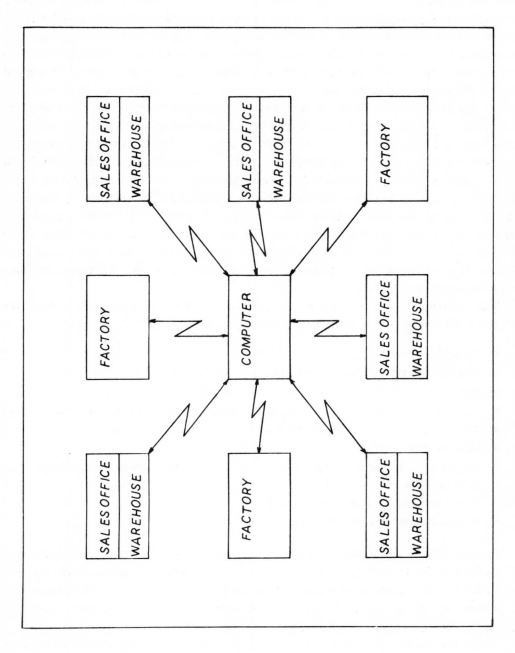

Figure 2-3. *Factory-warehouse-computer system schematic.*

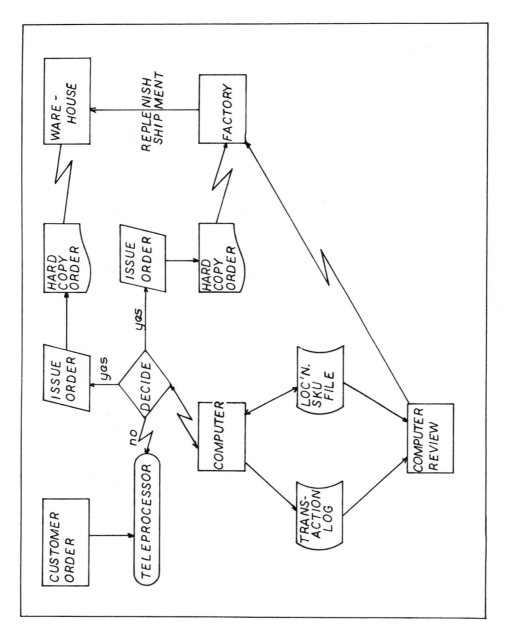

Figure 2-4. *Information flow network.*

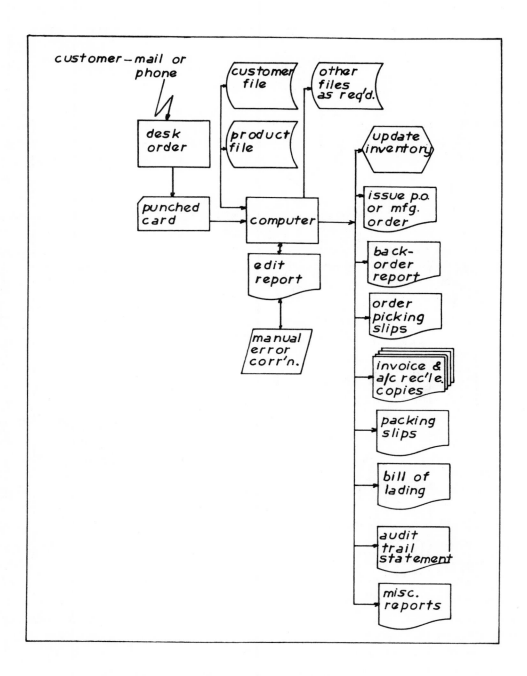

Figure 2-5. *Simplified order entry system.*

automated order entry and action system. A simplified flow diagram is shown in Figure 2-5 which covers everything described above, plus issuance of purchase and manufacturing orders, invoices, packing slips, picking sheets, bills of lading, audit trail, warehouse release notices, etc.

Physical Book Stock Reconciliation

Inventories may be checked on an annual basis, using all available manpower to make a complete physical check and tally of all items on hand. The physical check is a means of learning of, and correcting, bookkeeping errors. It may also serve to uncover theft or fraudulent practices. Since many persons are used for the counting operation who have little real interest in the activity, reconciliation of book and physical count may be prolonged. The new book inventory may be no more accurate than the old record.

Where the system has been largely computerized, it is probably easier to have counts made throughout the year. For example, with items which move very slowly — say two or three transactions per year — the computer can be programmed to issue a count ticket when the demand occurs. Count would be made immediately. On faster-moving items, it is simple enough to set up a schedule for the daily count and reconciliation of a few items. There is less confusion with such a procedure, and the need for the annual 100% count and its attendant confusion is eliminated.

Inventory Replenishment

We have briefly discussed replenishment of warehouse stocks above. Stock levels at a warehouse are subject to more erratic demands than is the case at the main factory from which replenishment is drawn. The variation at the warehouse may be due to a single customer (for a given stock item) who buys the greater part of the local stock, but at uneven intervals. Weather may be a factor with water-treating chemicals or air-conditioner refrigerant gases. However, when the demands of a number of warehouses are consolidated back to the factory level, the demand against the factory may be very well behaved for many items.

An automated warehouse replenishment system can function on either an imprest system or a statistical system. An imprest system establishes a maximum stock and reorder points for each item. Replenishment is secured at suitable intervals for all the goods sold since the previous replenishment. The imprest level should take into account the length of time (lead time) between the sale of the first item in the replenished stock and the arrival of the next replenishment, the average level of sales, the variability of sales, and special cases such as the customer who comes in occasionally but always wants a certain amount which may be higher than the average sales. It is a time-consuming operation to set initial imprest values accurately and equally time-consuming to update periodically. As a result, increases in imprest levels in the field will be made quickly when poor customer service occurs, but imprest levels are reduced only by a major effort. The net result is excessive field stocks.

With a computerized record-keeping system for warehouse stocks such as described above, there is a solid base for a statistically controlled system. In Figure 2-4, an SKU record for each stocking location and a transaction file are shown as a part of the system. The SKU file contains a product code which identifies the SKU plus an alphabetic description of the product.

In first setting up a computerized system for planning and control of inventories at warehouses, it is necessary to analyze daily sales transaction records for a period of months, preferably about a year. It may be necessary to dig this information out of shipping order or invoice hard copy files. If you are fortunate, it may be stored on magnetic tapes. The analysis would provide, for each SKU carried by the warehouse and the maximum and average demands during a specified lead time. The data required to establish economic safety stocks would be obtained at the same time. To make our calculations, we need for each warehouse not only the SKU and transaction files already mentioned, but also the replenishment lead time ex factory, the length of time required to sell enough goods to constitute a replenishment quantity, the level of service we intend to offer for the various SKU's, and a value for the "cost of holding" stock.

TABLE 2-1
Index of Terms

DEMANDS

X	= any single demand.
$\overline{X}$	= any average demand.
X_1	= demand during the interval between reaching an order point and delivery of replenishment shipment.
$\overline{X}_1$	= average demand during the interval between reaching an order point and delivery of replenishment shipment.
X_2	= demand during the time required to sell a replenishment quantity.
$\overline{X}_2$	= Average demand during the time required to sell a replenishment quantity.
X_d	= Daily demand.
$\overline{X}_d$	= Average daily demand.
X_{max}	= Maximum demand.
X_{acc}	= Accumulated demand.
X_{ann}	= Annual demand.

LEAD TIME

T	= any time period.
T_1	= Time for replenishment between OP and delivery — days.

$\overline{T}_1$ = Average time for replenishment between OP and delivery — days.

T_2 = Time to sell a replenishment quantity.

$\overline{T}_2$ = Average time to sell a replenishment quantity.

T_{max} = Maximum replenishment lead time — days.

$T_{2\,max}$ = Maximum time to sell a replenishment quantity — days.

$T_{1\,max}$ = Maximum time for replenishment between OP and delivery — days.

OTHER TERMS

p = probability of, expressed as a decimal in range 0.0 to 1.0.

k = a constant.

= a replenishment weight.

I_s = safety stock.

UNLI = unit normal loss integral.

C_b = cost of a back order — imputed.

C_h = cost of handling.

C_o = cost of ordering.

I_s index = safety stock index.

ϕ = protection level expressed as a decimal.

σ = standard deviation of any variable.

θ = $\overline{X}_1 \overline{T}_1$.

γ_1 = coefficient of variability.

γ_2 = coefficient of protection.

$\triangle$ = Maximum lead time demand/average lead time.

λ = Maximum lead time/average lead time.

Ω = $\overline{T}_2 / \overline{\overline{T}}_1$.

Establishing Cost of Holding, C_h

Cost of holding, C_h, can be obtained by three methods. First, it can be built up from a number of inventory related costs; second, it can be equated to the return on investment of the average capitalization of the business; and third, it can be taken as the same value as desired R.O.I. for a new investment.

In the first method we look at:

Interest Costs. In recent years, prime rate for borrowed money has risen steadily. But whatever the current rate, internally generated funds should be valued at the same level.

Insurance. Rates will vary with the hazards involved. When risk is low, the rates are low — and vice versa. As a percentage of inventory, the rates can fluctuate between

1% and 4%. The total billing will vary with the amount of goods in inventory, although the billing rate will be adjusted only once a year.

Storage. If goods are stored in a public warehouse and have a variable inventory, space charges will be assessed on the basis of floor space (or cube) in use at a given time in the month, frequently at month's end. In this case, space charge is variable and is a changeable factor in your costs. If you rent a fixed amount of space, regardless of your stock levels, the cost is nonvariable. Likewise, in owned space, if you have plenty of unused space, the cost is nonvariable, but if you are hard up for space, or could use the space tied up with inventory for some other profitable use, then the value of the space is a variable cost. In the same way, warehouse labor, warehouse clerks, janitors, heat and light, etc., can be evaluated. If the cost can be varied with the inventory, then it is a factor in the cost of holding; thus, value of storage space and labor can vary from nothing to 3-4%.

Breakage and Pilferage. Breakage is partly attributable to the carelessness of workers and partially to the loading in the warehouse. When goods are jammed in, the possibility of breakage increases greatly. Pilferage is also related to the amount and kind of goods on hand. If there is a high stock level, desirable goods may disappear and their loss may not be immediately noticeable. This factor can equate to 1-2%.

Obsolescence. This varies widely. With style goods, the whim and caprice of the marketplace can destroy demand almost overnight, and inventories can be sold only at distress prices. With foodstuffs, drugs, and some chemicals, there is a definite shelf-life limitation. Milk and bread, saleable today, have only a limited market as stale goods. Most items do not fall into these categories and so obsolescence is a small factor. For these a 1% charge is quite conservative. Where there is a style or shelf-life problem, rates up to 20% or more are not unreasonable.

Taxes. Many localities have personal property or floor taxes, based upon the inventory on hand, usually on a specified day of the year. For any given warehouse, this can usually be obtained from the accounting records, and will be found to run 1-3%.

From the foregoing, a cost of holding will calculate to be in the range 13½-40%. This is fairly wide, and perhaps it is not too valuable to you as stated. Your own analysis will narrow these figures to a more useful range.

The second method, involves examination of the corporate balance sheet and comparing annual earnings before taxes with the investments in fixed property, inventory, marketable securities, and other items. Depending upon the company and how well it is managed, this may show the overall investment is earning up to 25% before taxes. This value is C_h.

The third method depends upon internal policies concerning new capital investment. Desired return on investment can vary considerably. If the investment in fixed facilities is tied to a long-term contract for a standard product with a good customer, and there is plenty of internal capital available, a return before taxes of 18-

20% might be acceptable. On the other hand, if the facilities are for an entirely new product, with uncertainty as to customer and volume, a much higher rate of return might be required as a kind of insurance against the risk involved. If capital is in tight supply, management may raise the desired rate of return on new investments to a high level in order to make best use of available money. Perhaps a 25-35% return before taxes might be an acceptable rule-of-thumb. This value can be taken as C_h.

A figure of 20-25% is very commonly used in inventory calculations. Later in this chapter, we will see that extreme accuracy in arriving at C_h and the related cost of setup is not critical. As long as the estimates of these two costs are approximately correct, any error has minimal effect on calculations.

Establishing Replenishment Lead Time, T

Warehouse lead time consists of two parts: (1) the time required to sell enough material to constitute a "shipping weight"; (2) the resupply time from the factory. The time required to sell a shipping weight is influenced not only by the usual shipping quantity, which may be a carload, truckload, or lesser quantity, but also by the accumulated customer demand against the warehouse. The usual shipping weight can be established: (1) by assuming the shipping weight to be that which gives the minimum unit shipping cost compatible with warehouse space available and any shelf-life restrictions; (2) by using some optimal weight model — i.e., minimum truckload, maximum truckload, or other combination.

Using the shipping weight, $\#$, and the forecast of the customer demand for all stock items, X_{acc}, for planning period T, we can calculate the time to sell an average replenishment weight, $\overline{T}_2$; thus:

$$\overline{T}_2 = \#T/X_{acc}.$$

Example: If $\#$ = 30,000 lbs.
T = 30 days
X_{acc} = 90,000 lbs.
then $\overline{T}_2$ = 30,000 x 30 / 90,000 = 10 days.

Maximum $\overline{T}_2$ can be established by determining the demand during the slowest month of the year.

Resupply time will usually include warehouse response time, communication time to the factory, factory response time, factory to warehouse in-transit time, and unloading time at the warehouse. Since we are examining a computerized system, we could review the depletion of warehouse stocks every day, and when $\#$ is reached, print out a shipping order at the factory by telecommunication. It is probable this review would be made at the end of the day, and warehouse response time plus communication time would be minimal. Time required by the factory to assemble goods for shipment will vary, depending upon the variety of items in the replenishment shipment and ability to schedule a carrier. In-transit time is dependent upon distance, the quantity being shipped (*T/L* or *L/T/L*) if by motor truck, and lesser factors such as weekends, holidays, and weather. Note that if less than full legal weight is loaded on a common carrier truck, the carrier has the option of loading additional freight for others moving in the same direction. This can introduce a wide variance to the in-transit time. In any event, it is not too difficult to establish an average and maximum in-transit time. Unloading at the warehouse may be insignificant, but if multi-items are being replenished, the time required to sort and place them in the warehouse may be substantial. The whole cycle should be studied and an effort made to bring average cycle and variability to an optimum value. When this is done, we shall have values of average resupply time, $\bar{T}_1$, and maximum supply time, T_{max}. Now we can state that average lead time, $\bar{T}$, is:

$$\bar{T} = \bar{T}_{2_{max}} + T_{1_{max}}.$$

Calculation of Safety Stocks—Fast-Moving Items

We will first look at safety stock levels where the lead time demands are normally distributed, which is close to the case with fast-moving items. Where demands are slow moving or lumpy, a different approach is taken in figuring safety stocks; this procedure will be discussed later on. Immediately following, is a mathematical derivation of the factors needed to determine safety stocks for fast movers. Readers who are more interested in the application may skip to page 69 for the practical method.

Before proceeding with the development of the safety stock formulas, we need to familiarize ourselves with certain definitions:

(a) Service protection level = ϕ (Greek letter phi) = a decimal between 0 and 1.00.

(b) $\Delta = \dfrac{\text{Maximum replenishment lead time demand}}{\text{Average replenishment lead time demand}} = \dfrac{X_{max}\,\bar{T}_1}{\bar{X}_1\,\bar{T}_1}.$ (2-1)

(c) $\lambda = \dfrac{\text{Maximum replenishment lead time}}{\text{Average replenishment lead time}} = \dfrac{T_{max}.}{\bar{T}_1}$ (2-2)

(d) $\gamma_1 = \dfrac{\text{Replenishment lead time demand – average lead time demand}}{\text{Standard deviation of replenishment lead time demand}}$ (2-3)

$= \dfrac{X_1 T_1 - \bar{X}_1 \bar{T}_1}{\sigma\, X_1 T_1}.$

(e) $\gamma_2 = \dfrac{\text{Safety stock - average replenishment lead time demand}}{\text{Standard deviation of replenishment lead time demand}}$ (2-4)

$$= \frac{I_s - \bar{X}_1 \bar{T}_1}{X_1 T_1} \ .$$

(f) $V_{X_1 T_1} = \dfrac{\text{Standard deviation of replenishment lead time demand}}{\text{Average replenishment lead time demand}}$ (2-5)

$$= \frac{\sigma \, X_1 T_1}{\bar{X}_1 \, \bar{T}_1} \ .$$

In the above:

ϕ = Service protection level.

$\triangle$ = Measure of variability of demand.

λ = Measure of variability of lead time.

γ_1 = Demand factor.

γ_2 = Service protection factor.

$V_{X_1 T_1}$ = Random variable variation factor.

Given the service protection level, ϕ, we can write an equation in which ϕ and safety stock I_s both appear:

$$\int_{I_s}^{\infty} (X_1 T_1 - I_s)\, f X_1 T_1\, dX_1 T_1 \leqslant (1-\phi)\bar{X}_2 \bar{T}_2 \ , \qquad (2\text{-}6)$$

where $X_1 T_1$ = demand during replenishment lead time and $\bar{X}_2 \bar{T}_2$ = average demand during average replenishment lead time.

Since we have stated that lead time demands are normally distributed, we can rewrite the term $f X_1 T_1$ in eq. 2-6, using normal distribution mathematics:

$$f X_1 T_1 = \left(\frac{1}{\sigma X_1 T_1 \sqrt{2\pi}}\right) e^{-\frac{1}{2}\left(\dfrac{X_1 T_1 - \bar{X}_1 \bar{T}_1}{\sigma X_1 T_1}\right)^2}. \qquad (2\text{-}7)$$

With eq. 2-7, we can rewrite eq. 2-6:

$$\frac{1}{\sigma X_1 T_1 \sqrt{2\pi}} = \int_{I_s}^{\infty} (X_1 T_1 - I_s)\, e^{-\frac{1}{2}\left(\dfrac{X_1 T_1 - \bar{X}_1 \bar{T}^1}{\sigma X_1 T_1}\right)^2} dX_1 T_1 \qquad (2\text{-}8)$$

$$= (1-\phi)\,\bar{X}_2 \bar{T}_2 \ .$$

If we combine eqs. 2-3 and 2-4, we have:

$$\sigma X_1 T_1 (\gamma_1 - \gamma_2) = (X_1 T_1 - \bar{X}_1 \bar{T}_1) - (I_s - \bar{X}_1 \bar{T}_1), \tag{2-9}$$

and

$$dX_1 T_1 = (\sigma X_1 T_1) d\gamma_2 . \tag{2-10}$$

Now if we substitute eqs. 2-9 and 2-10 in eq. 2-8 and simultaneously assume the distribution has a zero mean and standard deviation of one, we will have the equation for the unit normal loss integral or UNLI:

$$\text{UNLI} = \frac{1}{\sqrt{2\pi}} \int_{I_s}^{\infty} (\gamma_1 - \gamma_2) e^{-\frac{1}{2} \gamma_1} d\gamma_1$$

$$= (1 - \phi) (\bar{X}_2 \bar{T}_2) / \sigma X_1 T_1 . \tag{2-11}$$

Eq. 2-11 has only one value for any value of γ_2. If we rearrange eq. 2-4, we can solve it for I_s, thus:

$$I_s = \bar{X}_1 \bar{T}_1 + \gamma_2 \sigma X_1 T_1 . \tag{2-12}$$

Eq. 2-5 may also be transposed to read:

$$\sigma X_1 T_1 = \bar{X}_1 \bar{T}_1 (V_{X_1 T_1}). \tag{2-13}$$

We know that the average demand during the average time to sell a replenishment quantity is equal to the average daily demand during the same period multiplied by the number of days in the period, and that the average demand during the average replenishment lead time is equal to average daily demand during the same period multiplied by the number of days in the period; hence:

$$\frac{\bar{X}_2 \bar{T}_2}{\bar{X}_1 \bar{T}_1} = \frac{\bar{X}_d \bar{T}_2}{\bar{X}_d T_1} = \frac{\bar{T}_2}{\bar{T}_1} , \tag{2-14}$$

where $\bar{X}_d$ = daily demand average.

If we now substitute eqs. 2-13 and 2-14 in eqs. 2-11 and 2-12, we find that

$$\text{UNLI} \; = \; \frac{1 - \phi}{V_{X_1 T_1} \, (\bar{T}_2 / \bar{T}_1)} \tag{2-15}$$

and

$$I_s = \bar{X}_1 \bar{T}_1 \, (1 + \gamma_2 V_{X_1 T_1}) \, . \tag{2-16}$$

Lead time varies independently of the variation of daily demand, thus lead time demand may be represented as

$$\bar{X}_1 \bar{T}_1 = \sum_{i=1}^{T_1} d_i \, . \tag{2-17}$$

The average lead time demand is

$$\bar{X}_1 \bar{T}_1 = \bar{d} \, \bar{T}_1 \, , \tag{2-18}$$

and standard deviation is

$$\sigma \bar{X}_1 \bar{T}_1 = \sqrt{\bar{T} \, \sigma^2 d + d^2 \, \sigma^2 \, T_1} \, . \tag{2-19}$$

Repeating eq. 2-5 and substituting eqs. 2-18 and 2-19, we have

$$V_{X_1 T_1} = \sigma X_1 T_1 / \bar{X}_1 \bar{T}_1$$

$$= \frac{\sqrt{\bar{T} \, \sigma^2 d + d^2 \sigma^2 T_1}}{\bar{d} \bar{T}_1}$$

$$= \sqrt{(1/T_1) \, (\sigma^2) \, (d/\bar{d}) + \sigma^2 T_1 / (\bar{T}_1)^2} \, . \tag{2-20}$$

But if we look only at demand during the average lead time, we can write eq. 2-17 as

$$\bar{X}_1 \bar{T}_1 = \sum_{i=1}^{\bar{T}_1} d_i \, , \tag{2-21}$$

with an average of

$$\bar{X}_1 \bar{T}_1 = \bar{T}_1 d, \text{ which is the same as eq. 2-18} \tag{2-22}$$

and standard deviation

$$\sigma X_1 T_1 = \sqrt{\bar{T}_1 \sigma^2 d}. \tag{2-23}$$

From eqs. 2-5, 2-17, 2-18, and 2-23, we get for the case of simple demand during the average lead time

$$V_{X_1 T_1} = \sigma X_1 T_1 / X_1 \bar{T}_1$$

$$\sqrt{V^2_{X_1 \bar{T}_1} + V^2_{T^1}}. \tag{2-24}$$

We can now substitute eq. 2-24 in eqs. 2-15 and 2-16 to get

$$\text{UNLI} = 3(1 - \phi)(\bar{T}_2 / \bar{T}_1) \tag{2-25}$$

$$\sqrt{V^2_{X \bar{T}_1} + V^2_{T_1}}$$

and

$$I_s = \bar{X}_1 \bar{T}_1 (1 + \gamma_2) \sqrt{V^2_{X \bar{T}_1} + V^2_{T_1}}. \tag{2-26}$$

A basic premise of these calculations is that lead time demand is normally distributed. With a normal distribution, over 99% of the observed values of the variable, X, will be within +3 or -3 standard deviations of the mean*, so that we can write:

$$\sigma X_1 T_1 = 1/3 (X_{max} \bar{T}_1 - \bar{X}_1 \bar{T}_1) \tag{2-27}$$
$$\text{and}$$
$$\sigma \bar{T}_1 = 1/3 (T_{max} - \bar{T}_1). \tag{2-28}$$

Substituting eqs. 2-1, 2-2, 2-27, and 2-28 in eq. 2-24, we get first

$$V_{X_1 T_1} = 1/3 (\Delta - 1), \tag{2-29}$$

---

*Watch out for the truly abnormal demands, such as special one-time orders or abnormal lead times caused by strikes or storms. In such cases, second highest values should be used.

and similarly

$$V_{T_1} = 1/3 \ (\lambda - 1). \tag{2-30}$$

Then from eq. 2-24

$$V_{X_1 T_1} = 1/3 \ \sqrt{(\Delta - 1)^2 + (\lambda - 1)^2}, \tag{2-31}$$

and eq. 2-25 becomes

$$\text{UNLI} = \frac{3 \ (1 - \phi) \ (\overline{T}_2 / \overline{T}_1)}{\sqrt{(\Delta - 1)^2 + (\lambda - 1)^2}} \tag{2-32}$$

Safety stock for fast-moving items can thus be calculated from $\phi, \Delta, \lambda, \overline{X}_1 \overline{T}_1$, and $\overline{T}_2 / \overline{T}_1$.

EXAMPLE:

For Product A, $\overline{T}_2 = 12$ days.

$\overline{T}_1 = 12$ days.

$T_{max} = 15$ days.

$\overline{X}_1 \overline{T}_1 = 23$ units.

$X_{max} \overline{T}_1 = 50$ units.

$\phi = 0.95$.

Then

$\overline{T}_2 / \overline{T}_1 = 1.0$

$\lambda = 15/12 = 1.25$

$\Delta = 50/12 = 4.17$

$V_{X_1 T_1} = 1/3 \sqrt{(3.17)^2 + (0.25)^2} = 1.06$

$\text{UNLI} = (1 - .95) \times 1/1.06 = 0.0472.$

Going to the unit normal loss table, Table 2-2 below, we find the value at the intersections of line 1.2 (in the left-hand column) and the column headed 0.8, where we find the value closest to our calculated value of 0.0472 — thus $\gamma_2 = 1.28$. Now we can calculate the safety stock using eq. 2-16:

$$I_s = 23\,[\,1 + (1.28 \times 1.06)\,]$$

$$= 31.2 \text{ units.}$$

TABLE 2-2
Unit Normal Loss Integral
$$G(u) = P'_N(u) - uP_N(\tilde{u} > u)$$

u	.00	.01	.02	.03	.04	.05	.06	.07	.08	.09
.0	.3989	.3940	.3890	.3841	.3793	.3744	.3697	.3649	.3602	.3556
.1	.3509	.3464	.3418	.3373	.3328	.3284	.3240	.3197	.3154	.3111
.2	.3069	.3027	.2986	.2944	.2904	.2863	.2824	.2784	.2745	.2706
.3	.2668	.2630	.2592	.2555	.2518	.2481	.2445	.2409	.2374	.2339
.4	.2304	.2270	.2236	.2203	.2169	.2137	.2104	.2072	.2040	.2009
.5	.1978	.1947	.1917	.1887	.1857	.1828	.1799	.1771	.1742	.1714
.6	.1687	.1659	.1633	.1606	.1580	.1554	.1528	.1503	.1478	.1453
.7	.1429	.1405	.1381	.1358	.1334	.1312	.1289	.1267	.1245	.1223
.8	.1202	.1181	.1160	.1140	.1120	.1100	.1080	.1061	.1042	.1023
.9	.1004	.09860	.09680	.09503	.09328	.09156	.08986	.08819	.08654	.08491
1.0	.08332	.08174	.08019	.07866	.07716	.07568	.07422	.07279	.07138	.06999
1.1	.06862	.06727	.06595	.06465	.06336	.06210	.06086	.05964	.05844	.05726
1.2	.05610	.05496	.05384	.05274	.05165	.05059	.04954	.04851	.04750	.04650
1.3	.04553	.04457	.04363	.04270	.04179	.04090	.04002	.03916	.03831	.03748
1.4	.03667	.03587	.03508	.03431	.03356	.03281	.03208	.03137	.03067	.02998
1.5	.02931	.02865	.02800	.02736	.02674	.02612	.02552	.02494	.02436	.02380
1.6	.02324	.02270	.02217	.02165	.02114	.02064	.02015	.01967	.01920	.01874
1.7	.01829	.01785	.01742	.01699	.01658	.01617	.01578	.01539	.01501	.01464
1.8	.01428	.01392	.01357	.01323	.01290	.01257	.01226	.01195	.01164	.01134
1.9	.01105	.01077	.01049	.01022	$.0^2 9957$	$.0^2 9698$	$.0^2 9445$	$.0^2 9198$	$.0^2 8957$	$.0^2 8721$
2.0	$.0^2 8491$	$.0^2 8266$	$.0^2 8046$	$.0^2 7832$	$.0^2 7623$	$.0^2 7418$	$.0^2 7219$	$.0^2 7024$	$.0^2 6835$	$.0^2 6649$
2.1	$.0^2 6468$	$.0^2 6292$	$.0^2 6120$	$.0^2 5952$	$.0^2 5788$	$.0^2 5628$	$.0^2 5472$	$.0^2 5320$	$.0^2 5172$	$.0^2 5028$
2.2	$.0^2 4887$	$.0^2 4750$	$.0^2 4616$	$.0^2 4486$	$.0^2 4358$	$.0^2 4235$	$.0^2 4114$	$.0^2 3996$	$.0^2 3882$	$.0^2 3770$
2.3	$.0^2 3662$	$.0^2 3556$	$.0^2 3453$	$.0^2 3352$	$.0^2 3255$	$.0^2 3159$	$.0^2 3067$	$.0^2 2977$	$.0^2 2889$	$.0^2 2804$
2.4	$.0^2 2720$	$.0^2 2640$	$.0^2 2561$	$.0^2 2484$	$.0^2 2410$	$.0^2 2337$	$.0^2 2267$	$.0^2 2199$	$.0^2 2132$	$.0^2 2067$
2.5	$.0^2 2004$	$.0^2 1943$	$.0^2 1883$	$.0^2 1826$	$.0^2 1769$	$.0^2 1715$	$.0^2 1662$	$.0^2 1610$	$.0^2 1560$	$.0^2 1511$
2.6	$.0^2 1464$	$.0^2 1418$	$.0^2 1373$	$.0^2 1330$	$.0^2 1288$	$.0^2 1247$	$.0^2 1207$	$.0^2 1169$	$.0^2 1132$	$.0^2 1095$
2.7	$.0^2 1060$	$.0^2 1026$	$.0^3 9928$	$.0^3 9607$	$.0^3 9295$	$.0^3 8992$	$.0^3 8699$	$.0^3 8414$	$.0^3 8138$	$.0^3 7870$
2.8	$.0^3 7611$	$.0^3 7359$	$.0^3 7115$	$.0^3 6879$	$.0^3 6650$	$.0^3 6428$	$.0^3 6213$	$.0^3 6004$	$.0^3 5802$	$.0^3 5606$
2.9	$.0^3 5417$	$.0^3 5233$	$.0^3 5055$	$.0^3 4883$	$.0^3 4716$	$.0^3 4555$	$.0^3 4398$	$.0^3 4247$	$.0^3 4101$	$.0^3 3959$
3.0	$.0^3 3822$	$.0^3 3689$	$.0^3 3560$	$.0^3 3436$	$.0^3 3316$	$.0^3 3199$	$.0^3 3087$	$.0^3 2978$	$.0^3 2873$	$.0^3 2771$
3.1	$.0^3 2673$	$.0^3 2577$	$.0^3 2485$	$.0^3 2396$	$.0^3 2311$	$.0^3 2227$	$.0^3 2147$	$.0^3 2070$	$.0^3 1995$	$.0^3 1922$
3.2	$.0^3 1852$	$.0^3 1785$	$.0^3 1720$	$.0^3 1657$	$.0^3 1596$	$.0^3 1537$	$.0^3 1480$	$.0^3 1426$	$.0^3 1373$	$.0^3 1322$
3.3	$.0^3 1273$	$.0^3 1225$	$.0^3 1179$	$.0^3 1135$	$.0^3 1093$	$.0^3 1051$	$.0^3 1012$	$.0^4 9734$	$.0^4 9365$	$.0^4 9009$
3.4	$.0^4 8666$	$.0^4 8335$	$.0^4 8016$	$.0^4 7709$	$.0^4 7413$	$.0^4 7127$	$.0^4 6852$	$.0^4 6587$	$.0^4 6331$	$.0^4 6085$

TABLE 2-2 (Cont'd)
Unit Normal Loss Integral
$$G(u) = P'_N(u) - uP_N(\tilde{u} > u)$$

u	.00	.01	.02	.03	.04	.05	.06	.07	.08	.09
3.5	$.0^4 5848$	$.0^4 5620$	$.0^4 5400$	$.0^4 5188$	$.0^4 4984$	$.0^4 4788$	$.0^4 4599$	$.0^4 4417$	$.0^4 4242$	$.0^4 4073$
3.6	$.0^4 3911$	$.0^4 3755$	$.0^4 3605$	$.0^4 3460$	$.0^4 3321$	$.0^4 3188$	$.0^4 3059$	$.0^4 2935$	$.0^4 2816$	$.0^4 2702$
3.7	$.0^4 2592$	$.0^4 2486$	$.0^4 2385$	$.0^4 2287$	$.0^4 2193$	$.0^4 2103$	$.0^4 2016$	$.0^4 1933$	$.0^4 1853$	$.0^4 1776$
3.8	$.0^4 1702$	$.0^4 1632$	$.0^4 1563$	$.0^4 1498$	$.0^4 1435$	$.0^4 1375$	$.0^4 1317$	$.0^4 1262$	$.0^4 1208$	$.0^4 1157$
3.9	$.0^4 1108$	$.0^4 1061$	$.0^4 1016$	$.0^5 9723$	$.0^5 9307$	$.0^5 8908$	$.0^5 8525$	$.0^5 8158$	$.0^5 7806$	$.0^5 7469$
4.0	$.0^5 7145$	$.0^5 6835$	$.0^5 6538$	$.0^5 6253$	$.0^5 5980$	$.0^5 5718$	$.0^5 5468$	$.0^5 5227$	$.0^5 4997$	$.0^5 4777$
4.1	$.0^5 4566$	$.0^5 4364$	$.0^5 4170$	$.0^5 3985$	$.0^5 3807$	$.0^5 3637$	$.0^5 3475$	$.0^5 3319$	$.0^5 3170$	$.0^5 3027$
4.2	$.0^5 2891$	$.0^5 2760$	$.0^5 2635$	$.0^5 2516$	$.0^5 2402$	$.0^5 2292$	$.0^5 2188$	$.0^5 2088$	$.0^5 1992$	$.0^5 1901$
4.3	$.0^5 1814$	$.0^5 1730$	$.0^5 1650$	$.0^5 1574$	$.0^5 1501$	$.0^5 1431$	$.0^5 1365$	$.0^5 1301$	$.0^5 1241$	$.0^5 1183$
4.4	$.0^5 1127$	$.0^5 1074$	$.0^5 1024$	$.0^6 9756$	$.0^6 9296$	$.0^6 8857$	$.0^6 8437$	$.0^6 8037$	$.0^6 7655$	$.0^6 7290$
4.5	$.0^6 6942$	$.0^6 6610$	$.0^6 6294$	$.0^6 5992$	$.0^6 5704$	$.0^6 5429$	$.0^6 5167$	$.0^6 4917$	$.0^6 4679$	$.0^6 4452$
4.6	$.0^6 4236$	$.0^6 4029$	$.0^6 3833$	$.0^6 3645$	$.0^6 3467$	$.0^6 3297$	$.0^6 3135$	$.0^6 2981$	$.0^6 2834$	$.0^6 2694$
4.7	$.0^6 2560$	$.0^6 2433$	$.0^6 2313$	$.0^6 2197$	$.0^6 2088$	$.0^6 1984$	$.0^6 1884$	$.0^6 1790$	$.0^6 1700$	$.0^6 1615$
4.8	$.0^6 1533$	$.0^6 1456$	$.0^6 1382$	$.0^6 1312$	$.0^6 1246$	$.0^6 1182$	$.0^6 1122$	$.0^6 1065$	$.0^6 1011$	$.0^7 9588$
4.9	$.0^7 9096$	$.0^7 8629$	$.0^7 8185$	$.0^7 7763$	$.0^7 7362$	$.0^7 6982$	$.0^7 6620$	$.0^7 6276$	$.0^7 5950$	$.0^7 5640$

$$G(-u) = u + G(u)$$
Examples: $G(3.57) = .0^4 4417 = .00004417$
$$G(-3.57) = 3.57004417$$

Calculation of Safety Stocks—Slow Movers

With slow-moving products, calculation of safety stocks moves along another path. The distribution of lead time demand follows a different distribution pattern called the Poisson distribution. To arrive at safety stock levels, we must derive parameters related to that distribution of demand patterns. Again the reader not interested in derivations is invited to skip to page 74, where the use of the method begins.

Before proceeding with the development of the safety stock formulas, we will again set up certain needed definitions:

(1) In terms of our problem, the Poisson probability function is

$$pX_1 T_1 = e^{-\theta}\theta^{X_1} / X_1!, \tag{2-33}$$

where for convenience in writing future equations we have substituted θ for $X_1 T_1$.

(2) For a Poisson distribution, the variance is equal to the mean, and thus the standard deviation is

$$\sigma = \sqrt{X_1 T_1}. \tag{2-34}$$

(3) The service protection level is again ϕ, a decimal lying between 0 and 1.00.

To start the derivation, we shall state:

$$\sum_{I_s+1}^{\infty} (\theta - I_s)p\theta \leq (1 - \phi) \bar{X}_1 \bar{T}_1 \leq \theta - (I_s + 1)p\theta, \tag{2-35}$$

which says that probability of a given lead time demand times that lead time demand minus safety stock is equal to or less than one minus the protection level times the average demand during the average time to sell a replenishment quantity, which in turn is less than or equal to the probability of a lead time demand times that lead time demand minus safety stock plus one unit. Since we do not know I_s, we must proceed to convert eq. 2-35 to a form that we can use. The terms in eq. 2-35 will be referred to as left-hand (LH) member for the portion of the equation to the left of the first $\leq$ sign, as central member (CM) for the portion between $\leq$ signs, and the right-hand (RH) member:

$$\text{LH} = \sum_{I_s+1}^{\infty} (\theta - I_s)p\theta = \sum_{I_s+1}^{\infty} \theta\, p\theta - I_s \sum_{I_s}^{\infty} p\theta. \tag{2-36}$$

The term $\sum_{I_s+1}^{\infty} \theta\, p\theta$ can be expanded to:

$$(I_s + 1)p(I_s + 1) + (I_s + 2)p(I_s + 2) + \ldots\ldots (I_s + n)p(I_s + n). \tag{2-37}$$

With eq. 2-33 and factorial theory we can write

$$p(I_s + 1) = \frac{e^{-\theta} \theta^{(I_s + 1)}}{(I_s + 1)!}$$

$$= (e^{-\theta})\,(\theta^{I_s}/I_s!) = \theta\,/(I_s + 1)pI_s; \tag{2-38}$$

thus,

$$(I_s + 1)p(I_s + 1) = \theta\, pI_s. \tag{2-39}$$

All terms in eq. 2-38 may be similarly treated so that

$$\sum_{I_s+1}^{\infty} \theta\, p\theta = \theta\, pI_s + \theta\, p\,(I_s + 1)\ldots = \theta \sum_{I_s}^{\infty} p\theta, \qquad (2\text{-}40)$$

while

$$\sum_{I_s+1}^{\infty} p\theta = \sum_{I_s+1}^{\infty} p\theta - pI_s . \qquad (2\text{-}41)$$

We can now write LH member of eq. 2-35 as

$$\text{LH} = \theta \sum_{I_s}^{\infty} p\theta - I_s \sum_{I_s}^{\infty} p\theta - pI_s$$

$$= (\theta - I_s) \sum_{I_s}^{\infty} \theta\, p\theta - (I_s + 1) \sum_{I_s}^{\infty} p\theta . \qquad (2\text{-}42)$$

The right-hand member of eq. 2-35 is handled in the same manner and becomes

$$\text{RH} = (\theta - I_s + 1) \sum_{I_s}^{\infty} p\theta + I_s pI_s . \qquad (2\text{-}43)$$

The middle term can be changed if we remember that

$$\overline{X}_2 \overline{T}_2 = \overline{d}\,\overline{T}_2 = \overline{d}\,\overline{T}_2 (\overline{T}_1/\overline{T}_1) = \overline{d}\,\overline{T}_1 (\overline{T}_2/\overline{T}_1) = \theta\ (\overline{T}_2/\overline{T}_1). \qquad (2\text{-}44)$$

The values of the "right-hand" tail of the Poisson distribution are published in many statistical handbooks and we will use them. In order to make it easy, we will define

$$p' = \sum_{I_s}^{\infty} p\theta = p(\theta \geqslant I_s) = (1 - \phi)\,(I_s + 1). \qquad (2\text{-}45)$$

Now with eqs. 2-40, 2-41, 2-44, and 2-45, we can rewrite 2-35:

$$(\theta - I_s)p'I_s + I_s pI_s \leqslant (1 - \phi)\theta\,(\overline{T}_2/\,\overline{T}_1) \leqslant (\theta - I_s + 1)p'I_s + I_s p\,I_s \qquad (2\text{-}46)$$

or

$$\text{LH} \leqslant \text{CM} \leqslant \text{RH}.$$

This equation can be solved by trial-and-error methods, which will be demonstrated. It can be seen that slow-mover safety stocks are defined by θ, $\overline{T}_2/\overline{T}_1$, and ϕ.

We need fewer factors because of the nature of the Poisson distribution properties. The standard deviation and coefficient of variation are known when we have θ; hence, there is no need for Δ and λ. An inequality, such as eq. 2-46, is solved by selecting consecutive values of I_s and then choosing that value which satisfies it.

Use of Slow-Mover Method

We are now ready to calculate safety stock for a slow mover. Let us reconsider the data in the previous example above, except that lead time demand is now Poisson distribution with θ = 4. The other data remain unchanged; i.e., $\overline{T}_2$ = 12, $\overline{T}_1$ = 12, T_{max} + 15 and ϕ = 0.97. In that case, $\overline{T}_2/\overline{T}_1$ = 1.0.

Since $\sigma = \theta = 4$ and this yields a ϕ of 0.50, we must try higher values of I_s to reach a ϕ of 0.97. We will first try I_s = 5. Then:

$$\theta - I_s = 4 - 5 = -1$$

$$p'I_s = p' = 0.3712 \text{ from Table 2-3*}$$

$$\theta - I_s p' I_s = -1 \, (.3712) = -.3712$$

$$pI_s \qquad = p5 = 0.1563 \text{ from Table 2-4*}$$

$$I_s p I_s \qquad = 5 \times 0.1563 = 0.7815.$$

Then LH = -.3712 + .7815 = .4103

CM = (1 - 0.97) x 4 x 1 = .1200

RH = .4103 + .1563 = .5666.

Then $.4103 \nleq .1200 \leq .5666$ and the requirements of eq. 2-46 are not met. We must repeat the calculation, using I_s = 6, 7, 8, etc., until we find a value to satisfy eq. 2-48.

The various values are shown in Table 2-5, from which we see that safety stock level is 7 units.

---

*To use Table 2-3, look in the horizontal group heads opposite x' for 4.0 and in the vertical column below x' for 5. Where row 5 and column 4 intersect, find 0.3712. Use Table 2-4 in the same manner.

TABLE 2-3
Cumulative Terms, Poisson Distribution

λ

x'	0.1	0.2	0.3	0.4	0.5	0.6	0.7	0.8	0.9	1.0
0	1.0000	1.0000	1.0000	1.0000	1.0000	1.0000	1.0000	1.0000	1.0000	1.0000
1	.0952	.1813	.2592	.3297	.3935	.4512	.5034	.5507	.5934	.6321
2	.0047	.0175	.0369	.0616	.0902	.1219	.1558	.1912	.2275	.2642
3	.0002	.0011	.0036	.0079	.0144	.0231	.0341	.0474	.0629	.0803
4	.0000	.0001	.0003	.0008	.0018	.0034	.0058	.0091	.0135	.0190
5	.0000	.0000	.0000	.0001	.0002	.0004	.0008	.0014	.0023	.0037
6	.0000	.0000	.0000	.0000	.0000	.0000	.0001	.0002	.0003	.0006
7	.0000	.0000	.0000	.0000	.0000	.0000	.0000	.0000	.0000	.0001

λ

x'	1.1	1.2	1.3	1.4	1.5	1.6	1.7	1.8	1.9	2.0
0	1.0000	1.0000	1.0000	1.0000	1.0000	1.0000	1.0000	1.0000	1.0000	1.0000
1	.6671	.6988	.7275	.7534	.7769	.7981	.8173	.8347	.8504	.8647
2	.3010	.3374	.3732	.4082	.4422	.4751	.5068	.5372	.5663	.5940
3	.0996	.1205	.1429	.1665	.1912	.2166	.2428	.2694	.2963	.3233
4	.0257	.0338	.0431	.0537	.0656	.0788	.0932	.1087	.1253	.1429
5	.0054	.0077	.0107	.0143	.0186	.0237	.0296	.0364	.0441	.0527
6	.0010	.0015	.0022	.0032	.0045	.0060	.0080	.0104	.0132	.0166
7	.0001	.0003	.0004	.0006	.0009	.0013	.0019	.0026	.0034	.0045
8	.0000	.0000	.0001	.0001	.0002	.0003	.0004	.0006	.0008	.0011
9	.0000	.0000	.0000	.0000	.0000	.0000	.0001	.0001	.0002	.0002

λ

x'	2.1	2.2	2.3	2.4	2.5	2.6	2.7	2.8	2.9	3.0
0	1.0000	1.0000	1.0000	1.0000	1.0000	1.0000	1.0000	1.0000	1.0000	1.0000
1	.8775	.8892	.8997	.9093	.9179	.9257	.9328	.9392	.9450	.9502
2	.6204	.6454	.6691	.6916	.7127	.7326	.7513	.7689	.7854	.8009
3	.3504	.3773	.4040	.4303	.4562	.4816	.5064	.5305	.5540	.5768
4	.1614	.1806	.2007	.2213	.2424	.2640	.2859	.3081	.3304	.3528
5	.0621	.0725	.0838	.0959	.1088	.1226	.1371	.1523	.1682	.1847
6	.0204	.0249	.0300	.0357	.0420	.0490	.0567	.0651	.0742	.0839
7	.0059	.0075	.0094	.0116	.0142	.0172	.0206	.0244	.0287	.0335
8	.0015	.0020	.0026	.0033	.0042	.0053	.0066	.0081	.0099	.0119
9	.0003	.0005	.0006	.0009	.0011	.0015	.0019	.0024	.0031	.0038
10	.0001	.0001	.0001	.0002	.0003	.0004	.0005	.0007	.0009	.0011
11	.0000	.0000	.0000	.0000	.0001	.0001	.0001	.0002	.0002	.0003
12	.0000	.0000	.0000	.0000	.0000	.0000	.0000	.0000	.0001	.0001

TABLE 2-3 (Cont'd)
Cumulative Terms, Poisson Distribution

					λ					
x'	3.1	3.2	3.3	3.4	3.5	3.6	3.7	3.8	3.9	4.0
0	1.0000	1.0000	1.0000	1.0000	1.0000	1.0000	1.0000	1.0000	1.0000	1.0000
1	.9550	.9592	.9631	.9666	.9698	.9727	.9753	.9776	.9798	.9817
2	.8153	.8288	.8414	.8532	.8641	.8743	.8838	.8926	.9008	.9084
3	.5988	.6201	.6406	.6603	.6792	.6973	.7146	.7311	.7469	.7619
4	.3752	.3975	.4197	.4416	.4634	.4848	.5058	.5265	.5468	.5665
5	.2018	.2194	.2374	.2558	.2746	.2936	.3128	.3322	.3516	.3712
6	.0943	.1054	.1171	.1295	.1424	.1559	.1699	.1844	.1994	.2149
7	.0388	.0446	.0510	.0579	.0653	.0733	.0818	.0909	.1005	.1107
8	.0142	.0168	.0198	.0231	.0267	.0308	.0352	.0401	.0454	.0511
9	.0047	.0057	.0069	.0083	.0099	.0117	.0137	.0160	.0185	.0214
10	.0014	.0018	.0022	.0027	.0033	.0040	.0048	.0058	.0069	.0081
11	.0004	.0005	.0006	.0008	.0010	.0013	.0016	.0019	.0023	.0028
12	.0001	.0001	.0002	.0002	.0003	.0004	.0005	.0006	.0007	.0009
13	.0000	.0000	.0000	.0001	.0001	.0001	.0001	.0002	.0002	.0003
14	.0000	.0000	.0000	.0000	.0000	.0000	.0000	.0000	.0001	.0001

					λ					
x'	4.1	4.2	4.3	4.4	4.5	4.6	4.7	4.8	4.9	5.0
0	1.0000	1.0000	1.0000	1.0000	1.0000	1.0000	1.0000	1.0000	1.0000	1.0000
1	.9834	.9850	.9864	.9877	.9889	.9899	.9909	.9918	.9926	.9933
2	.9155	.9220	.9281	.9337	.9389	.9437	.9482	.9523	.9561	.9596
3	.7762	.7898	.8026	.8149	.8264	.8374	.8477	.8575	.8667	.8753
4	.5858	.6046	.6228	.6406	.6577	.6743	.6903	.7058	.7207	.7350
5	.3907	.4102	.4296	.4488	.4679	.4868	.5054	.5237	.5418	.5595
6	.2307	.2469	.2633	.2801	.2971	.3142	.3316	.3490	.3665	.3840
7	.1214	.1325	.1442	.1564	.1689	.1820	.1954	.2092	.2233	.2378
8	.0573	.0639	.0710	.0786	.0866	.0951	.1040	.1133	.1231	.1334
9	.0245	.0279	.0317	.0358	.0403	.0451	.0503	.0558	.0618	.0681
10	.0095	.0111	.0129	.0149	.0171	.0195	.0222	.0251	.0283	.0318
11	.0034	.0041	.0048	.0057	.0067	.0078	.0090	.0104	.0120	.0137
12	.0011	.0014	.0017	.0020	.0024	.0029	.0034	.0040	.0047	.0055
13	.0003	.0004	.0005	.0007	.0008	.0010	.0012	.0014	.0017	.0020
14	.0001	.0001	.0002	.0002	.0003	.0003	.0004	.0005	.0006	.0007
15	.0000	.0000	.0000	.0001	.0001	.0001	.0001	.0001	.0002	.0002
16	.0000	.0000	.0000	.0000	.0000	.0000	.0000	.0000	.0001	.0001

TABLE 2-3 (Cont'd)
Cumulative Terms, Poisson Distribution

λ

x'	5.1	5.2	5.3	5.4	5.5	5.6	5.7	5.8	5.9	6.0
0	1.0000	1.0000	1.0000	1.0000	1.0000	1.0000	1.0000	1.0000	1.0000	1.0000
1	.9939	.9945	.9950	.9955	.9959	.9963	.9967	.9970	.9973	.9975
2	.9628	.9658	.9686	.9711	.9734	.9756	.9776	.9794	.9811	.9826
3	.8835	.8912	.8984	.9052	.9116	.9176	.9232	.9285	.9334	.9380
4	.7487	.7619	.7746	.7867	.7983	.8094	.8200	.8300	.8396	.8488
5	.5769	.5939	.6105	.6267	.6425	.6579	.6728	.6873	.7013	.7149
6	.4016	.4191	.4365	.4539	.4711	.4881	.5050	.5217	.5381	.5543
7	.2526	.2676	.2829	.2983	.3140	.3297	.3456	.3616	.3776	.3937
8	.1440	.1551	.1665	.1783	.1905	.2030	.2159	.2290	.2424	.2560
9	.0748	.0819	.0894	.0974	.1056	.1143	.1234	.1328	.1426	.1528
10	.0356	.0397	.0441	.0488	.0538	.0591	.0648	.0708	.0772	.0839
11	.0156	.0177	.0200	.0225	.0253	.0282	.0314	.0349	.0386	.0426
12	.0063	.0073	.0084	.0096	.0110	.0125	.0141	.0160	.0179	.0201
13	.0024	.0028	.0033	.0038	.0045	.0051	.0059	.0068	.0078	.0088
14	.0008	.0010	.0012	.0014	.0017	.0020	.0023	.0027	.0031	.0036
15	.0003	.0003	.0004	.0005	.0006	.0007	.0009	.0010	.0012	.0014
16	.0001	.0001	.0001	.0002	.0002	.0002	.0003	.0004	.0004	.0005
17	.0000	.0000	.0000	.0001	.0001	.0001	.0001	.0001	.0001	.0002
18	.0000	.0000	.0000	.0000	.0000	.0000	.0000	.0000	.0000	.0001

λ

x'	6.1	6.2	6.3	6.4	6.5	6.6	6.7	6.8	6.9	7.0
0	1.0000	1.0000	1.0000	1.0000	1.0000	1.0000	1.0000	1.0000	1.0000	1.0000
1	.9978	.9980	.9982	.9983	.9985	.9986	.9988	.9989	.9990	.9991
2	.9841	.9854	.9866	.9877	.9887	.9897	.9905	.9913	.9920	.9927
3	.9423	.9464	.9502	.9537	.9570	.9600	.9629	.9656	.9680	.9704
4	.8575	.8658	.8736	.8811	.8882	.8948	.9012	.9072	.9129	.9182
5	.7281	.7408	.7531	.7649	.7763	.7873	.7978	.8080	.8177	.8270
6	.5702	.5859	.6012	.6163	.6310	.6453	.6594	.6730	.6863	.6993
7	.4098	.4258	.4418	.4577	.4735	.4892	.5047	.5201	.5353	.5503
8	.2699	.2840	.2983	.3127	.3272	.3419	.3567	.3715	.3864	.4013
9	.1633	.1741	.1852	.1967	.2084	.2204	.2327	.2452	.2580	.2709
10	.0910	.0984	.1061	.1142	.1226	.1314	.1404	.1498	.1505	.1695
11	.0469	.0514	.0563	.0614	.0668	.0726	.0786	.0849	.0916	.0985
12	.0224	.0250	.0277	.0307	.0339	.0373	.0409	.0448	.0490	.0534
13	.0100	.0113	.0127	.0143	.0160	.0179	.0199	.0221	.0245	.0270
14	.0042	.0048	.0055	.0063	.0071	.0080	.0091	.0102	.0115	.0128

TABLE 2-3 (Cont'd)
Cumulative Terms, Poisson Distribution

					λ					
x'	6.1	6.2	6.3	6.4	6.5	6.6	6.7	6.8	6.9	7.0
15	.0016	.0019	.0022	.0026	.0030	.0034	.0039	.0044	.0050	.0057
16	.0006	.0007	.0008	.0010	.0012	.0014	.0016	.0018	.0021	.0024
17	.0002	.0003	.0003	.0004	.0004	.0005	.0006	.0007	.0008	.0010
18	.0001	.0001	.0001	.0001	.0002	.0002	.0002	.0003	.0003	.0004
19	.0000	.0000	.0000	.0000	.0001	.0001	.0001	.0001	.0001	.0001

					λ					
x'	7.1	7.2	7.3	7.4	7.5	7.6	7.7	7.8	7.9	8.0
0	1.0000	1.0000	1.0000	1.0000	1.0000	1.0000	1.0000	1.0000	1.0000	1.0000
1	.9992	.9993	.9993	.9994	.9994	.9995	.9995	.9996	.9996	.9997
2	.9933	.9939	.9944	.9949	.9953	.9957	.9961	.9964	.9967	.9970
3	.9725	.9745	.9764	.0781	.9797	.9812	.9826	.9839	.9851	.9862
4	.9233	.9281	.9326	.9368	.9409	.9446	.9482	.9515	.9547	.9576
5	.8359	.8445	.8527	.8605	.8679	.8751	.8819	.8883	.8945	.9004
6	.7119	.7241	.7360	.7474	.7586	.7693	.7797	.7897	.7994	.8088
7	.5651	.5796	.5940	.6080	.6218	.6354	.6486	.6616	.6743	.6866
8	.4162	.4311	.4459	.4607	.4754	.4900	.5044	.5188	.5330	.5470
9	.2840	.2973	.3108	.3243	.3380	.3518	.3657	.3796	.3935	.4075
10	.1798	.1904	.2012	.2123	.2236	.2351	.2469	.2589	.2710	.2834
11	.1058	.1133	.1212	.1293	.1378	.1465	.1555	.1648	.1743	.1841
12	.0580	.0629	.0681	.0735	.0792	.0852	.0915	.0980	.1048	.1119
13	.0297	.0327	.0358	.0391	.0427	.0464	.0504	.0546	.0591	.0638
14	.0143	.0159	.0176	.0195	.0216	.0238	.0261	.0286	.0313	.0342
15	.0065	.0073	.0082	.0092	.0103	.0114	.0127	.0141	.0156	.0173
16	.0028	.0031	.0036	.0041	.0046	.0052	.0059	.0066	.0074	.0082
17	.0011	.0013	.0015	.0017	.0020	.0022	.0026	.0029	.0033	.0037
18	.0004	.0005	.0006	.0007	.0008	.0009	.0011	.0012	.0014	.0016
19	.0002	.0002	.0002	.0003	.0003	.0004	.0004	.0005	.0006	.0006
20	.0001	.0001	.0001	.0001	.0001	.0001	.0002	.0002	.0002	.0003
21	.0000	.0000	.0000	.0000	.0000	.0000	.0001	.0001	.0001	.0001

					λ					
x'	8.1	8.2	8.3	8.4	8.5	8.6	8.7	8.8	8.9	9.0
0	1.0000	1.0000	1.0000	1.0000	1.0000	1.0000	1.0000	1.0000	1.0000	1.0000
1	.9997	.9997	.9998	.9998	.9998	.9998	.9998	.9998	.9999	.9999
2	.9972	.9975	.9977	.9979	.9981	.9982	.9984	.9985	.9987	.9988
3	.9873	.9882	.9891	.9900	.9907	.9914	.9921	.9927	.9932	.9938
4	.9604	.9630	.9654	.9677	.9699	.9719	.9738	.9756	.9772	.9788

TABLE 2-3 (Cont'd)
Cumulative Terms, Poisson Distribution

λ

x'	8.1	8.2	8.3	8.4	8.5	8.6	8.7	8.8	8.9	9.0
5	.9060	.9113	.9163	.9211	.9256	.9299	.9340	.9379	.9416	.9450
6	.8178	.8264	.8347	.8427	.8504	.8578	.8648	.8716	.8781	.8843
7	.6987	.7104	.7219	.7330	.7438	.7543	.7645	.7744	.7840	.7932
8	.5609	.5746	.5881	.6013	.6144	.6272	.6398	.6522	.6643	.6761
9	.4214	.4353	.4493	.4631	.4769	.4906	.5042	.5177	.5311	.5443
10	.2959	.3085	.3212	.3341	.3470	.3600	.3731	.3863	.3994	.4126
11	.1942	.2045	.2150	.2257	.2366	.2478	.2591	.2706	.2822	.2940
12	.1193	.1269	.1348	.1429	.1513	.1600	.1689	.1780	.1874	.1970
13	.0687	.0739	.0793	.0850	.0909	.0971	.1035	.1102	.1171	.1242
14	.0372	.0405	.0439	.0476	.0514	.0555	.0597	.0642	.0689	.0739
15	.0190	.0209	.0229	.0251	.0274	.0299	.0325	.0353	.0383	.0415
16	.0092	.0102	.0113	.0125	.0138	.0152	.0168	.0184	.0202	.0220
17	.0042	.0047	.0053	.0059	.0066	.0074	.0082	.0091	.0101	.0111
18	.0018	.0021	.0023	.0027	.0030	.0034	.0038	.0043	.0048	.0053
19	.0008	.0009	.0010	.0011	.0013	.0015	.0017	.0019	.0022	.0024
20	.0003	.0003	.0004	.0005	.0005	.0006	.0007	.0008	.0009	.0011
21	.0001	.0001	.0002	.0002	.0002	.0002	.0003	.0003	.0004	.0004
22	.0000	.0000	.0001	.0001	.0001	.0001	.0001	.0001	.0002	.0002
23	.0000	.0000	.0000	.0000	.0000	.0000	.0000	.0000	.0001	.0001

λ

x'	9.1	9.2	9.3	9.4	9.5	9.6	9.7	9.8	9.9	10
0	1.0000	1.0000	1.0000	1.0000	1.0000	1.0000	1.0000	1.0000	1.0000	1.0000
1	.9999	.9999	.9999	.9999	.9999	.9999	.9999	.9999	1.0000	1.0000
2	.9989	.9990	.9991	.9991	.9992	.9993	.9993	.9994	.9995	.9995
3	.9942	.9947	.9951	.9955	.9958	.9962	.9965	.9967	.9970	.9972
4	.9802	.9816	.9828	.9840	.9851	.9862	.9871	.9880	.9889	.9897
5	.9483	.9514	.9544	.9571	.9597	.9622	.9645	.9667	.9688	.9707
6	.8902	.8959	.9014	.9065	.9115	.9162	.9207	.9250	.9290	.9329
7	.8022	.8108	.8192	.8273	.8351	.8426	.8498	.8567	.8634	.8699
8	.6877	.6990	.7101	.7208	.7313	.7416	.7515	.7612	.7706	.7798
9	.5574	.5704	.5832	.5958	.6082	.6204	.6324	.6442	.6558	.6672
10	.4258	.4389	.4521	.4651	.4782	.4911	.5040	.5168	.5295	.5421
11	.3059	.3180	.3301	.3424	.3547	.3671	.3795	.3920	.4045	.4170
12	.2068	.2168	.2270	.2374	.2480	.2588	.2697	.2807	.2919	.3032
13	.1316	.1393	.1471	.1552	.1636	.1721	.1809	.1899	.1991	.2084
14	.0790	.0844	.0900	.0958	.1019	.1081	.1147	.1214	.1284	.1355

TABLE 2-3 (Cont'd)
Cumulative Terms, Poisson Distribution

λ

x'	9.1	9.2	9.3	9.4	9.5	9.6	9.7	9.8	9.9	10
15	.0448	.0483	.0520	.0559	.0600	.0643	.0688	.0735	.0784	.0835
16	.0240	.0262	.0285	.0309	.0335	.0362	.0391	.0421	.0454	.0487
17	.0122	.0135	.0148	.0162	.0177	.0194	.0211	.0230	.0249	.0270
18	.0059	.0066	.0073	.0081	.0089	.0098	.0108	.0119	.0130	.0143
19	.0027	.0031	.0034	.0038	.0043	.0048	.0053	.0059	.0065	.0072
20	.0012	.0014	.0015	.0017	.0020	.0022	.0025	.0028	.0031	.0035
21	.0005	.0006	.0007	.0008	.0009	.0010	.0011	.0013	.0014	.0016
22	.0002	.0002	.0003	.0003	.0004	.0004	.0005	.0005	.0006	.0007
23	.0001	.0001	.0001	.0001	.0001	.0002	.0002	.0002	.0003	.0003
24	.0000	.0000	.0000	.0000	.0001	.0001	.0001	.0001	.0001	.0001

λ

x'	11	12	13	14	15	16	17	18	19	20
0	1.0000	1.0000	1.0000	1.0000	1.0000	1.0000	1.0000	1.0000	1.0000	1.0000
1	1.0000	1.0000	1.0000	1.0000	1.0000	1.0000	1.0000	1.0000	1.0000	1.0000
2	.9998	.9999	1.0000	1.0000	1.0000	1.0000	1.0000	1.0000	1.0000	1.0000
3	.9988	.9995	.9998	.9999	1.0000	1.0000	1.0000	1.0000	1.0000	1.0000
4	.9951	.9977	.9990	.9995	.9998	.9999	1.0000	1.0000	1.0000	1.0000
5	.9849	.9924	.9963	.9982	.9991	.9996	.9998	.9999	1.0000	1.0000
6	.9625	.9797	.9893	.9945	.9972	.9986	.9993	.9997	.9998	.9999
7	.9214	.9542	.9741	.9858	.9924	.9960	.9979	.9990	.9995	.9997
8	.8568	.9105	.9460	.9684	.9820	.9900	.9946	.9971	.9985	.9992
9	.7680	.8450	.9002	.9379	.9626	.9780	.9874	.9929	.9961	.9979
10	.6595	.7576	.8342	.8906	.9301	.9567	.9739	.9846	.9911	.9950
11	.5401	.6528	.7483	.8243	.8815	.9226	.9509	.9696	.9817	.9892
12	.4207	.5384	.6468	.7400	.8152	.8730	.9153	.9451	.9653	.9786
13	.3113	.4240	.5369	.6415	.7324	.8069	.8650	.9083	.9394	.9610
14	.2187	.3185	.4270	.5356	.6368	.7255	.7991	.8574	.9016	.9339
15	.1460	.2280	.3249	.4296	.5343	.6325	.7192	.7919	.8503	.8951
16	.0926	.1556	.2364	.3306	.4319	.5333	.6285	.7133	.7852	.8435
17	.0559	.1013	.1645	.2441	.3359	.4340	.5323	.6250	.7080	.7789
18	.0322	.0630	.1095	.1728	.2511	.3407	.4360	.5314	.6216	.7030
19	.0177	.0374	.0698	.1174	.1805	.2577	.3450	.4378	.5305	.6186
20	.0093	.0213	.0427	.0765	.1248	.1878	.2637	.3491	.4394	.5297
21	.0047	.0116	.0250	.0479	.0830	.1318	.1945	.2693	.3528	.4409
22	.0023	.0061	.0141	.0288	.0531	.0892	.1385	.2009	.2745	.3563
23	.0010	.0030	.0076	.0167	.0327	.0582	.0953	.1449	.2069	.2794
24	.0005	.0015	.0040	.0093	.0195	.0367	.0633	.1011	.1510	.2125

TABLE 2-3 (Cont'd)
Cumulative Terms, Poisson Distribution

					λ					
x'	11	12	13	14	15	16	17	18	19	20
25	.0002	.0007	.0020	.0050	.0112	.0223	.0406	.0683	.1067	.1568
26	.0001	.0003	.0010	.0026	.0062	.0131	.0252	.0446	.0731	.1122
27	.0000	.0001	.0005	.0013	.0033	.0075	.0152	.0282	.0486	.0779
28	.0000	.0001	.0002	.0006	.0017	.0041	.0088	.0173	.0313	.0525
29	.0000	.0000	.0001	.0003	.0009	.0022	.0050	.0103	.0195	.0343
30	.0000	.0000	.0000	.0001	.0004	.0011	.0027	.0059	.0118	.0218
31	.0000	.0000	.0000	.0001	.0002	.0006	.0014	.0033	.0070	.0135
32	.0000	.0000	.0000	.0000	.0001	.0003	.0007	.0018	.0040	.0081
33	.0000	.0000	.0000	.0000	.0000	.0001	.0004	.0010	.0022	.0047
34	.0000	.0000	.0000	.0000	.0000	.0001	.0002	.0005	.0012	.0027
35	.0000	.0000	.0000	.0000	.0000	.0000	.0001	.0002	.0006	.0015
36	.0000	.0000	.0000	.0000	.0000	.0000	.0000	.0001	.0003	.0008
37	.0000	.0000	.0000	.0000	.0000	.0000	.0000	.0001	.0002	.0004
38	.0000	.0000	.0000	.0000	.0000	.0000	.0000	.0000	.0001	.0002
39	.0000	.0000	.0000	.0000	.0000	.0000	.0000	.0000	.0000	.0001
40	.0000	.0000	.0000	.0000	.0000	.0000	.0000	.0000	.0000	.0001

From *Handbook of Tables for Probability and Statistics.*
The Chemical Rubber Co., Cleveland, Ohio. Copyright 1966, 1968. Used by permission.

TABLE 2-4
Individual Terms, Poisson Distribution

					λ					
x	0.1	0.2	0.3	0.4	0.5	0.6	0.7	0.8	0.9	1.0
0	.9048	.8187	.7408	.6703	.6065	.5488	.4966	.4493	.4066	.3679
1	.0905	.1637	.2222	.2681	.3033	.3293	.3476	.3595	.3659	.3679
2	.0045	.0164	.0333	.0536	.0758	.0988	.1217	.1438	.1647	.1839
3	.0002	.0011	.0033	.0072	.0126	.0198	.0284	.0383	.0494	.0613
4	.0000	.0001	.0003	.0007	.0016	.0030	.0050	.0077	.0111	.0153
5	.0000	.0000	.0000	.0001	.0002	.0004	.0007	.0012	.0020	.0031
6	.0000	.0000	.0000	.0000	.0000	.0000	.0001	.0002	.0003	.0005
7	.0000	.0000	.0000	.0000	.0000	.0000	.0000	.0000	.0000	.0001

TABLE 2-4 (Cont'd)
Individual Terms, Poisson Distribution

λ

x	1.1	1.2	1.3	1.4	1.5	1.6	1.7	1.8	1.9	2.0
0	.3329	.3012	.2725	.2466	.2231	.2019	.1827	.1653	.1496	.1353
1	.3662	.3614	.3543	.3452	.3347	.3230	.3106	.2975	.2842	.2707
2	.2014	.2169	.2303	.2417	.2510	.2584	.2640	.2678	.2700	.2707
3	.0738	.0867	.0998	.1128	.1255	.1378	.1496	.1607	.1710	.1804
4	.0203	.0260	.0324	.0395	.0471	.0551	.0636	.0723	.0812	.0902
5	.0045	.0062	.0084	.0111	.0141	.0176	.0216	.0260	.0309	.0361
6	.0008	.0012	.0018	.0026	.0035	.0047	.0061	.0078	.0098	.0120
7	.0001	.0002	.0003	.0005	.0008	.0011	.0015	.0020	.0027	.0034
8	.0000	.0000	.0001	.0001	.0001	.0002	.0003	.0005	.0006	.0009
9	.0000	.0000	.0000	.0000	.0000	.0000	.0001	.0001	.0001	.0002

λ

x	2.1	2.2	2.3	2.4	2.5	2.6	2.7	2.8	2.9	3.0
0	.1225	.1108	.1003	.0907	.0821	.0743	.0672	.0608	.0550	.0498
1	.2572	.2438	.2306	.2177	.2052	.1931	.1815	.1703	.1596	.1494
2	.2700	.2681	.2652	.2613	.2565	.2510	.2450	.2384	.2314	.2240
3	.1890	.1966	.2033	.2090	.2138	.2176	.2205	.2225	.2237	.2240
4	.0992	.1082	.1169	.1254	.1336	.1414	.1488	.1557	.1622	.1680
5	.0417	.0476	.0538	.0602	.0668	.0735	.0804	.0872	.0940	.1008
6	.0146	.0174	.0206	.0241	.0278	.0319	.0362	.0407	.0455	.0504
7	.0044	.0055	.0068	.0083	.0099	.0118	.0139	.0163	.0188	.0216
8	.0011	.0015	.0019	.0025	.0031	.0038	.0047	.0057	.0068	.0081
9	.0003	.0004	.0005	.0007	.0009	.0011	.0014	.0018	.0022	.0027
10	.0001	.0001	.0001	.0002	.0002	.0003	.0004	.0005	.0006	.0008
11	.0000	.0000	.0000	.0000	.0000	.0001	.0001	.0001	.0002	.0002
12	.0000	.0000	.0000	.0000	.0000	.0000	.0000	.0000	.0000	.0001

λ

x	3.1	3.2	3.3	3.4	3.5	3.6	3.7	3.8	3.9	4.0
0	.0450	.0408	.0369	.0334	.0302	.0273	.0247	.0224	.0202	.0183
1	.1397	.1304	.1217	.1135	.1057	.0984	.0915	.0850	.0789	.0733
2	.2165	.2087	.2008	.1929	.1850	.1771	.1692	.1615	.1539	.1465
3	.2237	.2226	.2209	.2186	.2158	.2125	.2087	.2046	.2001	.1954
4	.1734	.1781	.1823	.1858	.1888	.1912	.1931	.1944	.1951	.1954
5	.1075	.1140	.1203	.1264	.1322	.1377	.1429	.1477	.1522	.1563
6	.0555	.0608	.0662	.0716	.0771	.0826	.0881	.0936	.0989	.1042
7	.0246	.0278	.0312	.0348	.0385	.0425	.0466	.0508	.0551	.0595
8	.0095	.0111	.0129	.0148	.0169	.0191	.0215	.0241	.0269	.0298
9	.0033	.0040	.0047	.0056	.0066	.0076	.0089	.0102	.0116	.0132

TABLE 2-4 (Cont'd)
Individual Terms, Poisson Distribution

λ

x	3.1	3.2	3.3	3.4	3.5	3.6	3.7	3.8	3.9	4.0
10	.0010	.0013	.0016	.0019	.0023	.0028	.0033	.0039	.0045	.0053
11	.0003	.0004	.0005	.0006	.0007	.0009	.0011	.0013	.0016	.0019
12	.0001	.0001	.0001	.0002	.0002	.0003	.0003	.0004	.0005	.0006
13	.0000	.0000	.0000	.0000	.0001	.0001	.0001	.0001	.0002	.0002
14	.0000	.0000	.0000	.0000	.0000	.0000	.0000	.0000	.0000	.0001

λ

x	4.1	4.2	4.3	4.4	4.5	4.6	4.7	4.8	4.9	5.0
0	.0166	.0150	.0136	.0123	.0111	.0101	.0091	.0082	.0074	.0067
1	.0679	.0630	.0583	.0540	.0500	.0462	.0427	.0395	.0365	.0337
2	.1393	.1323	.1254	.1188	.1125	.1063	.1005	.0948	.0894	.0842
3	.1904	.1852	.1798	.1743	.1687	.1631	.1574	.1517	.1460	.1404
4	.1951	.1944	.1933	.1917	.1898	.1875	.1849	.1820	.1789	.1755
5	.1600	.1633	.1662	.1687	.1708	.1725	.1738	.1747	.1753	.1755
6	.1093	.1143	.1191	.1237	.1281	.1323	.1362	.1398	.1432	.1462
7	.0640	.0686	.0732	.0778	.0824	.0869	.0914	.0959	.1002	.1044
8	.0328	.0360	.0393	.0428	.0463	.0500	.0537	.0575	.0614	.0653
9	.0150	.0168	.0188	.0209	.0232	.0255	.0280	.0307	.0334	.0363
10	.0061	.0071	.0081	.0092	.0104	.0118	.0132	.0147	.0164	.0181
11	.0023	.0027	.0032	.0037	.0043	.0049	.0056	.0064	.0073	.0082
12	.0008	.0009	.0011	.0014	.0016	.0019	.0022	.0026	.0030	.0034
13	.0002	.0003	.0004	.0005	.0006	.0007	.0008	.0009	.0011	.0013
14	.0001	.0001	.0001	.0001	.0002	.0002	.0003	.0003	.0004	.0005
15	.0000	.0000	.0000	.0000	.0001	.0001	.0001	.0001	.0001	.0002

λ

x	5.1	5.2	5.3	5.4	5.5	5.6	5.7	5.8	5.9	6.0
0	.0061	.0055	.0050	.0045	.0041	.0037	.0033	.0030	.0027	.0025
1	.0311	.0287	.0265	.0244	.0225	.0207	.0191	.0176	.0162	.0149
2	.0793	.0746	.0701	.0659	.0618	.0580	.0544	.0509	.0477	.0446
3	.1348	.1293	.1239	.1185	.1133	.1082	.1033	.0985	.0938	.0892
4	.1719	.1681	.1641	.1600	.1558	.1515	.1472	.1428	.1383	.1339
5	.1753	.1748	.1740	.1728	.1714	.1697	.1678	.1656	.1632	.1606
6	.1490	.1515	.1537	.1555	.1571	.1584	.1594	.1601	.1605	.1606
7	.1086	.1125	.1163	.1200	.1234	.1267	.1298	.1326	.1353	.1377
8	.0692	.0731	.0771	.0810	.0849	.0887	.0925	.0962	.0998	.1033
9	.0392	.0423	.0454	.0486	.0519	.0552	.0586	.0620	.0654	.0688

TABLE 2-4 (Cont'd)
Individual Terms, Poisson Distribution

λ

x	5.1	5.2	5.3	5.4	5.5	5.6	5.7	5.8	5.9	6.0
10	.0200	.0220	.0241	.0262	.0285	.0309	.0334	.0359	.0386	.0413
11	.0093	.0104	.0116	.0129	.0143	.0157	.0173	.0190	.0207	.0225
12	.0039	.0045	.0051	.0058	.0065	.0073	.0082	.0092	.0102	.0113
13	.0015	.0018	.0021	.0024	.0028	.0032	.0036	.0041	.0046	.0052
14	.0006	.0007	.0008	.0009	.0011	.0013	.0015	.0017	.0019	.0022
15	.0002	.0002	.0003	.0003	.0004	.0005	.0006	.0007	.0008	.0009
16	.0001	.0001	.0001	.0001	.0001	.0002	.0002	.0002	.0003	.0003
17	.0000	.0000	.0000	.0000	.0000	.0000	.0001	.0001	.0001	.0001

λ

x	6.1	6.2	6.3	6.4	6.5	6.6	6.7	6.8	6.9	7.0
0	.0022	.0020	.0018	.0017	.0015	.0014	.0012	.0011	.0010	.0009
1	.0137	.0126	.0116	.0106	.0098	.0090	.0082	.0076	.0070	.0064
2	.0417	.0390	.0364	.0340	.0318	.0296	.0276	.0258	.0240	.0223
3	.0848	.0806	.0765	.0726	.0688	.0652	.0617	.0584	.0552	.0521
4	.1294	.1249	.1205	.1162	.1118	.1076	.1034	.0992	.0952	.0912
5	.1579	.1549	.1519	.1487	.1454	.1420	.1385	.1349	.1314	.1277
6	.1605	.1601	.1595	.1586	.1575	.1562	.1546	.1529	.1511	.1490
7	.1399	.1418	.1435	.1450	.1462	.1472	.1480	.1486	.1489	.1490
8	.1066	.1099	.1130	.1160	.1188	.1215	.1240	.1263	.1284	.1304
9	.0723	.0757	.0791	.0825	.0858	.0891	.0923	.0954	.0985	.1014
10	.0441	.0469	.0498	.0528	.0558	.0588	.0618	.0649	.0679	.0710
11	.0245	.0265	.0285	.0307	.0330	.0353	.0377	.0401	.0426	.0452
12	.0124	.0137	.0150	.0164	.0179	.0194	.0210	.0227	.0245	.0264
13	.0058	.0065	.0073	.0081	.0089	.0098	.0108	.0119	.0130	.0142
14	.0025	.0029	.0033	.0037	.0041	.0046	.0052	.0058	.0064	.0071
15	.0010	.0012	.0014	.0016	.0018	.0020	.0023	.0026	.0029	.0033
16	.0004	.0005	.0005	.0006	.0007	.0008	.0010	.0011	.0013	.0014
17	.0001	.0002	.0002	.0002	.0003	.0003	.0004	.0004	.0005	.0006
18	.0000	.0001	.0001	.0001	.0001	.0001	.0001	.0002	.0002	.0002
19	.0000	.0000	.0000	.0000	.0000	.0000	.0000	.0001	.0001	.0001

λ

x	7.1	7.2	7.3	7.4	7.5	7.6	7.7	7.8	7.9	8.0
0	.0008	.0007	.0007	.0006	.0006	.0005	.0005	.0004	.0004	.0003
1	.0059	.0054	.0049	.0045	.0041	.0038	.0035	.0032	.0029	.0027
2	.0208	.0194	.0180	.0167	.0156	.0145	.0134	.0125	.0116	.0107
3	.0492	.0464	.0438	.0413	.0389	.0366	.0345	.0324	.0305	.0286
4	.0874	.0836	.0799	.0764	.0729	.0696	.0663	.0632	.0602	.0573

TABLE 2-4 (Cont'd)
Individual Terms, Poisson Distribution

λ

x	7.1	7.2	7.3	7.4	7.5	7.6	7.7	7.8	7.9	8.0
5	.1241	.1204	.1167	.1130	.1094	.1057	.1021	.0986	.0951	.0916
6	.1468	.1445	.1420	.1394	.1367	.1339	.1311	.1282	.1252	.1221
7	.1489	.1486	.1481	.1474	.1465	.1454	.1442	.1428	.1413	.1396
8	.1321	.1337	.1351	.1363	.1373	.1382	.1388	.1392	.1395	.1396
9	.1042	.1070	.1096	.1121	.1144	.1167	.1187	.1207	.1224	.1241
10	.0740	.0770	.0800	.0829	.0858	.0887	.0914	.0941	.0967	.0993
11	.0478	.0504	.0531	.0558	.0585	.0613	.0640	.0667	.0695	.0722
12	.0283	.0303	.0323	.0344	.0366	.0388	.0411	.0434	.0457	.0481
13	.0154	.0168	.0181	.0196	.0211	.0227	.0243	.0260	.0278	.0296
14	.0078	.0086	.0095	.0104	.0113	.0123	.0134	.0145	.0157	.0169
15	.0037	.0041	.0046	.0051	.0057	.0062	.0069	.0075	.0083	.0090
16	.0016	.0019	.0021	.0024	.0026	.0030	.0033	.0037	.0041	.0045
17	.0007	.0008	.0009	.0010	.0012	.0013	.0015	.0017	.0019	.0021
18	.0003	.0003	.0004	.0004	.0005	.0006	.0006	.0007	.0008	.0009
19	.0001	.0001	.0001	.0002	.0002	.0002	.0003	.0003	.0003	.0004
20	.0000	.0000	.0001	.0001	.0001	.0001	.0001	.0001	.0001	.0002
21	.0000	.0000	.0000	.0000	.0000	.0000	.0000	.0000	.0001	.0001

λ

x	8.1	8.2	8.3	8.4	8.5	8.6	8.7	8.8	8.9	9.0
0	.0003	.0003	.0002	.0002	.0002	.0002	.0002	.0002	.0001	.0001
1	.0025	.0023	.0021	.0019	.0017	.0016	.0014	.0013	.0012	.0011
2	.0100	.0092	.0086	.0079	.0074	.0068	.0063	.0058	.0054	.0050
3	.0269	.0252	.0237	.0222	.0208	.0195	.0183	.0171	.0160	.0150
4	.0544	.0517	.0491	.0466	.0443	.0420	.0398	.0377	.0357	.0337
5	.0882	.0849	.0816	.0784	.0752	.0722	.0692	.0663	.0635	.0607
6	.1191	.1160	.1128	.1097	.1066	.1034	.1003	.0972	.0941	.0911
7	.1378	.1358	.1338	.1317	.1294	.1271	.1247	.1222	.1197	.1171
8	.1395	.1392	.1388	.1382	.1375	.1366	.1356	.1344	.1332	.1318
9	.1256	.1269	.1280	.1290	.1299	.1306	.1311	.1315	.1317	.1318
10	.1017	.1040	.1063	.1084	.1104	.1123	.1140	.1157	.1172	.1186
11	.0749	.0776	.0802	.0828	.0853	.0878	.0902	.0925	.0948	.0970
12	.0505	.0530	.0555	.0579	.0604	.0629	.0654	.0679	.0703	.0728
13	.0315	.0334	.0354	.0374	.0395	.0416	.0438	.0459	.0481	.0504
14	.0182	.0196	.0210	.0225	.0240	.0256	.0272	.0289	.0306	.0324
15	.0098	.0107	.0116	.0126	.0136	.0147	.0158	.0169	.0182	.0194
16	.0050	.0055	.0060	.0066	.0072	.0079	.0086	.0093	.0101	.0109

TABLE 2-4 (Cont'd)
Individual Terms, Poisson Distribution

					λ					
x	8.1	8.2	8.3	8.4	8.5	8.6	8.7	8.8	8.9	9.0
17	.0024	.0026	.0029	.0033	.0036	.0040	.0044	.0048	.0053	.0058
18	.0011	.0012	.0014	.0015	.0017	.0019	.0021	.0024	.0026	.0029
19	.0005	.0005	.0006	.0007	.0008	.0009	.0010	.0011	.0012	.0014
20	.0002	.0002	.0002	.0003	.0003	.0004	.0004	.0005	.0005	.0006
21	.0001	.0001	.0001	.0001	.0001	.0002	.0002	.0002	.0002	.0003
22	.0000	.0000	.0000	.0000	.0001	.0001	.0001	.0001	.0001	.0001

					λ					
x	9.1	9.2	9.3	9.4	9.5	9.6	9.7	9.8	9.9	10
0	.0001	.0001	.0001	.0001	.0001	.0001	.0001	.0001	.0001	.0000
1	.0010	.0009	.0009	.0008	.0007	.0007	.0006	.0005	.0005	.0005
2	.0046	.0043	.0040	.0037	.0034	.0031	.0029	.0027	.0025	.0023
3	.0140	.0131	.0123	.0115	.0107	.0100	.0093	.0087	.0081	.0076
4	.0319	.0302	.0285	.0269	.0254	.0240	.0226	.0213	.0201	.0189
5	.0581	.0555	.0530	.0506	.0483	.0460	.0439	.0418	.0398	.0378
6	.0881	.0851	.0822	.0793	.0764	.0736	.0709	.0682	.0656	.0631
7	.1145	.1118	.1091	.1064	.1037	.1010	.0982	.0955	.0928	.0901
8	.1302	.1286	.1269	.1251	.1232	.1212	.1191	.1170	.1148	.1126
9	.1317	.1315	.1311	.1306	.1300	.1293	.1284	.1274	.1263	.1251
10	.1198	.1210	.1219	.1228	.1235	.1241	.1245	.1249	.1250	.1251
11	.0991	.1012	.1031	.1049	.1067	.1083	.1098	.1112	.1125	.1137
12	.0752	.0776	.0799	.0822	.0844	.0866	.0888	.0908	.0928	.0948
13	.0526	.0549	.0572	.0594	.0617	.0640	.0662	.0685	.0707	.0729
14	.0342	.0361	.0380	.0399	.0419	.0439	.0459	.0479	.0500	.0521
15	.0208	.0221	.0235	.0250	.0265	.0281	.0297	.0313	.0330	.0347
16	.0118	.0127	.0137	.0147	.0157	.0168	.0180	.0192	.0204	.0217
17	.0063	.0069	.0075	.0081	.0088	.0095	.0103	.0111	.0119	.0128
18	.0032	.0035	.0039	.0042	.0046	.0051	.0055	.0060	.0065	.0071
19	.0015	.0017	.0019	.0021	.0023	.0026	.0028	.0031	.0034	.0037
20	.0007	.0008	.0009	.0010	.0011	.0012	.0014	.0015	.0017	.0019
21	.0003	.0003	.0004	.0004	.0005	.0006	.0006	.0007	.0008	.0009
22	.0001	.0001	.0002	.0002	.0002	.0002	.0003	.0003	.0004	.0004
23	.0000	.0001	.0001	.0001	.0001	.0001	.0001	.0001	.0002	.0002
24	.0000	.0000	.0000	.0000	.0000	.0000	.0000	.0001	.0001	.0001

					λ					
x	11	12	13	14	15	16	17	18	19	20
0	.0000	.0000	.0000	.0000	.0000	.0000	.0000	.0000	.0000	.0000
1	.0002	.0001	.0000	.0000	.0000	.0000	.0000	.0000	.0000	.0000

TABLE 2-4 (Cont'd)
Individual Terms, Poisson Distribution

					λ					
x	11	12	13	14	15	16	17	18	19	20
2	.0010	.0004	.0002	.0001	.0000	.0000	.0000	.0000	.0000	.0000
3	.0037	.0018	.0008	.0004	.0002	.0001	.0000	.0000	.0000	.0000
4	.0102	.0053	.0027	.0013	.0006	.0003	.0001	.0001	.0000	.0000
5	.0224	.0127	.0070	.0037	.0019	.0010	.0005	.0002	.0001	.0001
6	.0411	.0255	.0152	.0087	.0048	.0026	.0014	.0007	.0004	.0002
7	.0646	.0437	.0281	.0174	.0104	.0060	.0034	.0018	.0010	.0005
8	.0888	.0655	.0457	.0304	.0194	.0120	.0072	.0042	.0024	.0013
9	.1085	.0874	.0661	.0473	.0324	.0213	.0135	.0083	.0050	.0029
10	.1194	.1048	.0859	.0663	.0486	.0341	.0230	.0150	.0095	.0058
11	.1194	.1144	.1015	.0844	.0663	.0496	.0355	.0245	.0164	.0106
12	.1094	.1144	.1099	.0984	.0829	.0661	.0504	.0368	.0259	.0176
13	.0926	.1056	.1099	.1060	.0956	.0814	.0658	.0509	.0378	.0271
14	.0728	.0905	.1021	.1060	.1024	.0930	.0800	.0655	.0514	.0387
15	.0534	.0724	.0885	.0989	.1024	.0992	.0906	.0786	.0650	.0516
16	.0367	.0543	.0719	.0866	.0960	.0992	.0963	.0884	.0772	.0646
17	.0237	.0383	.0550	.0713	.0847	.0934	.0963	.0936	.0863	.0760
18	.0145	.0256	.0397	.0554	.0706	.0830	.0909	.0936	.0911	.0844
19	.0084	.0161	.0272	.0409	.0557	.0699	.0814	.0887	.0911	.0888
20	.0046	.0097	.0177	.0286	.0418	.0559	.0692	.0798	.0866	.0888
21	.0024	.0055	.0109	.0191	.0299	.0426	.0560	.0684	.0783	.0846
22	.0012	.0030	.0065	.0121	.0204	.0310	.0433	.0560	.0676	.0769
23	.0006	.0016	.0037	.0074	.0133	.0216	.0320	.0438	.0559	.0669
24	.0003	.0008	.0020	.0043	.0083	.0144	.0226	.0328	.0442	.0557
25	.0001	.0004	.0010	.0024	.0050	.0092	.0154	.0237	.0336	.0446
26	.0000	.0002	.0005	.0013	.0029	.0057	.0101	.0164	.0246	.0343
27	.0000	.0001	.0002	.0007	.0016	.0034	.0063	.0109	.0173	.0254
28	.0000	.0000	.0001	.0003	.0009	.0019	.0038	.0070	.0117	.0181
29	.0000	.0000	.0001	.0002	.0004	.0011	.0023	.0044	.0077	.0125
30	.0000	.0000	.0000	.0001	.0002	.0006	.0013	.0026	.0049	.0083
31	.0000	.0000	.0000	.0000	.0001	.0003	.0007	.0015	.0030	.0054
32	.0000	.0000	.0000	.0000	.0001	.0001	.0004	.0009	.0018	.0034
33	.0000	.0000	.0000	.0000	.0000	.0001	.0002	.0005	.0010	.0020
34	.0000	.0000	.0000	.0000	.0000	.0000	.0001	.0002	.0006	.0012
35	.0000	.0000	.0000	.0000	.0000	.0000	.0000	.0001	.0003	.0007
36	.0000	.0000	.0000	.0000	.0000	.0000	.0000	.0001	.0002	.0004
37	.0000	.0000	.0000	.0000	.0000	.0000	.0000	.0000	.0001	.0002
38	.0000	.0000	.0000	.0000	.0000	.0000	.0000	.0000	.0000	.0001
39	.0000	.0000	.0000	.0000	.0000	.0000	.0000	.0000	.0000	.0001

From *Handbook of Tables for Probability and Statistics.*
The Chemical Rubber Co., Cleveland, Ohio. Copyright 1966, 1968. Used by permission.

TABLE 2-5
Sample Safety Stock Calculation, Slow Mover

I_s	$p'I_s$	$\theta-I_s$	$(\theta-I_s)p'I_s$	pI_s	I_spI_s	LH	RH	CM
5	.3712	-1	-.3712	.1563	.7815	.4103	.5666	.1200
6	.2149	-2	-.4298	.1043	.6252	.1954	.2997	.1200
7	.1107	-3	-.3321	.0595	.4165	.0844	.1439	.1200
8	.0540	-4	-.2044	.0298	.2384	.0340	.0638	.1200
9	.0214	-5	-.1070	.0132	.1188	.0118	.0250	.1200

Solution
I_s

5	.4103	$\nleqslant$	.1200	$\leqslant$	.7815	
6	.1954	$\nleqslant$	.1200	$\leqslant$	.2997	
7	.0844	$\leqslant$	.1200	$\leqslant$	.1439	← Only this value satisfies equation 21
8	.0340	$\leqslant$	.1200	$\nleqslant$	.0638	Therefore safety stock = 7 units
9	.0118	$\leqslant$	.1200	$\nleqslant$	.0250	

Notice that for normally distributed lead time demand at 95% protection against stock-out, the safety stock level is 30 units, while with the Poisson distributed lead time demand and 97% protection, the safety stock level is only 7. The importance of recognizing the difference in lead time demand distribution is plain. If you decide that all products have a normally distributed lead time demand, your inventories will be substantially higher than required for good customer service. On the other hand, if all calculations are based on the slow-moving formula, there will be too many stock-outs. Unfortunately, there are no easy solutions to managing inventory; however, see Chapter 7 for more on recognizing normal and Poisson distributions.

Setting Service Levels

In the foregoing discussion, protection levels of 95% and 97% were used. For the examples, the values were literally picked out of the air. With a real system, a more logical method is needed, and to do this, we need to know what it will cost to provide any given level of protection of customer service. Previously, we found that safety stock level could be derived from five factors: (1) desired protection level; (2) maximum average demand ratio; (3) maximum average lead time ratio; (4) average demand during average lead time; (5) the ratio of T_2/T_1. Factors two, three, four, and five can be obtained from historical data, but factor one must be reached through a set of calculations involving determination of $V_{X_1T_1}$, UNLI, and I_s. From these we can get the safety stock multiplier, $kV_{X_1T_1}$, and from a table of normal probability values (see

Table 2-6) look up the corresponding I_s index. With this index, we can calculate the imputed value of a back-ordered item:

$$C_b = C_h \, (\overline{T}_2 / T) \, / I_s \text{ index,}$$

where C_b = imputed dollar cost of a delayed item and the other terms are as already defined.

TABLE 2-6
Normal Probability Values*

t	$p(t)$	$P(t)$	$U(t)$	t	$p(t)$	$P(t)$	$U(t)$
0.00	0.399	0.500	0.399	.32	.379	.626	.259
.01	.399	.504	.393	.33	.378	.629	.255
.02	.399	.508	.389	.34	.377	.633	.252
.03	.399	.512	.384	.35	.375	.637	.248
.04	.399	.516	.379	.36	.374	.641	.245
.05	.398	.520	.374	.37	.373	.644	.241
.06	.398	.524	.370	.38	.371	.648	.237
.07	.398	.528	.365	.39	.370	.652	.234
.08	.398	.532	.360	.40	.368	.655	.230
.09	.397	.536	.356	.41	.367	.659	.227
.10	.397	.540	.351	.42	.365	.663	.224
.11	.397	.544	.346	.43	.364	.666	.220
.12	.396	.548	.341	.44	.362	.670	.217
.13	.396	.552	.337	.45	.361	.674	.214
.14	.395	.556	.333	.46	.359	.677	.210
.15	.395	.560	.328	.47	.357	.681	.207
.16	.394	.564	.324	.48	.356	.684	.204
.17	.393	.568	.320	.49	.354	.688	.201
.18	.393	.571	.315	.50	.352	.692	.198
.19	.392	.575	.311	.51	.350	.695	.195
.20	.391	.579	.307	.52	.349	.699	.192
.21	.390	.583	.303	.53	.347	.702	.189
.22	.389	.587	.299	.54	.345	.705	.186
.23	.389	.591	.294	.55	.343	.709	.183
.24	.388	.595	.290	.56	.341	.712	.180
.25	.387	.599	.286	.57	.339	.716	.177
.26	.386	.603	.282	.58	.337	.719	.174
.27	.385	.607	.278	.59	.335	.722	.171
.28	.384	.610	.274	.60	.333	.726	.169
.29	.383	.614	.271	.61	.331	.729	.166
.30	.381	.618	.267	.62	.329	.732	.163
.31	.380	.622	.263	.63	.327	.736	.161

*Columns t, p(t) and P(t) are from *Handbook of Tables for Probability and Statistics*, The Chemical Rubber Co., Cleveland, Ohio. Copyright 1966, 1968. Used by permission.
Column U(t) is from Prichard and Engle, *Modern Inventory Management*, John Wiley and Sons, Inc., New York, N.Y. Copyright 1965. Used by permission.

TABLE 2-6 (Cont'd)
Normal Probability Values

t	p(t)	P(t)	U(t)	t	p(t)	P(t)	U(t)
.64	.325	.739	.158	1.08	.223	.860	.071
.65	.323	.742	.155	1.09	.220	.862	.070
.66	.321	.745	.153	1.10	.218	.864	.069
.67	.319	.749	.150	1.11	.216	.867	.067
.68	.317	.752	.148	1.12	.213	.869	.066
.69	.314	.755	.145	1.13	.211	.871	.065
.70	.312	.758	.143	1.14	.208	.873	.063
.71	.310	.761	.141	1.15	.206	.875	.062
.72	.308	.764	.138	1.16	.204	.877	.061
.73	.306	.767	.136	1.17	.202	.879	.060
.74	.303	.770	.134	1.18	.199	.881	.059
.75	.301	.773	.131	1.19	.197	.883	.057
.76	.299	.776	.129	1.20	.194	.885	.056
.77	.297	.779	.127	1.21	.192	.887	.055
.78	.294	.782	.125	1.22	.190	.889	.054
.79	.292	.785	.122	1.23	.187	.891	.053
.80	.290	.788	.120	1.24	.185	.893	.052
.81	.287	.791	.118	1.25	.183	.894	.051
.82	.285	.794	.116	1.26	.180	.896	.050
.83	.283	.797	.114	1.27	.178	.898	.049
.84	.280	.800	.112	1.28	.176	.900	.048
.85	.278	.802	.110	1.29	.174	.902	.047
.86	.276	.805	.108	1.30	.171	.903	.046
.87	.273	.808	.106	1.31	.169	.905	.045
.88	.271	.811	.104	1.32	.167	.907	.044
.89	.269	.813	.102	1.33	.165	.908	.043
.90	.266	.816	.100	1.34	.163	.910	.042
.91	.264	.819	.099	1.35	.160	.912	.041
.92	.261	.821	.097	1.36	.158	.913	.040
.93	.259	.824	.095	1.37	.156	.915	.039
.94	.257	.826	.093	1.38	.154	.916	.038
.95	.254	.829	.092	1.39	.152	.918	.037
.96	.252	.832	.090	1.40	.150	.919	.037
.97	.249	.834	.088	1.41	.148	.921	.036
.98	.247	.837	.087	1.42	.146	.922	.035
.99	.244	.839	.085	1.43	.144	.924	.034
1.00	.242	.841	.083	1.44	.142	.925	.034
1.01	.240	.844	.082	1.45	.139	.927	.033
1.02	.237	.846	.080	1.46	.137	.928	.032
1.03	.235	.849	.079	1.47	.135	.929	.031
1.04	.232	.851	.077	1.48	.133	.931	.031
1.05	.230	.853	.076	1.49	.132	.932	.030
1.06	.228	.855	.074	1.50	.1295	.9332	.0293
1.07	.225	.857	.073	1.51	.1276	.9345	.0287

t	p(t)	P(t)	U(t)	t	p(t)	P(t)	U(t)
1.52	.1257	.9357	.0280	1.60	.1109	.9452	.0232
1.53	.1238	.9370	.0274	1.61	.1092	.9463	.0227
1.54	.1219	.9382	.0267	1.62	.1074	.9474	.0222
1.55	.1200	.9394	.0261	1.63	.1057	.9485	.0217
1.56	.1182	.9406	.0255	1.64	.1040	.9495	.0212
1.57	.1163	.9418	.0249	1.65	.1023	.9505	.0206
1.58	.1145	.9430	.0244	1.66	.1006	.9515	.0201
1.59	.1127	.9441	.0238	1.67	.0989	.9525	.0196

TABLE 2-6 (Cont'd)
Normal Probability Values

t	p(t)	P(t)	U(t)	t	p(t)	P(t)	U(t)
1.68	.0973	.9535	.0192	2.04	.0498	.9793	.0076
1.69	.0957	.9545	.0188	2.05	.0488	.9798	.0074
1.70	.0941	.9554	.0183	2.06	.0478	.9803	.0072
1.71	.0925	.9564	.0179	2.07	.0468	.9808	.0070
1.72	.0909	.9573	.0175	2.08	.0459	.9812	.0068
1.73	.0893	.9582	.0170	2.09	.0449	.9817	.0067
1.74	.0878	.9591	.0166	2.10	.0440	.9821	.0065
1.75	.0863	.9599	.0162	2.11	.0431	.9826	.0064
1.76	.0848	.9608	.0158	2.12	.0422	.9830	.0062
1.77	.0833	.9616	.0154	2.13	.0413	.9834	.0060
1.78	.0818	.9625	.0150	2.14	.0404	.9838	.0058
1.79	.0804	.9633	.0147	2.15	.0396	.9842	.0056
1.80	.0790	.9641	.0143	2.16	.0387	.9846	.0054
1.81	.0775	.9649	.0140	2.17	.0379	.9850	.0053
1.82	.0761	.9659	.0136	2.18	.0371	.9854	.0052
1.83	.0748	.9664	.0133	2.19	.0363	.9857	.0050
1.84	.0734	.9671	.0129	2.20	.0355	.9861	.0049
1.85	.0721	.9678	.0126	2.21	.0347	.9865	.0048
1.86	.0707	.9686	.0123	2.22	.0339	.9868	.0046
1.87	.0694	.9693	.0120	2.23	.0332	.9871	.0044
1.88	.0681	.9700	.0117	2.24	.0325	.9875	.0043
1.89	.0669	.9706	.0114	2.25	.0317	.9878	.0042
1.90	.0656	.9713	.0111	2.26	.0310	.9881	.0041
1.91	.0644	.9719	.0108	2.27	.0303	.9884	.0040
1.92	.0632	.9726	.0106	2.28	.0297	.9887	.0039
1.93	.0620	.9732	.0103	2.29	.0290	.9890	.0038
1.94	.0608	.9738	.0100	2.30	.0283	.9893	.0037
1.95	.0596	.9744	.0097	2.31	.0277	.9896	.0036
1.96	.0584	.9750	.0094	2.32	.0271	.9898	.0035
1.97	.0573	.9756	.0092	2.33	.0264	.9901	.0034
1.98	.0562	.9762	.0090	2.34	.0258	.9904	.0033
1.99	.0551	.9767	.0087	2.35	.0252	.9906	.0032
2.00	.0540	.9773	.0085	2.36	.0246	.9909	.0031
2.01	.0529	.9778	.0083	2.37	.0241	.9911	.0030
2.02	.0519	.9783	.0081	2.38	.0235	.9913	.0029
2.03	.0508	.9788	.0078	2.39	.0229	.9916	.0028

t	p(t)	P(t)	U(t)	t	p(t)	P(t)	U(t)
2.40	.0224	.9918	.0027	2.56	.0151	.9948	.0017
2.41	.0219	.9920	.0026	2.57	.0147	.9949	.0016
2.42	.0213	.9922	.0025	2.58	.0143	.9951	.0016
2.43	.0208	.9925	.0024	2.59	.0139	.9952	.0015
2.44	.0203	.9927	.0023	2.60	.0136	.9953	.0015
2.45	.0198	.9929	.0023	2.61	.0132	.9955	.0014
2.46	.0194	.9931	.0022	2.62	.0129	.9956	.0014
2.47	.0189	.9932	.0021	2.63	.0126	.9957	.0013
2.48	.0184	.9934	.0021	2.64	.0122	.9959	.0013
2.49	.0180	.9936	.0020	2.65	.0119	.9960	.0012
2.50	.0175	.9938	.0020	2.66	.0116	.9961	.0012
2.51	.0171	.9940	.0019	2.67	.0113	.9962	.0012
2.52	.0167	.9941	.0019	2.68	.0110	.9963	.0011
2.53	.0163	.9943	.0018	2.69	.0107	.9964	.0011
2.54	.0159	.9945	.0018	2.70	.0104	.9965	.0011
2.55	.0155	.9946	.0017	2.71	.0101	.9966	.0010

TABLE 2-6 (Cont'd)
Normal Probability Values

t	$p(t)$	$P(t)$	$U(t)$	t	$p(t)$	$P(t)$	$U(t)$
2.72	.0099	.9967	.0010	2.87	.0065	.9980	.0006
2.73	.0096	.9968	.0010	2.88	.0063	.9980	.0006
2.74	.0094	.9969	.0009	2.89	.0061	.9981	.0006
2.75	.0091	.9970	.0009	2.90	.0060	.9981	.0005
2.76	.0089	.9971	.0009	2.91	.0058	.9982	.0005
2.77	.0086	.9972	.0008	2.92	.0056	.9983	.0005
2.78	.0084	.9973	.0008	2.93	.0055	.9983	.0005
2.79	.0081	.9974	.0008	2.94	.0053	.9984	.0005
2.80	.0079	.9974	.0008	2.95	.0051	.9984	.0005
2.81	.0077	.9975	.0007	2.96	.0050	.9985	.0005
2.82	.0075	.9976	.0007	2.97	.0049	.9985	.0004
2.83	.0073	.9977	.0007	2.98	.0047	.9986	.0004
2.84	.0071	.9977	.0007	2.99	.0046	.9986	.0004
2.85	.0069	.9978	.0006	3.00	.0044	.9987	.0004
2.86	.0067	.9979	.0006				

For example, Product X has a unit inventory value of $17.60. The annual holding cost rate is 25%, giving us an annual dollar cost of holding a single unit of $4.40. The warehouse characteristics are:

T = 365 days.

$\overline{T}_2$ = 25 days.

$\overline{T}_1$ = 36 days.

$\overline{T}_2/\overline{T}_1$ = 0.7.

λ = 1.3.

T_{max} = 47.

X_{ann} = 132 units.

$\overline{X}_1 \overline{T}_1$ = 13 units.

Δ = 3.1.

$X_{max} \overline{T}_1$ = 40 units.

By calculation and reference tables, the following values are obtained:

ϕ	$V_{X_1 T_1}$	UNLI	k^*	$kV_{X_1 T_1}$	I_s index*	I_s	C_b
.999	0.77	.0009	2.75	2.12	.006	41	$48.39
.99	0.77	.0091	1.98	1.52	.028	33	$10.71
.97	0.77	.0273	1.53	1.18	.059	28	$ 5.08
.95	0.77	.0455	1.30	1.00	.083	26	$ 3.61
.90	0.77	.0909	.95	.73	.136	22	$ 2.21
.80	0.77	.1818	.55	.42	.224	18	$ 1.34

Now let's consider the various types of customers and their reactions to the warehouse being out of stock. The percentage breakdowns will have to be evaluated for your own situation, but for the example they are:

a. 25% of customers will wait until the next regular stock replenishment.

b. 20% of customers will accept suitable substitute, with added cost absorbed by vendor.

c. 40% of customers willing to accept shipment from more remote stocking point; freight to vendor account.

d. 5% of customers will pay freight from more remote point.

e. 10% of customers will place order elsewhere this time.

f. No customer will take his account elsewhere. (In this example, this type customer is ignored, as it usually takes persistent lack of service to drive a customer away.)

Following is a table which summarizes the preceding list:

Customer type	% demand	Estimated stock-out cost per unit
a	25	0
b	20	$ 5.00
c	40	$ 7.00
d	5	0
e	10	$12.00

The weighted stock-out cost = (.25 x 0) + (.20 x 5.00) + (.40 x 7.00) + (.05 x 0) + (.10 x 12.00) = $5.00.

Returning to our previous Product X example, we see that our weighted stock-out cost compares best with the 97% level of protection. However, suppose that a

*To find values of k and I_s, proceed as follows. In Table 2-6, look for the value UNLI = 0.0009 in the fourth column, and in the first column read 2.75 as the value of k. Calculate $kV_{X_1 T_1}$. Then look up the value .2.12 in column 1, and in column 4 read 0.0062 — the value of the I_s index. From the equation $C_b = C_h(T_2/T_1)I_s$ index, calculate the cost of a back order. Note that in the table there has been some rounding in the calculations.

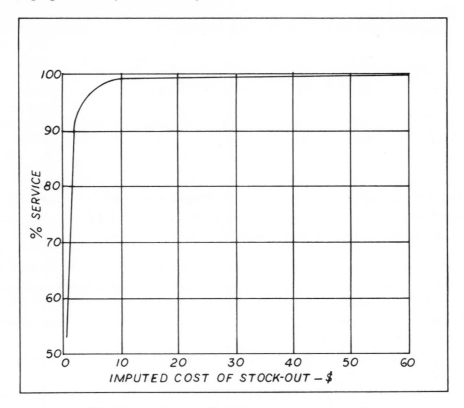

Figure 2-6. *Service level vs. stock-out cost, C_h.*

95% level of protection is selected. At the 97% level, we would expect to be short
(1 - .97) x 132 = 4 units, while at the 95% level we would have (1 - .95) x 132 = 6.6 units
less. Safety stock would decrease 2 units for an annual savings of 2 x $4.40 = $8.80,
while stock-out costs would increase 2.6 x $3.61 = $9.38. On the other hand, if a 99%
level were chosen, a similar calculation would show a 5-unit increase in inventory with
$22 cost, while the decrease in stock-outs (2.7) would save only $13.71. The same
reasoning applies to slow movers also.

Figure 2-6 shows the relationship between service level and the imputed cost of
stock-out. At low levels of service, the imputed stock-out costs are very low. One
might infer that low levels of service are more economical, but we have already put
together an analysis showing a per-unit stock-out cost for Product X of $5. Thus, im-
puted stock-out costs lower than this value must be considered unreal.

Figure 2-7 shows the relationship between service level and the cost of holding,
C_h, for Product X. Since the C_h has been taken as 25%, the full inventory value of safety
stock follows the same curve but with dollar values multiplied by four. It can be seen
that safety stock required to improve service from the 60% level to the 95% level is
about the same as that required to move from the 95 to the 99.9% level. The latter
investment is not very attractive.

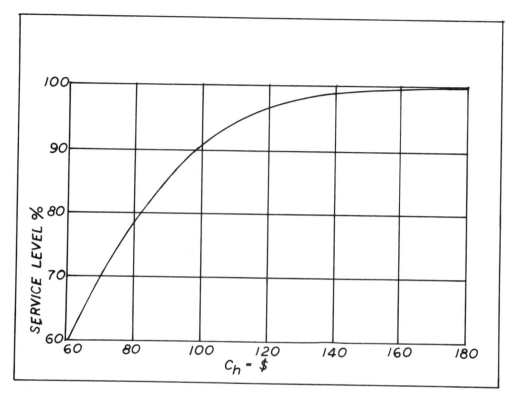

Figure 2-7. *Service level vs. C_h of safety stock.*

Going through these calculations for every item in a multi-SKU inventory will be very time-consuming. Practically, the inventory is categorized into a number of groups, say with monthly sales at up to $25, $26 to $100, $101 to $500, $501 to $2,000, etc. Then a sampling of calculations is made for each group, which is averaged. In this way, a group level of service can be determined.

If a general rule-of-thumb can be cited, it would be that the higher-volume products would have higher safety stock protection; i.e., 97-98-99%, and the slow-moving items would be in the 80-90% range. The reason for this is that typically 15% of the products account for 65-75% of the warehouse volume and there should be stock available to meet practically all demands. Where the volume is high enough and there are many warehouses, most of the safety stock may in effect be held at the factory for all locations and a pipeline resupply concept adopted. For slow-moving items, we have already seen that safety stocks are typically low, but if low levels of service are acceptable, it might pay to try even lower levels.

In reviewing actual service levels at a number of large warehousing operations, it was found that service levels averaged between 88% and 92% across the whole line of products. For the whole line, service will drop to the 88% level when demand is very high and rise to the 92% level when demand slows. Within this range, inventory managers have attempted to maintain high availability for their fast movers, and they have not worried too much about stock-outs on their slow-moving items. Many inventory managers have private goals of 95% service levels, but all confess that management is generally reluctant to invest the added working capital to achieve that goal.

Reorder Point

Since we have established the safety stock level and we know the average demand during the average lead time, the reorder point is:

$$\text{OP} = I_s + \bar{X}_1/\bar{T}_1 .$$

Returning to our Product X example, at 95% service level, I_s is 26 and $\bar{X}_1|\bar{T}_1 = 13$. The order point is $26 + 13 = 39$ units.

Replenishment (Order) Quantity

If we consider a warehouse which handles a substantial number of SKU's obtained from a single factory, and stock is being replenished at some fairly regular interval in truckload quantities, the order quantity is merely the average quantity sold between the receipt of shipments, plus any depletion of the safety stock or minus any short fall of actual sales, vs. $\bar{X}_1/\bar{T}_1$. However, it is not unusual to find in a warehouse receiving the bulk of its replenishment from one factory that some items are replenished from several other sources. The order point for these items will again be $I_s + \bar{X}_1/\bar{T}_1$, but it is likely that replenishment quantity is something less than a full truckload. To determine the best order quantity — i.e., the quantity which is most economical to obtain — we must resort to the economic order quantity formula. This is written:

$$\text{EOQ} = \sqrt{2C_o \bullet X_{ann}/C_h} .$$

C_o = Cost of placing an order.

X_{ann} = Annual demand in units.

C_h = Dollar cost of holding one unit in stock for one year.

The cost of ordering, C_o, includes:

a. Salaries of clerks involved in the preparation of replenishment orders.
b. Salaries of clerks at factory who process the order.

c. Salaries of order pickers, packers, and shippers. N.B.—b and c apply only where replenishment is drawn against an owned source.

d. Salary of stock record clerk at warehouse.

e. Wages of receivers and material handlers to store item.

f. Salaries in central accounting of personnel who make records for cross-checking warehouse stocks, pay bills for goods and freight, etc.

g. In-bound freights.

The cost of holding C_h consists of two parts:

a. The dollar value of a single unit.

b. The percentage of that cost required to hold a single unit on hand for one year.

To simplify the calculations when done manually, notice that the cost of ordering and the percentage factor of the cost of holding, as well as the multiplier two, are all constant so that the calculation can be reduced to $\text{EOQ} = k \sqrt{D/\text{unit value of SKU.}}$ This does make calculations easier. With a computer, there is no problem.

The cost of processing a replenishment order through an internal paper channel is probably a little cheaper than when goods are purchased from an outside vendor, but the difference in cost is probably not all that great. Extreme accuracy in determining these costs are not critical, in that a square root will be taken — but an effort should be made to establish a reasonable estimate. Considering all of the handling of paper and material involved in processing a replenishment, it is probable C_o will not be less than about \$8-\$10 and may run up to \$25 or more.

If we return to Product X once more and use C_o = \$12.50 and C_h = .25 x \$17.60 and assume that Product X is obtained by itself from a separate source, then

$$\text{EOQ} = \sqrt{2 \times \$12.50 \times 132 / .25 \times \$17.60} = 27 \text{ units.}$$

Thus, the maximum stock of Product X will be 26 + 27 = 53 units, and the average inventory will be 26 + 27/2 = 39½ units.

Earlier in this chapter, it was stated that the effect of variation in holding cost would be examined further. In Figure 2-8, the effect of changing holding cost fraction by 5% increments from 10% to 40% on the cost of a stock-out, C_D, is shown. It can be seen that the range of C_D at levels below 95% is only nominal.

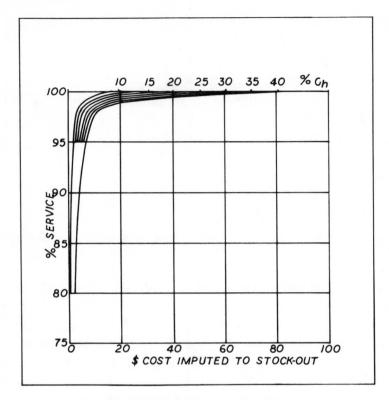

Figure 2-8. *Effect of C_h on C_b .*

Using the same holding cost fractions as above, it is seen in Figure 2-9 that increased C_h reduces EOQ, but more and more slowly. Thus from an infinite EOQ at zero C_h, we drop very quickly to a value of 43 at $C_h = 10\%$. Doubling C_h to 20% reduces EOQ to 31, and redoubling to 40% reduces EOQ to about 22. From the shape of the curve, further redoublings of C_h will drop EOQ only slightly.

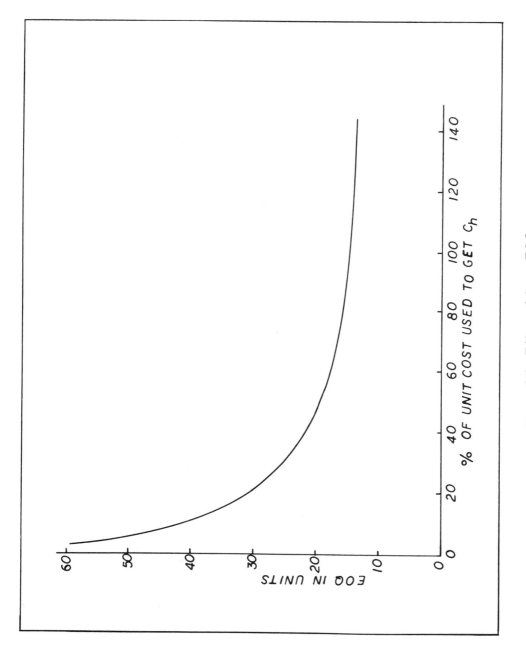

Figure 2-9. *Effect of C_h on EOQ.*

BIBLIOGRAPHY AND FURTHER READING

(1) Brown, R.G., *Smoothing, Forecasting and Prediction of Discrete Time Series*, Englewood Cliffs, N.J., Prentice-Hall, Inc., 1963. A presentation of mathematical concepts as applied to forecasting as related to inventory. Exponential smoothing techniques are thoroughly discussed.

(2) Brown, R.G., *Statistical Forecasting for Inventory Control*, New York, N.Y., McGraw-Hill Book Co., Inc., 1959.

(3) Buchan, J. and Koenigsberg, E., *Scientific Inventory Management*, Englewood Cliffs, N.J., Prentice-Hall, Inc., 1962. An extensive series of case studies illustrating various phases of inventory management.

(4) D'Anna, J.P., *Inventory and Profit*, New York, N.Y., American Management Association, 1966. Profitability techniques applied to inventory management. A short, practical work.

(5) Magee, J.F. and Boodman, D.M., *Production Planning and Inventory Control*, *2nd Ed.*, New York, N.Y., McGraw-Hill Book Co., 1967. Production planning as related to inventory management.

(6) Morse, P.M., *Queues, Inventories and Maintenance*, New York, N.Y., John Wiley and Sons, Inc., 1958. Chapter 10 covers application of queueing methods to inventory control. A mathematical approach.

(7) Prichard, J.W. and Eagle, R.H., *Modern Inventory Management*, New York, N.Y., John Wiley and Sons, Inc., 1965. Excellent coverage of many details in inventory management.

(8) Starr, M.K. and Miller, D.W., *Inventory Control: Theory and Practice*, Englewood Cliffs, N.J., Prentice-Hall, Inc., 1962. A technical discussion of inventory control.

(9) Stelzer, W., *Materials Management*, Englewood Cliffs, N.J., Prentice-Hall, Inc., 1970. In Chapter 6, the author covers the relationships between purchasing and inventory.

(10) Weast, R.C. and Selby, S.M., *Handbook of Tables for Probability and Statistics*, *2nd Ed.*, Cleveland, Ohio, The Chemical Rubber Co., 1968. Handbook of mathematical tables.

Chapter 3

The concept of a Materials Management Department as a separate function in a business is one which has been gaining momentum in recent years. Stature comparable to manufacturing, marketing, and accounting is beginning to develop. Even today, however, there are companies unaware of the problems in this area. Historically, manufacturing companies have been started to make a specific product. It is not unusual for one, two, or three men to go into the manufacturing business. Initially, they may all work in the manufacturing and sales function and may even handle record keeping. But if the business survives

BUILDING A PROFITABLE MATERIALS MANAGEMENT DEPARTMENT

and grows, the entrepreneurs will specialize or will secure the help of others to concentrate specifically on the areas of manufacturing, sales, accounting, purchasing, personnel, etc. This pattern has been repeated over and over and will continue.

As long as the organization is small, it is possible for its management to keep informed on all phases of the business. If aware of the various alternatives available, the management group can make business decisions which are optimal or close to it. Businesses have a way of growing, however, and along with the business, management grows also. As an example, rate and routing problems are turned over to a specialist. With continued growth, this job can grow and require the services of several specialists — for rates and routings, rail problems, private rail and truck carriage, common-carrier motor truck carriage, marine transport, etc. Other departments of the business grow in a similar way, with employees who are very knowledgeable about small pieces of the business. These specialists make decisions which to them appear to be economic, to be money-savers. But the decision which shows a benefit to the costs in their area of responsibility may have negative effects on the costs in another area. Frequently, no one is aware of the reason for the cost increases. Examples of these kinds of decisions have already been cited.

Materials management, in the sense used in this book, commonly is not the responsibility of a single group. Indeed, the direct opposite is the case. Forecasting may be a marketing responsibility and sometimes is limited to a projection of anticipated demand for major items in the line and a total dollar projection — sometimes only a total dollar projection. However, a forecast should also serve manufacturing, warehousing, transportation, purchasing, and financial groups; the indicated type of forecast does not help them, so they may in fact try to make their own projections to meet their own needs.

Inventory management may be shared by manufacturing, sales, and accounting. As a result, no one will be really responsible for the stocks on hand around the company. A great many functions, closely related to each other, are in fact so dispersed through an organization, especially a large one, that optimal decisions cannot be, and are not, obtained. Table 3-1 lists various materials management functions.

All of these functions (and there may be others) are part and parcel in the materials management area. If there is not an established organization to coordinate these activities, it is almost certain that best costs are not being achieved. For example, a rate man in the traffic area might see the opportunity to save $1 per hundred-weight on freights between East and West Coast locations by shipping maximum carloads of 120,000 pounds. Current practice is to ship 40,000 pounds or about four months' supply. Valued at 25¢ per pound, the average inventory of 20,000 pounds is worth $5,000. At 25% cost of possession, the holding cost is $1,250 per year. With 120,000-pound shipments, the average inventory is worth $15,000 and the cost of possession is now $3,750 per year. To save $1,200 per year in freights, we have increased our cost of possession by $2,500. Remember well that "cost of possession" is often called a

TABLE 3-1
Materials Management Functions

Sales forecasting.

Inventory management.

Purchasing interface.

Traffic interface.

Rates and routings.

Packaging interface for product protection.

Private carriage-Motor truck.

-Rail operations.

-Marine.

Warehouse design, location, operations.

Order entry and related accounting interfaces.

Production planning.

Systems and data-processing interface.

Manpower planning.

Equipment load planning.

Sales interface for customer service, expediting, and small orders.

"foregone profit opportunity" and as such it does not show on the accounting record. Note that we have not even considered whether there is floor space available in the West Coast warehouse or if there were competing demands for all of the space, floor taxes, obsolescence, product damage, possible loss of the market, etc., as other negative factors.

The need to coordinate and reconcile the conflicting demands of customer service, inventory levels, production rates, production runs, field stocks, transportation costs, etc., demands that all of these functions be brought under single management. The reduction in freight rates will not then be obtained as the result of greatly increased inventory investment; reduction in inventories will not be made at the cost of reducing effectiveness of customer service; factory runs will not be lengthened at the expense of inventory and customer service for other items; and other conflicts will be avoided or lessened. Provision of this single coordination function is the prime reason for the existence of a Materials Management Department.

Selling the Materials Management Concept

How can you proceed to sell the idea of establishing a Materials Management Department? If you are high up in the organization, you can direct that preliminary studies be made. But suppose you are not in that position; how do you stir up interest at those levels?

It is sometimes not appreciated just how much money is spent in delivering goods to customers, in warehousing costs, in purchasing, in planning, in pilferage and damage, in inventory, and in the various supervisory and management efforts related to these activities. During the early 1960's, these costs were evaluated for several broad types of industry, and the findings were eye-openers. (See Bibliography #2 for details.) With all distribution costs fairly well-covered, it was found that from 10% to 25% or more of net sales went into distribution expenses. I have seen no data more recent, but it would not be surprising to find today that freights, warehousing costs, other handling and shipping costs, etc., are in the 15%-20% range for many companies. For starters, you could bring these figures to the attention of your management with the recommendation that an evaluation of these costs in your own company might be in order, and that results could lead to a major cost reduction opportunity.

The mechanics of establishing the size of the materials management problem in your company will in all likelihood be different than in another organization. In my experience, the appointment of an ad hoc study team by the chief executive to analyze the scope of the problem was successful. The team was headed by a management engineer from the corporate level and was staffed at the division level with a senior buyer, an assistant sales manager, a manufacturing manager, a product manager, a traffic manager, the general warehouse supervisor, the manager of industrial engineering, accounting representatives, and a systems and data-processing representative.

Depending upon their expertise, these men were assigned to smaller project teams to study various phases of the business, such as:

- Sales forecasting methods.
- Factory inventory control.
- Warehouse inventory control.
- Purchasing interface with inventory control.
- Private trucking.

- Railroad car operations.
- Marine operations.
- Traffic interfaces with other groups.
- Warehouse locations.
- Labor utilization at warehouses.
- Production planning routines.
- Order processing and invoicing.
- Others.

Team assignments were to examine current practices, establish the size of the expenditures involved in the various phases of the distribution system as it existed, and make an appraisal of the potential for cost reduction through optimization of the interlocking activities. This latter goal may prove to be a difficult chore. In some cases, the only conclusion to be reached at the survey stage is that expenditures in certain areas are relatively large, or moderate, or small and that potential cost reductions are in the same order.

Establishing expenditures in various areas may also provide intriguing problems. As an example, determination of annual freight costs may show that freights on inbound raw materials are charged into the cost of manufacture; freights on finished goods to warehouses are charged to selling expense; private truck costs to a third account; and prepaid freights to customers to a fourth account. Establishing responsibility for forecasts of raw material needs, production plans, and customer demand for major and minor product items may show very shadowy areas of authority and responsibility. The trail in establishing responsibility for inventory control may be equally elusive.

The exercise of developing this data is worth the effort and time. It may, and probably will, bring into the open how badly scattered the materials management responsibility is, and also show how little true coordination exists between the various steps from the end of manufacture through the various paths for movement of goods to the user, the flow of cash back into the till, and the closing of the cycle with procurement and delivery of raw materials back into the manufacturing operations. Upon the completion of the survey as indicated, the magnitude of expenditures in the materials management part of the business will be reasonably well defined. There will also be an indication of some fairly firm cost reduction potentials, intuitive judgments of other potentials, and some judgments which will be of the "if" type — "If we can reduce a block of costs by a certain modest percentage, we may be able to save so many dollars."

Deadlines were set for the accomplishment of the studies. The project was completed and reported to the chief executive in eight months. Identifiable distribution expenditures were between 10% and 15% of net sales. An estimate of indirect costs was judged to be in the general area of 5% of net sales. The total of these costs was in the range of $35-40,000,000.

As a result of the studies, a decision was made to proceed on a corporate-wide basis and to establish a Materials Management Department. Implementation was started first in the division initiating the studies. Later, further studies were made to determine which members of the central office staff were specifically engaged in materials management type activities and the extent of their involvement. From these studies a good idea was obtained of the probable size of the staff for the new department, and in many cases the staff members were selected from these other departments on the basis of the degree of their involvement.

There are many difficulties in implementing such a major change. Reallocation of duties and responsibilities is resisted in subtle ways, more perhaps because of a fear of losing contact with the day-to-day situation than resistance to the change itself. There may have been some of this, but it was not apparent. Then there is delay in getting people released to their new assignments. There is also a time requirement to develop an understanding of the materials management concept and to develop the procedures for managing the new systems.

The organization initially established at the corporate level was essentially staff specialists to advise the line groups at the division level. An experienced corporate department director was engaged, and specialists in forecasting, inventory, traffic, computer usage, warehouse operations, and other lesser functions were made members of his staff. At the division level, there was a parallel line organization with day-to-day authority and responsibility to manage the materials system.

Assuming that your studies lead to the conclusion that a materials management group is needed as a new department in your company, the question arises, "How should it be structured?" In the example above, it is seen that a mixture of line and staff seemed to be the right combination. On the line side were such things as warehouse operations, private truck and rail operations, marine operations, inventory management, and production planning. On the staff side were sales forecasting, traffic, cost analysis, and methods research. There would also be a functional relation with other departments — such as control over quantities purchased; liaison with the packaging engineers to assure adequate protection for the finished product during transportation and warehousing, with sales in the area of unusually small orders and customer service, with accounting on costs and budgets, with systems and data processing on computer applications, and with any other departmental areas interfacing with materials management.

The organizational setup you finally adopt will be determined by the size of your company and the annual volume of sales. For a company faced with the functions outlined in the preceding paragraphs, an organization similar to that shown in Figure 3-1 would be appropriate. There will be variations from the chart in the assignment of functions shown, especially when the scope of the overall activity is at modest levels, or where the functions are not pertinent.

The head of the department should be at the same level in the organization as the

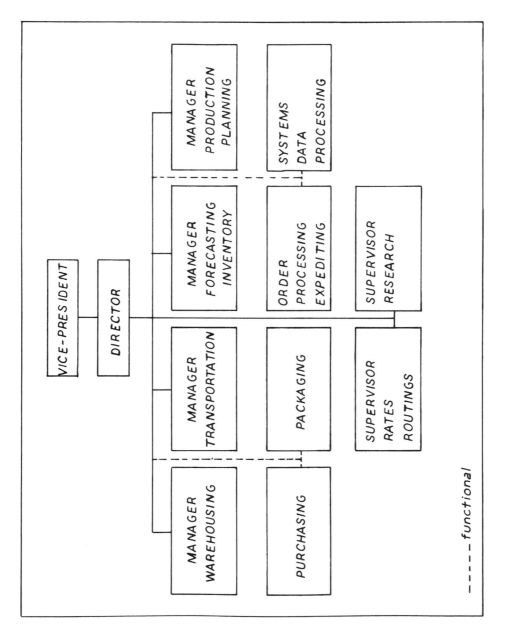

Figure 3-1. *Organization of a Materials Management Department.*

heads of other major departments. The various managers and supervisors of functions should also be at the same level organizationally as managers and supervisors of comparable responsibility in other areas. Clerical and stenographic assistance would be supplied as needed.

BIBLIOGRAPHY AND FURTHER READING

(1)   Oppengart, A., "The Challenge of Physical Distribution," N.Y., N.Y., *The Journal of Industrial Engineering*, published by A.I.I.E., April, 1968. Thoughts on the potentials of physical distribution activity.

(2)   Snyder, R.E., "Physical Distribution Cost Survey," Bala Cynwyd, Pa.; "Distribution Age," published by the Chilton Co.; a series printed during the spring and summer of 1962.

(3)   Stelzer, W.R., Jr., *Materials Management*, Englewood Cliffs, N.J., Prentice-Hall, Inc., 1970. The author discusses centralized vs. decentralized materials management in Chapter 1.

(4)   Stolle, J.F., "How to manage Physical Distribution," Boston, Mass., *The Harvard Business Review*, July-August, 1967. Arguments pro and con on staff vs. line relationships in a physical distribution department. Equally applicable to materials management.

Chapter 4

Establishment of a new warehouse is often decided on an almost casual basis. "Zeta Corporation is enjoying almost 100% of the market for Product B in the Detroit area. If we have as much as 5% of it we are lucky. We should also have a warehouse in Detroit so we can increase our share of that market." Warehouse space is built or rented in Detroit. More of Product B is sold in that city and the share of the market is improved. But somehow or other, the increases in volume do not reflect back into the profit statements for Product B. Yes, there was an increase in dollars' worth of goods sold, but the profit has not changed. What happened?

STRATEGIC LOCATION
AND INTELLIGENT DESIGN
OF THE WAREHOUSE

If Zeta knew what they were doing when they moved into Detroit, and if, in fact, Zeta had a profitable Detroit warehouse operation, then imitation of Zeta might be a good move. However, Zeta may have moved in with sketchy reasons also. Truly, if a warehouse in Detroit is being considered, it should be given the benefit of a thorough study that will relate the Detroit potential to the total business. A number of factors should be taken into consideration, such as:

- What is the best location for our warehouse?
- What kinds of transportation service are available for in-bound and out-bound shipments?
- What is the tax structure for the various sites?
- Is there an adequate and economical labor pool?
- What will the total cost of operations be for selected alternate sites?
- What will the future bring?

In picking a site, the last thing you should do, literally, is go looking for land or available buildings. First, you should consider where the present and potential customers are located. For the potential customers, an estimate of the probability of getting some specific portion of their business is required. While doing this it is well to look at a fairly wide area, perhaps to a radius of 200 miles. In the Detroit example, this would take in nearly all of lower Michigan, Ontario Province as far east as Toronto, the northwest corner of Pennsylvania, and the northern portions of Ohio and Indiana. Even a 100-mile radius would encompass Cleveland, Toledo, and the industrialized southeast of Michigan.

Location Methods and Availability of Transportation

The tabulation of actual customer locations within 100 and 200 miles of Detroit provides a base from which to start. Next add the volumes taken by these existing customers. Then tabulate the potential new customers, with an optimistic and pessimistic estimate of quantities you might sell to them. With this data and a map, it is possible to make an eyeball selection of potential sites for the 100- and 200-mile market areas. More accurate methods of pinpointing the center of gravity of the market are available. One of the simplest has been described by Follet (Bibliography #3). In essence this analog method uses a map, some fishing line, and some weights to represent tonnage moving to customers, together with a ring to tie all the customers together. As the weights are changed, the center of gravity moves to reflect the varied conditions. This method also can be used for re-evaluating present warehouse locations. Linear programming, described in a later chapter, is a far more powerful tool, but the little analog does very well in locating a single warehouse.

Whichever method you use, whether the eyeball, analog, or mathematical, a general area of some 15-20 miles diameter has been identified. To close in on a specific site, we would next look at the availability of transportation services. Is there rail service in the area? Perhaps the need for rail service is not visualized now, but it may be needed later. It would help to sell the property later if its use were to be discontinued. For a redistribution warehouse, trucking service is more significant. Get hold of a trucking guide book, such as *Leonard's Guide,* and find out how many carriers have operating rights in the general area of the proposed warehouse.

Example

A study has been made to determine the location of a new warehouse to serve the New England states. Center of gravity of the market was approximately 10 miles north of Concord, New Hampshire. This area was served by only one carrier, which also served the areas where the customers were. To get the variety of carriers needed to handle in-bound and out-bound shipments directly, it was necessary to shift the location of the warehouse to an area where many carriers had rights. After looking at several other sites, each further away from the center of gravity, a site was chosen some 60 miles from the original selection. This site had both rail service and access to many motor carriers, thus avoiding the frustrations and delays inherent in multi-line movement. Consideration should be given also to the commercial delivery zones that surround all cities of any size. If many customers are within this zone, it may be better to have the warehouse within the zone than just outside of it, because of the freight savings.

Taxes

Your company may have to pay corporate franchise taxes, income taxes, real estate taxes, sales taxes, personal property taxes, inventory taxes, and others. Investigation of all of these should be painstaking. If internal specialists are not available, get a consultant. There are such things as "free ports" and "local option laws" and special treatment of finished-goods inventories, all of which alter the tax burden.

Inventory taxes are a way of life with taxing authorities. Practically every state, many major cities, and other political subdivisions assess taxes against goods in storage. Assessment dates are most often December 31 or January 1, but may be at any time of the year. It is often found that assessment is based on an "average inventory" for the preceding 12 months rather than for a single date. Taxing rates by themselves are almost meaningless, as they range from about 1% to as high as 65% of the assessed valuation of stored goods. Assessed valuation in most cases is less than the fair market value of the goods and may be as low as 10%. Valuations in the range 35% to 65% are more commonly found.

Tax exemptions on stored goods also vary widely. Some states exempt personal property, goods stored "in transit" (i.e., originating and to be sold outside of the state where stored), agricultural commodities, manufacturer's stocks, goods in interstate commerce, and others. As already noted, some states allow local options to counties in exempting inventory from taxation. Detailing the variations of inventory taxes is beyond the scope of this book and, in any event, would be quickly obsolete because of the frequent changes in laws. An annual digest is available. (See Bibliography #1.)

A careful analysis of alternate locations (city, county, adjoining counties, and even adjoining states) is a must. Some kind of estimate of future revenue needs of the communities involved will give an indication of future tax burdens. Will there be major changes in the area population which will entail new schools, sewer and water expansions, and other service needs?

Labor Availability

The fourth area to investigate is manpower availability to staff the warehouse. There will be a need for material handlers, fork-lift operators, and clerical help. Before settling on a site for a new facility, it is of critical importance to evaluate the labor availability for the several alternate locations. It is often assumed that help can be obtained, but discretion dictates that an evaluation be made. To do this, first stop in at the local state employment service office. Discussion with the head of this service will quickly reveal whether there is a pool of qualified personnel, but do not accept general statements of availability. Personally examine the file records of the people who are awaiting employment. Check on their previous work experience, age, residence, and other germane information. If the applicant is not interested in the type of work you have to offer, lacks experience of use to you, or has held too many jobs, he may be weeded out. Those left are an indication of availability of help. Also check on the list of unfilled openings; if there are many for the type of labor you are seeking, help availability is probably low.

A second place to look is in the want-ad section of newspapers. A sampling over a period of two or three years will give strong indications of availability of the type help you need. If there are few ads for material handlers, checkers, truck drivers, inventory clerks, etc., it is an indication that help may be available. However, if there are continuing ads for this kind of help, it is an indication that little surplus help is in the marketplace.

A factor in recruiting help is the distance between where they live and where they will work. Is there frequent and dependable public transportation? Is your location reasonably close in time and distance? Are the areas through which your help will have to travel to get to the job such that help will not be reluctant to pass through?

An attempt should be made to forecast what labor availability will be in the years ahead. This is without doubt a difficult chore and the answers may be based on purely subjective data, but there may be some assistance available from the state employment service or from other warehouse managers.

Cost Analysis

Following design of the warehouse proper, including probable site development costs and the cost of warehouse equipment, office space, parking arrangements, staffing etc., a total cost projection is the final step. Transportation costs in and out, taxes, payroll with fringes, building and equipment maintenance, utility costs, depreciation and lease costs, telephone, mail, supplies, insurance, and other costs are combined to arrive at a total cost of operation. These figures are compared for alternate locations and a decision reached for a specific area to locate the warehouse. Cost figures can be compared with anticipated revenue to determine whether the warehouse will add to the overall profitability of the business. Assuming that it does, search for a site upon which to build or for an existing warehouse to purchase or rent.

Site Factors

As touched on already, it is usually desirable to select a site which has access to a railroad. It is also advantageous to have ready access to a freeway. Consideration should be given to the possibility of flooding of sites located near rivers or on low-lying ground. Historical records can provide evidence of flooding conditions in the past. Underground conditions may be a source of difficulty. Load-bearing capacity of land may be impaired because of quicksand or boggy conditions and requires expensive corrective measures or heavy piling. On the other hand, solid rock makes installation of sewers, depressed loading docks, or underground storage very expensive. Filled land can also cause difficulty if heavy refuse has been buried. Most sites do not have these problems, but it is well to be aware of the possibilities and to avoid unpleasant surprises.

Warehouse Design

Many of the warehouses built today are of one-story construction, typically a square (cheapest) building with about 20 to 22 feet clear from floor to trusses. Column spacing tends to be about 40 to 50 feet. Even though this is the popular design, there are advantages to two-story structures, especially where fast- and slow-moving stocks are handled. The slow-moving items would be moved to and from the second floor with a high-speed platform elevator or belt conveyor. Service facilities, cafeterias, locker rooms, and office space can all be on the second level, leaving the first floor for the heavy handling operations. Offices and such are peripheral to the main purpose of a warehouse, and the ultimate decision to have them on a first or second level depends upon further analysis.

Establishing Space Requirements

To establish warehouse space requirements, the following factors must be considered:

- Estimation of material volumes to be stored.
- Conversion of volumes to cube requirements.
- Determination of height to which goods can be stacked.
- Determination of floor area required for storage.
- Allowances for inability to tight-stack.
- Allowances for aisles, staging areas, shipping and receiving docks.
- Space requirements for offices, locker rooms, lunchrooms, and other services.
- Tentative expansion plan.

Volumes to Be Stored

From preliminary studies, an estimate of the volume to move through the warehouse has been established and broken down by product. From manufacturing schedules, frequency of manufacture can be determined and from this a replenishment interval established also. If the factory maintains reserve stocks at all times, then replenishment can be obtained at any time. Assuming that the factory does carry reserve stocks, the warehouse stocks need to be only large enough to cover the replenishment period demand plus a safety stock to cover the occasional high demand during the replenishment cycle. Thus, if the replenishment cycle is two weeks, the safety stock is equivalent to one week, and the replenishment quantity equals two weeks' demand, then the maximum stock is theoretically:

$$\frac{\text{Safety stock + replenishment quantity}}{\text{Replenishment cycle}} = \frac{3}{2} = 1\frac{1}{2} \text{ weeks average stock.}$$

It seldom occurs that all items are at their maximum stock levels simultaneously. It will happen though since it is possible, and that is why you sometimes see the aisles filled. The practical approach is to assume that inventory for all items will be at the theoretical average at all times. This is the figure to use in calculating space requirements, even though we know that at times some items will be at their maximum levels. At the same time, others will be out of stock or at very low levels. For each of the stocked items, an average inventory has been determined. From this average inventory and the container dimensions, calculate the number of pallet loads to be stocked for each item. Then from knowledge of piling characteristics, determine which items can be stacked only one pallet high, two pallets high, etc.

Pallet Stacks

Allowable heights of pallet stacks can be determined only from experience, but some information can be offered. Where the shipping container is completely filled with rigid items, such as canned goods, pallets can be stacked very high. The limit would be the stability of the pile, crushing of cans at the bottom of the pile, or pallet failure. With corrugated and paperboard receptacles, we find cases where the container is not solidly filled; examples: soft goods, fiber drums not quite filled with granular materials, small items bulk-packed in the shipper. When these items are stacked, the container will gradually deform, with the distortion accelerated at times of high humidity. Pallet stacks under these conditions will slowly begin to tilt, and if left alone will fall. Container overhang beyond the edge of the pallet sometimes causes pallet stack instability also.

Taking the pallet dimension (or if there will be container overhang, use the larger dimension) and multiplying by the height of the pallet and load combined, and then summarizing for all palletized materials, will yield the cubic feet of space required to hold the inventory, tight-stacked. This is the net cubic volume required, with no allowances. It was mentioned previously that a record should be kept of the products which, when palletized, could be stacked two or more pallets high. Since design of the warehouse building will probably be based on stacking 20-22 feet high, we cannot economically allow a floor space to be tied up with a single pallet. This leads us to a consideration of rack systems.

Storage Racks

There are three principal types of fixed steel storage racks for palletized materials. The first consists of stringers between vertical posts, with vertical spacing of stringers adjusted to suit the height of pallet loads being stored. The stringers are horizontally spaced to support the pallet at front and back only. Stringers are usually long enough to hold three pallets. Pallets are only one deep in these racks. With racks back-to-back and an aisle on either side, two-deep storage can be had. This kind of rack is best used against a wall, and low-volume items or partial pallet loads are stored on it.

The second type is a drive-in rack. These are usually custom-made to desired height and depth. Entry is provided at each end of the pallet row, and at an appropriate spot towards the center of the bank of pallet rows there is bracing steel to provide additional stiffness to the structure. Stiffeners are located to suit the needs of the warehouse and may divide the row of stacks in half or into any other desired ratio. The third type of rack is called the drive-through rack. The row of pallets can be removed completely from either end. Necessary structural rigidity is obtained by ties to building members. The drive-through racks are of some help in maintaining turnover of goods.

In addition to the fixed racks, there are several types of demountable racks. These are specially designed single units which are bolted or otherwise attached to a pallet, with steel cornerposts and a connecting framework above the load which serves as a base on which to put another load. There are also stacking boxes and cages which are useful in some circumstances.

Utilization of racks permits greatly improved use of the cube for those items giving inherently unstable pallet stacks at maximum height. They are also valuable where materials are susceptible to damage from pressure, even though they would yield stable stacks. They are also effective in handling odd-shaped items, such as auto fenders. Space utilization is improved for these type items by racks, but with the added clearances required on both sides and above the pallet to permit negotiation of the pallet load within the rack, plus room for the steel rack itself, space utilization is lower than with straight-stacking.

Space Requirements

Let's now get back to determining space required. From the tabulation of items which must be rack-stored, pick off the number of pallets to be thus stored and determine how many will require stringer type racks or drive-in, drive-through racks. From manufacturers' specifications, calculate the floor area required to accommodate the racks. The cube requirement of the remaining pallets, which may be free-stacked, is converted to floor space by dividing the total cube of the remaining pallet loads by the cube of a typical pallet stack. This yields a quantity which is the number of pallet stacks required. By multiplying by the area of the pallet, the net free-stacking area is obtained.

Allowances

Additional space of 6-8 inches must be provided between rows of pallets, so that loads may be entered and removed without damage, for space blanked out by rows of columns, for access to fire doors and fire extinguishers, etc. As a quick measure, 20-25% additional space is often allowed for these elements.

Consider now that total space so far allowed is based on 100% utilization of the cube. Experience has shown that space utilization efficiency commonly runs in the 75-85% range in a well-loaded warehouse. To get a workable figure for floor space, the 100% utilization must be factored to bring utilization to the 75-85% range.

Aisles are needed to gain access to the stockpiles and move goods in and out. When using fork-lift trucks, aisles are usually 11-12 feet wide. Making them narrower will result in more damage to goods on turns and may slow down trucks when passing is required. Narrow aisles will also require more maneuvering on the part of the operator in order to enter the pallet slots, with more lost time. Aisle layout is dependent upon

Photo courtesy of McLean Trucking Co., Winston-Salem, N.C.

Photo 4-1. *Common-carrier terminal operation.*

the arrangement of racks and free-standing piles, the depth of the pallet piles, and other factors. A paper layout is the easiest way to find a workable solution. When the aisle layout is set, add this space to the previously calculated areas. Next, space for peripheral functions is added:

- Rail shipping-receiving dock.
- Truck receiving-shipping dock.
- Receiving stage area.
- Shipping stage area.
- Small-shipment packing area.
- *Elevator shaft, if used.
- *Toilet facilities.
- *Stairwells, if used.
- *Locker and washrooms.
- *Lunchroom.
- Office space.
- Battery-charging area.
- Repair shop area.
- Mechanical equipment area.
- *Garage.

---

*May be subject to municipal, state, or federal regulation. Space for these items are dictated by law and will not be discussed here.

Loading Docks—Rail

Receiving and shipping areas are of prime importance in a warehouse. Handling of rail shipments is fairly straightforward. The number of loading spots is limited by the length of the railroad track that can be installed next to the building, together with the length of rail cars. The dock itself can be outside the building with the track adjacent, or it can be just inside the building for an all-weather unloading operation. Another alternate is to have the track just outside the building wall with access doors suitably located so that they open directly into the cars.

The outside dock has an advantage in that cars can be spotted almost anywhere and at least part of the fork-truck traffic is kept out-of-doors. A couple of doors could serve a dock 300-400 feet long, thus conserving storage space inside. The disadvantages are open loading doors and a certain amount of exposure to cold weather and storms. With an inside dock, the exterior wall of the building has in essence been moved to enclose the exterior dock and track. The advantage lies in a fully protected loading area. The use of simple unloading doors is the cheapest method, but if there are a multiplicity of doors, there is a loss of storage space, and heat losses in winter can be severe.

Use of rail cars for in-bound shipments has the advantage of time flexibility. Twenty-four hours are allowed for unloading or loading, and if the installation has an "average" agreement with the railroad and a car is unloaded on the first day, a "credit" is obtained which may be used to offset "debits" on cars held for more than 48 hours, if enough cars are unloaded promptly. When cars are held until the time "arbitrary" charges are assessed, these charges must be made; there are no offsetting credits for arbitrary charges.

With mixed cars, goods can be sorted and palletized in the car and moved directly to storage. For shipments the advantage of time is also available, but sweeping, removal of protruding nails and strapping fasteners, and application of lining paper if needed is an expense. Unless "damage-free" or "bulkhead" cars are available, it will be found that provision of labor and materials to brace the shipment for movement may cost up to $200 per car.

Loading Docks—Trucks

In handling trucks, the problems are somewhat different from rail cars. To begin with, the truck carrier wants to back into the dock upon arrival. He wants to be loaded promptly and be on his way, especially when the shipment is very small. Even with full truckloads a quick turnaround is desired, but depending upon circumstances, up to three hours is allowed for loading full loads before detention time is assessed. But the warehouseman wants to keep his men busy, so to some extent he needs to have trucks backed up so that he can balance his workloads.

The problem here is the classic "waiting line," and it involves balancing the number of loaders and unloaders against the trucks arriving and tieing this in with the number of docks available, so that waiting time for the truckers and idle time for the warehousemen is at an optimum low level for both. If there are a great many small shipments, it may be possible to arrange with a local cartage company to drop a trailer at the dock for small shipments to be accumulated in. When the trailer is sufficiently full, the carter is called. He brings an empty trailer and leaves it in place of the full one. He then distributes the small shipments to the various principal carriers. This service is not available in all localities, however, but if it is, it does eliminate some of the turmoil and congestion around the shipping area.

A second action which helps to smooth out the dock operation is to plan when you will receive or ship your major loads. On major in-bound shipments, you arrange it so that the carrier's dispatcher will call you and ask at what hour you can accept the load. On out-bound shipments, you call the dispatcher and tell him when you want empty trailers to load. When you make these arrangements, play fair and handle the

Photo courtesy of McLean Trucking Co., Winston-Salem, N.C.

Photo 4-2. *A 166-bay common carrier terminal.*

trucks promptly as soon as they arrive. It is a good plan for both the warehouse and the trucker.

These two moves together will help to lessen the bunching of trucks at the dock. There will still be small deliveries at all times of the day depending upon the routes of the carrier's city trucks, but judicious scheduling is a tool for smoothing out the day's loads.

Determination of Loading Door Requirements

Even with these steps, there remains the problem of how many truck spots are needed. How much space is needed for staging in-bound and out-bound tonnage? How much space must be allowed in the immediate dock area and for the aprons beyond for trucks? For a new facility, it will be necessary to estimate the flow of traffic at the truck dock. Since the planning has included a projection of the business to flow through the warehouse, this volume can be converted into an estimate of the number of full and partial loads in-bound and out-bound, with an allowance made for any rail traffic. Do not overlook the small deliveries of supplies or of small emergency replenishments. For out-bound movements there will be a different pattern than in-bound, because customers will be apt to order smaller quantities than are being brought in on replenishment.

Keeping in mind the ability to schedule major receipts and shipments, make an estimate of the number of trucks arriving at the dock hour-by-hour throughout the day. To this add an estimate of the time that will be needed to load or unload each unit, based on the estimated weight each will handle. With this information, you will have the average arrival rate and the average service rate. With this data it is possible to use queueing theory and calculate loading door needs, but fortunately this has already been done for you, and the answers can be looked up in a table. See Bibliography #2, for source of tables. The tables cover loading/unloading rates from 2-4,000 pounds per hour for shipments running 150 pounds or less, up to 30,000 pounds per hour for palletized shipments.

Dock Aprons

Space required for docking and maneuvering trucks is readily determined. Doors should be spaced so that there is about 12 feet clearance for each vehicle. The space should be 4 or 5 feet longer than the longest truck expected. If an enclosed dock is planned, it might be wise to make some additional allowance in view of current agitation to legalize longer units. Beyond this parking area, there should be an apron equally as long to permit the vehicle to pull clear of adjacent vehicles or building structures before starting to turn. An adequate roadway to serve the dock area will be 20-25 feet wide.

Staging Areas

Within the building there should be space for staging in-bound and out-bound shipments, so that goods can be loaded or unloaded expeditiously. The movement of goods to and from storage can then be decoupled from the loading-unloading operation, thus obtaining some flexibility in use of manpower. From the estimates of arrivals and shipments, prepare a cumulative tabulation of weights to be moved across the dock area, together with a new balance on hand, hour-by-hour through the day. At some time during the day, the net balance in the staging area will be at a maximum. The stage must be sized to handle this peak load. Generally, goods are segregated by carrier, may be stacked on pallets, and if loads are stacked regularly, the pallets themselves may be stacked two or three high. Pallets must be readily accessible when the need to move them arises. Calculations of space requirements are similar to those for the warehouse proper.

Summary

Calculations have established floor space required for actual storage, aisles, rail and truck docks, and stages. Legal requirements have established the size of sanitary and service facilities. Miscellaneous utility and office areas are set by the requirements of the warehouse itself. Space for a sales group may possibly be included. In total, this is the square footage required under the roof. A layout to arrange the elements into a square configuration is next, and the project can then be turned over to the architect for final design.

Inflatable Buildings

The standard inflatable building is most often a half-cylinder, with end closures which are in effect quarter-spheres. Height of the structure is thus about half the width, while lengths can be to any desired value. The single wall fabric is usually nylon or Fiberglas or a combination and is coated on both sides with white or colored vinyl. The fabric is fireproof and waterproof, abrasion resistant, and not easily snagged The building is held to the ground by ground anchors, used in combination with a pipe or cable attached to the wall near ground level. A more sophisticated anchor uses a concrete curb and a system of clamps.

Inflatables can be set up on any fairly level plot of ground. Depending upon projected use, the ground may be paved or unpaved. Structures can be heated, but air conditioning is almost always prohibitively expensive. Lighting during the day is adequate with the natural transmission through the fabric (white), while at night a few electric lights will reflect illumination throughout. Internal air pressure supports the fabric, typically 0.02-0.05 psi supplied by an electric blower. With the anchorage

Photo courtesy of Birdair Structures, Inc., Buffalo, N.Y.

Photo 4-3. *Inflatable building ready for erection.*

Photo courtesy of Birdair Structures, Inc., Buffalo, N.Y.

Photo 4-4. *A long inflatable building on a concrete pad.*

Photo courtesy of Birdair Structures, Inc., Buffalo, N.Y.

Photo 4-5. *A processing operation within an inflatable building.*

provided, the structure will withstand winds up to 100 mph. The manufacturer usually recommends an auxiliary blower with automatic start-up in the event of power failure, to protect the fabric from wind damage if the weather is stormy.

Life of the building is dependent upon the weight of the fabric and thickness of the vinyl coating. A 15-mil vinyl coating appears to be optimum in inhibiting the effect of sunlight on the fabric. Manufacturers indicate a life of five to eight years under continuous usage, dependent upon climate. Fire rating is typically five-second flameout. Insurance rates run about $3 per $1,000 valuation. Inflatables have a two-year IRS write-off, and as a temporary structure are not usually taxed locally. In the 15-20,000 square foot sizes, cost including the fabric, anchorage, blower, a small entrance, and erection is in the neighborhood of $2 per square foot. Heating, lighting, fork-truck access door, paving, and other items are extras. If desired, the structure may be leased.

The advantages of inflatables include:

- Low first cost, with much of this cost recoverable through absence of local taxes.

Photo courtesy of Birdair Structures, Inc., Buffalo, N.Y.

Photo 4-6. *Start of a storage operation in an inflatable building.*

- Fast delivery. Building can be delivered and erected in as little as two weeks, if the site is ready and a standard unit ordered. Delivery is seldom longer than about eight weeks.
- No interior columns.
- When necessary, the structure can be taken down in a day and moved to another location at nominal expense.
- Low repair costs. Only the mechanical devices need periodic attention. Fabric tears are repaired by cementing a patch over the tear, without deflating the building.
- The air support system is continually forcing in fresh air, so that air is changed several times an hour.

Principal disadvantages are:

- There is no cost advantage for small inflatables, say under about 5,000 square feet, because of the higher cost contribution (proportionately) of air locks.
- Heating may be unduly expensive because of the continuing air flow. Air conditioning is prohibitively costly.
- Needs standby blowers. Probably not mandatory in a warehouse.

Photo courtesy of Birdair Structures, Inc., Buffalo, N.Y.

Photo 4-7. *Exterior view of an inflatable building and air-lock entry.*

Photo courtesy of Birdair Structures, Inc., Buffalo, N.Y.

Photo 4-8. *Air-lock doorway to inflatable building.*

- Lacks the physical security of a steel or masonry building as it is readily opened with a knife, but with an opening large enough to remove goods the structure will collapse with loss of air.

In summary, for quick, economical, flexible, and fairly durable warehousing, the inflatable building is very attractive.

Automatic Warehouses

Today it is rare to find a warehouse which is not at least partly mechanized, perhaps only with pallets and a lift truck of some sort. Mechanization has proceeded through various stages to the point of partial and complete automation. The Post Office Department, for instance, has been doing much work in the automated sorting and resorting of letters and packages with varying degrees of success.

An automatic warehouse has been developed for handling steel drums of chemicals. Production is brought from the manufacturing areas by motor truck and unloaded at a receiving stage. Drums are moved into storage by a conveyor passing an electronic coding station en route, where an operator keys in a stocking address. Each drum then moves to an automatic drum elevator and is transferred and lifted to the proper roll-through rack where it is discharged. The rack is equipped with retarders to ease the drum toward the discharge end of the rack until it comes to rest against another drum. When materials are to be withdrawn, an operator at another electronic station encodes the stocking location and number of drums needed for shipment. Drums are released one-by-one to the down elevator, thence to the conveyor system and the shipping stage.

A shoe manufacturer has installed a system of automated flow racks and conveyors for automatically picking and moving individual boxes of shoes to an order assembly and packing area. Racks in this instance are manually loaded. The electronic control system allows the operator to release a required size, style, color, and quantity of shoes and direct them to a specific order assembly area.

These two systems have one thing in common; the containers are standard units and are unlikely to be changed for marketing reasons. Once installed, the prospect of continuing use without modification is very high. The high cost of the automatic installation will have every opportunity to pay for itself. A successful and profitable automatic warehouse has several requirements:

- Volume to be handled must be high enough to keep the system operating steadily.
- There should be a fairly narrow range in the size and weight of units handled.

- Worker skills to operate and maintain the system are needed.
- Installation must be sturdy and reliable. There may be no way to get goods out of an automated system which has broken down.
- Installation must pay for itself in savings.

Before going ahead with an automatic warehouse system, present operations should be carefully scrutinized, especially in the areas of labor utilization, space utilization, and the ability to locate items in stock. If there is no management measure of labor performance in the existing warehouse, labor effectiveness may be very low. If remainders, dormant items, or very slow movers are held in the existing warehouse, cube utilization will be poor. If material cannot be found in the existing warehouse, a locater system is needed. Decisive action must be taken against these profit-eaters. On the other hand, if present labor performance is good, if dormant and slow-moving items are kept weeded out, and there is an effective locater system, then gains to be made by automating stand on their own feet. Advantages of an automatic warehouse include:

- Fewer workers at higher productivity.
- Storage area need be heated or cooled only to the extent required by the product.
- Aisle space is reduced.
- Stock racks are limited in height only by the economics of elevating the goods; 100-foot heights have been talked of.
- Possibility of maximum utilization of the enclosed cube.
- Decreased product damage due to handling.

Disadvantages are:

- Increased hazard of fire getting a good start in an essentially unattended storage area. A sophisticated fire-protection system is a must.
- Housekeeping in tightly constructed automatics may be difficult.
- Access to jams and hang-ups may be difficult. Clearing of jams may be equally difficult.
- Mechanical or electrical failure may make it impossible to either store or retrieve goods.

There is room for growth in automatic warehousing, and the growth will come. Where system requirements can be met, the returns are already quite attractive. It can be seen that as techniques and know-how continue to develop, the use of automation will also grow.

BIBLIOGRAPHY AND FURTHER READING

(1) "Digest of Tax Laws," Washington, D.C., "Distribution Management," published by The Traffic Service Corp., annually in August. A summary of laws pertaining to warehouse inventory taxation in all states.

(2) Drake, Sheahan, Sweeny and Hupp, Consultants, "Shipper-Motor Carrier Dock Planning Manual," Washington, D.C., Operations Council of American Trucking Associations, Inc., 1969. A practical application of waiting line theory for dock planning. Complete with tables of doors required vs. arrival and loading rates, plus data on staging areas and space required in the dock.

(3) Follet, E.C., "New Approach to an Old Problem," Bala-Cynwyd, Pa., "Distribution Manager," published by The Chilton Co., November, 1968. An analog method for establishing the location of warehouses.

(4) Haskell, R.H., "Recommended Yard and Dock Standards," Washington, D.C., "Distribution Management," published by The Traffic Service Corp., October, 1966. Another viewpoint on yard and dock layout.

(5) Hoch, L.C., "Ten Most Common Mistakes in Warehouse Location," Washington, D.C., "Distribution Management," published by The Traffic Service Corporation, August, 1967.

(6) "State Size and Weight Limits for Truck Trailer Combinations," Washington, D.C., Truck and Trailer Manufacturers Assn., periodic. Updating of legal limits in all states.

(7) Volpel, J.H., "Warehouse Space — How Much?", New York, N.Y., "Industrial Engineering," published by the American Institute of Industrial Engineers, January, 1969. A method for calculating space requirements for bulk mechanical goods.

(8) Zebrowski, E.R., "The Use of a Computer in the Development and Control of Warehousing," New York, N.Y., "Industrial Engineering," published by American Institute of Industrial Engineers, January, 1968. A computerized program for storage and retrieval of chemicals in a large warehouse.

Chapter 5

Warehouse operations are set up to handle many kinds of goods. A commodity warehouse would handle a single material; cotton or tobacco warehouses are examples. Bulk terminals warehouse grains, petroleum, chemicals. Cold storage is for perishables, and so on. General merchandise is the area to which the following discussions are addressed, as being perhaps more typical of the general run of warehousing.

Public warehousing is available to handle any of the foregoing and there are sometimes real advantages in doing so. Use of a public warehouse permits the

PROFESSIONAL MANAGEMENT OF WAREHOUSE OPERATIONS

testing of a market without tying up capital in real estate or making a lease commitment. If the market fails to materialize, it is easy to get out. If the market develops strongly, information is gathered that is useful in the design of an internally operated warehouse. Where volume is modest, the public warehouse is the most economical means of serving the trade. Responsibility of the public warehouseman in protecting goods against loss or damage is limited to his exercise of such care as a reasonably cautious man would exercise in the protection of his own goods. In the absence of specific agreement, he is not responsible for loss or damage which could not have been avoided by the exercise of such care. A directory of over 900 public warehouses is published annually (Bibliography #3) which covers merchandise and refrigerated and household goods warehouses in the U.S. and Canada, arranged by city, state or province, and company. A listing of services provided by each warehouse, such as repackaging, stock control reporting, pool car redistribution, and many others, are listed. This warehouse listing, while very extensive, is not claimed to be nor is it a listing of all available warehouse facilities.

Internally operated warehouses have their own set of advantages. Among others are improved control over stocks and customer service, flexibility to make changes without negotiations with another party, better feedback of sales information, possibility of using own trucks to make deliveries, lower costs of operation, and ability to handle any service that could be provided by an outside organization. Operation of a warehouse is as involved, in its own way, as any other phase of the business. Usually it is remotely located from the center of the business so that much reliance must be placed upon the man in charge in the field. At the same time, it is expected that suitable records will be maintained to provide a measure of control from headquarters. Basic to the control of a warehouse operation is a formal system for reporting costs, so that an analysis of expenditures can be made regularly and costs can be properly allocated to the various items being handled. The records should include:

Salaries	- Managers and supervision.
	- Clerical.
	- Premium pay.
Wages	- Clerical.
	- Warehousemen, by category.
	- Premium pay.
Payroll Fringes	- Hospital, medical, and surgical insurance.
	- Workmen's compensation insurance.
	- Life, accident, and sickness insurance.
	- Payroll taxes of various sorts.

- Major medical insurance.
- Union welfare costs.
- Miscellaneous items.

Mainte-nance

- Building and grounds.
- Equipment repair.

Delivery Costs

- Payroll and fringes.
- Repairs.
- Tires, batteries, etc.
- Fuel, oil, grease.
- Licenses and insurance.
- Garage expense.
- Out-bound freights.

Operating Supplies, Etc.

- Packaging supplies.
- Pallets.
- Container refurbishing.
- Uniforms and clothing.
- Heat, light, and power.
- Miscellaneous supplies.
- Expense for outside storage.

Admin-istrative Expense

- Stationery and supplies.
- Operating and sanitary supplies.
- Telephone, teletype, telegraph.
- Postage.
- Medical examinations.
- Temporary help; vacation accruals.
- Insurance and taxes, other.

Special Expenses

- Building rental or depreciation.
- Equipment rental or depreciation.

- Outside services; e.g., contract work.

- In-bound freights.

Measurement of Labor

Measuring the effective use of warehouse labor is not a simple problem because of the high variation of tasks in a warehouse. It is not uncommon to find order pickers working on line items varying from very small single items to solid pallet loads. In some instances, this range of line items may be found on a single-customer order. There are several methods, varying in sophistication, that may be used to get a greater or lesser degree of measured control over labor. Perhaps the simplest to install is the subjective standard. This can be used where there is not too great a variety of stockkeeping units. The procedure: select the SKU that is most commonly handled as the base unit and assign it a handling factor of unity. Persons knowledgeable in the warehouse handling of this item then evaluate the labor required to unload, store, retrieve, and ship the normal monthly volume of this item. The group then rates all other SKU's in percentage terms as being a greater or lesser consumer of labor. For example, if a 100-pound bag of Product A is the base SKU, the evaluating team might decide that a 450-pound drum of Product C would require 165% of the handling labor of Product A. The method can be extended over a considerable variety of items. The writer has seen it applied to units ranging from broken case items, lengths of pipe, bales, drums, carboys, cartons, and other types of containers. By keeping track of the number of each SKU sold (inventory records), the total movement through the warehouse is converted to a "standard" SKU. This number when multiplied by the evaluated time for the base SKU gives "earned" hours, which is then compared to actual hours and a performance figure calculated. The subjective standard is a crude tool by industrial engineering standards, but it is easily understood and is readily installed and used.

A second method is the use of work sampling. The concept was developed by Tippett in England when he was endeavoring to determine the causes for loom stoppages in a textile mill. As he studied the looms, he recognized that for any given instant, examination of all looms simultaneously gave an indication of stoppage experience in a short interval around the same observation point. By extension, examination of looms in sequence at intervals permitted simultaneous determination of cause of stoppage. This greatly facilitated his analysis of down time. Tippett called this method the "snapshot" method. Morrow brought the technique to the U.S. and called it "ratio delay." Later *Factory* magazine gave it the name "work sampling" because it saw the broad application to work measurement. Work sampling is based on the laws of probability in that a sample drawn at random from a large population (group of activities) will probably have about the same pattern of distribution of activities as the whole population. The statistical theories and mathematical derivations are thoroughly covered in the texts on work sampling (Bibliography #1 and 6) and will not be discussed here.

In making a work-sampling study of labor utilization in a warehouse, concern is with the effective use of manpower. What are the various activities in which the men might be engaged? Included might be the following:

Productive Work

- Loading and unloading carriers.
- Moving goods to and from storage.
- Picking and packing small items.
- Picking large items.
- Packaging materials from bulk.
- Rearranging stock.
- Walking (productive).
- Sweeping and housekeeping.
- Get or put away empty pallets.
- Talk to supervisor about work.
- Safety meeting, etc.

Nonproductive Work

- Personal needs.
- Coffee break.
- Wash-up time.
- Early quit and late start.
- Talking (personal).
- Walking empty-handed.
- Idle.

It is plain that this could be reduced to "work" and "not work," but if the not work is lumped into a single category and is high, there is no way to tell what is causing it. If, on the other hand, work is high, we might not be aware that "productive on the job" was low; i.e., there might be a lot of sweeping rather than material handling. If there are too many categories, many of them will not be observed often enough to have strong confidence in the true frequency of occurrence. Commonly, activities are grouped. Initial studies should be made with as many categories as possible, including a breakdown to types of packages handled, in order to find out where the activity is occurring before grouping. With this information, it may be found that loading and unloading, order picking, and packing account for most of the productive activity, while the remainder could be classified as "productive other." On the nonproductive side, idle, talking, and walking empty-handed might be the principal classification, with the remainder lumped together as "nonproductive other." However, the way that you categorize is dependent upon how you expect to use the observations.

Observation tours should be made in such a fashion that all working time during the day has an equal opportunity of being seen; i.e., from beginning to end of day. This means that you randomize the tour starting time so that over a period of a month or so, every interval during the day has equal opportunity of observation. Trips through the warehouse should follow a different path each time. A decision on worker activity is made at the instant each worker is seen. Usually, 1,500-2,000 observations (one worker seen once) are sufficient to assure the validity of the sample, especially when types of activity have been partially grouped. The number of productive observations are divided by the total number of observations to give a raw performance figure. If the result is in the 50-70% range, with about 2,000 observations, the probable maximum error is around plus or minus 2%. Let us say that the actual figure was 60% ±2%. Giving the workers the benefit of the doubt, take performance to be 62%. To this must be added a personal and a fatigue allowance. Fatigue allowance for warehouse work is typically about 10%. Personal is usually allowed at 5%. Thus total allowance is 15% and the effective performance is 62 x 1.15 = 71.30%. Performance in the 70-80% range in a general warehouse is an acceptable figure. In the absence of some measure of performance prior to work sampling, do not be astonished at a performance level in the 35-45% range.

If workloads in the warehouse are reasonably steady over time, work sampling studies need be made only two or three times a year, after performance has been brought to desired levels. At this frequency, control costs are kept at a modest level. Use of work sampling is not limited to measuring the performance of personnel, although this is perhaps its widest use. It may also be used for the analysis of equipment usage, loading on computers and office machinery, and many other studies limited only by the user's imagination.

Labor standards may also be set using regular time study techniques, together with frequency analysis and related analytical methods. Development may be through stop-watch time studies, or through use of predetermined time standards such as M-T-M, WOFAC, and others. Development of engineered time standards is time consuming, and measurement of performance on a continuing basis requires much clerical time. Setup and ongoing costs of this method militate against use of such standards except under special circumstances. Readers interested in the method are referred to Bibliography #5, 9, and 10.

Evaluation of Fork-Truck Needs

Fork-truck needs are directly related to the amount of handling to be done. To illustrate the method of evaluation, an aerosol filling line will be examined. Propellants and major product ingredients are received in bulk while other ingredients are in relatively small volume. The container components are cans, caps, valves, cartons, labels, etc. In a plant running six filling lines, we might find on a given typical day of 430 minutes that:

Line #1 averages* 160 x 4 oz. cans per minute.

Line #2 averages* 122 x 9 oz. cans per minute.

Line #3 averages* 180 x 13 oz. cans per minute.

Line #4 averages* 173 x 16 oz. cans per minute.

Line #5 averages* 192 x 13 oz. cans per minute.

Line #6 averages* 180 x 10 oz. cans per minute.

Container components are unloaded from trucks to a receiving stage area, moved to warehouse and stored, reclaimed from storage to the line staging area, and from line stage to the lines. Finished product is moved from lines to warehouse staging area (sometimes to shipping stage direct), warehoused, removed to shipping stage, and then loaded out. It can be seen that pallet loads of product and components are each handled four times. For #1 line, operating at 160 cans per minute, the number of pallet loads of components required to supply the line for the shift are:

Cans $\dfrac{160 \text{ cpm x } 430 \text{ minutes}}{4,600 \text{ cans/pallet}} = \dfrac{68,800}{4,600} = 15$ pallets.

Valves 68,800/2,000 per carton = 35 cartons = 1.1 pallets.

Caps 68,800/1,800 per carton = 38 cartons = 3.4 pallets.

Labels None—lithographed cans.

Product 68,800/288 cartons @ 12 cans each = 20 pallets.

Empty Cartons 288 x 20/720 on a pallet = 8 pallets.

Total = 47.5 pallets, rounding to 48 pallets.

---

*Lines are not identical, nor are products filled identical.

Similar calculations for the other lines show:

Line #2	= 60 pallets.
Line #3	= 98 pallets.
Line #4	= 110 pallets.
Line #5	= 111 pallets.
Line #6	= 73 pallets.
Grand total pallets	= 500 pallets.

But, since each pallet is handled four times, total number of pallets to be handled daily is 500 x 4 = 2,000.

Fork-truck data; from manufacturer's data, 4,000-pound capacity electric unit:

Lift speed, loaded = 40 fpm.	For average 15-foot lift = 22.5 seconds.
Lift speed, empty = 69 fpm.	For average 15-foot lift = 13.0 seconds.
Lower speed, loaded = 70 fpm.	For average 15-foot lift = 12.8 seconds.
Lower speed, empty = 80 fpm.	For average 15-foot lift = 11.2 seconds.
Lift loaded and lower empty	= 33.7 seconds.
Lift empty and lower loaded	= 25.8 seconds.
Travel speed—maximum, loaded	= 9.3 fps.
Travel speed—maximum, empty	= 9.7 fps.

Calculation of time to unload two pallet loads of empty cans to unloading stage — can pallets double-stacked in truck; average distance from stage to truck = 45 feet:

Back out of pallet at stage (5 feet at 1 fps)	= 5 seconds.
Back turn, then forward to truck (45 feet at 5 fps)	= 9 seconds.
Raise fork 6 inches	= 1 second.
Inch under pallet (5 feet at 1 fps)	= 5 seconds.
Lift pallet and ease out of position (5 feet at 1 fps)	= 5 seconds.
Travel to stage area and turn	= 9 seconds.
Position and set down	= 5 seconds
Total	= 39 seconds.

Because of interferences with other fork trucks, pedestrians, slowing at intersections, supervisory attention, personal needs, fatigue, and other allowances, it has been found that the theoretical 39 seconds to move a pallet from a truck to stage and return must be doubled to 78 seconds. With a daily requirement of 168 pallet loads of cans, the fork-truck requirement to unload cans to receiving stage is 168/2 x 78/60 = 109 minutes.

Calculation of time to move empty cans to storage in the warehouse — storage area is at an average distance of 360 feet from receiving stage:

Inch under pallets (2 high) at receiving	=	5 seconds.
Lift and turn	=	2 seconds.
Move to storage at 5 fps	=	72 seconds.
Raise load, average 15 feet	=	23 seconds.
Inch into position to drop	=	5 seconds.
Drop load on pile	=	2 seconds.
Back out	=	5 seconds.
Drop forks	=	11 seconds.
Return to stage area	=	72 seconds.
Lift forks 3-4 inches	=	1 second.
Total	=	198 seconds.
with allowances	=	396 seconds.
	=	6.6 minutes.

Total time to store 168 pallets = 168/2 x 6.6 = 554 minutes.

In a similar calculation, moving cans from warehouse to line stage area will require 260 minutes per day, and from line stage to depalletizing machines 285 minutes. For can handling alone, total time is 109 + 554 + 260 + 285 = 1,208 minutes per day, or at 405 minutes per shift = 2.98 fork trucks. Similar calculations show that other container components will require 7.00 trucks, and handling finished product, including shipping, will require 3.27 trucks for a total of 13.25 units.

This example is oriented towards a manufacturing warehouse, but it still involves receiving, storage, retrieval, and shipment. It illustrates the detail involved in analyzing fork-truck needs. In the example, the pallets were handled several times between receipt and shipment. In a straight warehousing operation, pallets might be taken directly from a truck to storage in the warehouse; with shipment, the reverse is true. To provide proper equipment, actual handling patterns must be known.

Selection of Fork Trucks

We will now take up the selection of fork-truck units. Initially, the features desired in the unit are established. Should it be gasoline, LPG, or electric? Should it be a sit-down or a stand-up rider? Should it be a straddle truck or a counterweighted unit? And so on. For this example, specifications call for:

- Spark-proof construction, electric units.

- 600-ampere-hour batteries.

- Rotating safety light.

- Hours-operated clock, on drive motor and on lift motors.

- 42-inch forks, 3,000-pound capacity at 24 inches, sit-down rider.

- 3-stage lift, 40-45 inches free lift.

- Overhead guards.

- Solid-state controls.

- Lock to prevent unauthorized use.

- Batteries.

- Cash price and lease costs.

- Service availability.

- Separate quote on preventive maintenance service.

As might be expected, quotations and related information did not come in exactly as requested from the bidders. Additional discussions were required with each company to resolve differences. Eventually all data was gathered and tabulated as in Table 5-1. It is interesting to note the variation in the handling of traded-in equipment and residual values, and to conjecture what this does to carrying charges under a lease or finance plan. With this kind of analysis, a sound economic decision is made without too much difficulty.

TABLE 5-1
Electric-Fork-Truck Cost Analysis

Manufacturer	X	Y	Z
Model	Z 40-266A-4	CE-30	Y 30-24
Capacity	3,000 pounds	3,000 pounds	3,000 pounds
Mast height	71 inches	83 inches	70 inches
Free lift	45 inches	42 inches	15 inches
Maximum lift	156-inch triple	189-inch triple	150-inch triple
Controls	Electronic	Electronic	Electronic
Type	Sit-down rider	Sit-down rider	Sit-down rider
Cost each - truck	$8,228	$9,197	$ not given
- battery	$2,096	$1,854	ʺ
- charger	$ 868	$ 895	ʺ
Total cost each - cash	$11,192	$11,946	$10,637
- lease	$13,458*	$12,740*	$12,870*
Maintenance cost on basis of 10,000 hours operation in five years.	$5,100	$5,800	$3,900
Total acquisition and maintenance cost — 2 units - cash****	$32,584	$35,492	$25,174
- lease	$37,116	$37,080	$29,640
Trade-in, 2 units - cash	$4,140	$2,670	$4,133
- lease	$5,060	$2,670	$4,133
Residual values	$2,225**	$5,205***	$1,773***
Net cost of units - cash	$12,832	$16,062	$12,265
- lease	$14,683	$16,856	$14,498

N.B.-Net Cost = cost each + maintenance - 7% investment credit - ½ trade-in, and, for Manufacturer X, an added deduction of ½ residual value.

    *Interest = prime rate + 2%.
   **Title passes to purchaser at no added cost.
  ***Title remains with vendor and may be purchased at indicated price or lease extended at much lower rate.
****Does not include interest on investment.

TABLE 5-1 (Cont'd)
Electric-Fork-Truck Cost Analysis

Manufacturer	X	Y	Z
Term of lease	60 months	60 months	60 months
Investment credit	To buyer	To buyer	To buyer
Freight and taxes	$505	$487	$543
Delivery	12 weeks	90 days	60 days
Maintenance includes:			
Monthly PM at customer	yes	yes	yes
Needed shop overhauls	yes	yes	yes
Emergency work	yes	yes	yes
Tire replacement	yes	yes	yes
Free loan equipment	yes	no	no
Fire and theft ins.	on lease only	no	on lease only
Battery replacement	on lease only up to 10,000 hrs.	on lease only up to 10,000 hrs.	on lease only up to 10,000 hrs.
Cost each	$1,020/year	$1,160/year	$780/year
Service center	Local, radio dispatched	Local, radio dispatched	Local, radio dispatched
Parts availability	75% local	93% local	97% local
Parts availability	97%, 24 hours ex factory	98%, 48 hours ex factory	100%, 7 days

Leasing of Equipment

Leasing has become very prominent in recent years, with many companies going into or expanding into this field. Many advantages for leasing are advanced to prospective clients. Some of these are:

(1) Client can secure the use of equipment that it cannot or does not want to buy; i.e., to meet seasonal needs. These are more often met by renting than leasing.

(2) Maintenance worries are eliminated. The lessor will often service or maintain equipment for a fee. The fee may be included in the lease cost or may be expressed separately.

(3) Small companies may be able to obtain equipment under either a straight lease or finance lease when it might be very difficult to get a bank loan for the same purpose.

(4) Fixed lease costs offer a degree of protection against inflation during the term of the lease.

(5) Lessor will allow trade-in allowance on old equipment and will dispose of the old equipment.

(6) No capital investment required. Parenthetically, accountants are beginning to consider leases as long-term obligations and to show these obligations on the balance sheet.

(7) Under some circumstances, lease payments may be tax deductible to the lessor who will, in turn, share a part of this benefit with the client.

Possible disadvantages are seldom mentioned, but there are some:

(1) It seldom occurs that equipment is entirely worn out beyond economical repair at the end of a lease; i.e., it is junk. There are values remaining that belong to the lessor. If the lease is extended, it should be at a sharply reduced rate, although maintenance charges will probably be higher.

(2) As indicated in the previous section, the interest rate was prime plus 2%. Other devices which inflate the interest cost are the occasional requirement to prepay several months' lease costs and inflated residual values.

(3) Outright ownership is usually (not always) cheaper than leasing.

Lease or Own Decisions

In deciding whether to lease or not, an analysis of costs under a lease plan vs. outright purchase is indicated, even in the circumstance where leasing is the only means to obtain the desired equipment. In the preceding evaluation of new equipment, there are substantial differences in the vendor's overall proposals even though cash cost for the trucks was essentially the same. There were differences in trade-in values on purchase and lease agreements, with a major difference in the offer by one company; a wide spread in residual values; and a difference in how residuals were handled at lease end. If a best buy is to be made, an analysis is required.

There are circumstances where leasing is cheaper. Perhaps the lessor has access to low-cost money and he will pass some of this saving along to the customer; the customer can borrow money only at very high interest rates; the lessor will share accelerated depreciation rates with the customer because of his own tax structure; and other special situations. If the customer can find situations like these so that leasing is really cheaper, why not take advantage of it? On the other hand, nonfinancial reasons may sway the decision to leasing where the difference in cost is not excessive.

Once equipment is leased, there are no special problems involved. Leases usually are of five or six years' duration but may be less if the indicated usage is expected to be extremely heavy. On the other hand, light usage does not bring leases of longer duration. Leasing of buildings or special rail equipment may run for periods approaching the economic life span.

Periodic payments against a lease are normally expensed in the current accounting records. Care must be exercised in drafting the lease so that it does not become subject to interpretation by Internal Revenue as a conditional sales contract. To avoid this difficulty, do not carry loss insurance on the lessor's equipment; steer clear of leases where the monthly payments plus residual option price is close to the original cost of the equipment; don't accept an automatic title transfer at the end of the lease.

Truck Leasing

There is the possibility of special difficulties in the use of leased or rented trucks in areas outside of a commercial delivery zone. This involves the supply of drivers with the equipment, either from the same or a closely allied source. If the lessee holds the necessary permits and operating rights between the points of loading and discharge of cargo, a single contract covering driver and vehicle is legal between common carriers; otherwise, the practice is illegal. A client can, however, enter into an exclusive agreement of substantial duration with the owner and operator of a single vehicle, as this is seen as contract hauling. The federal regulatory agencies look with deep suspicion upon the practice of getting a vehicle under lease from a leasing company with a driver from the same source. The criteria is that a single letter or telephone call will serve to bring the driver and vehicle to your service. The main thrust of federal suspicion lies in the concern that the leasing company is in effect offering common carriage at cut rates, without the benefit of operating rights or permits required of a common carrier and without published tariffs. A lessee participating in such practices may be judged guilty of law violation and appropriately penalized.

To avoid these troubles, lease vehicles from one source. If you need temporary drivers, obtain them from an independent agency specializing in truck drivers. The lessee then should exercise full control over the drivers as he would if they were on his own payroll. He must schedule the drivers' hours of work, see that driver logs are maintained, that safety regulations are obeyed, that hours spent in driving and on duty are in compliance with federal regulation, and so on. The area is grey and subject to the hazards of interpretation common to such grey areas.

It is permissible for private carriers to sublease equipment to others, but care should be exercised in trip or day leases, or very short-term leases, as again suspicion arises of illegal practices. Two-way leasing, two private carriers in effect exchange equipment, is definitely illegal. For example, a New York private carrier has many loads to Chicago but no return back and cannot afford to deadhead back. Fortuitously, he learns of a Chicago private carrier with the reverse problem. What is more natural than to swap equipment? Natural, maybe, but also illegal.

There are legitimate return hauls of commodities, probably 3-400 items, which are largely outside the regulatory format and can be carried for hire by private carriers. These are exempt agricultural commodities such as livestock, fish and shell-fish, and a host of fruit, vegetables, and similar materials. There are many complications. Cooked fish can be carried, but canned or otherwise preserved fish may not. It is beyond the scope of this book to explore this field in detail. The reader interested in this approach is referred to the Federal Bureau of Motor Carriers for up-to-date information. It does seem, though, that getting into this type of activity is pretty far afield from the main line of business enterprise. There are two other cautions: (a) get competent advice on what may be moved under the commodity exemptions; (b) do not mix exempt and nonexempt products — this is also against the law.

Stock-Locater Systems

In a warehouse with hundreds or even thousands of items in stock, finding stored goods can be a problem unless a system is used. High-volume items tend to be concentrated near the docks to reduce in-house transportation costs. Sometimes there is just not enough space to store everything where it "belongs"; goods are then slipped into any available slot and sometimes even the aisles are filled. In a small warehouse the stock handlers may remember where things were put, but in a large operation this method will not work.

Today, almost everything in inventory carries a stock number or product code. The idea of arranging SKU's in stock number sequence is appealing because of the ease in training stock handlers. But travel time will not be optimum under this arrangement, and cube utilization will be poor. Transportation is minimized if high-volume items are stored as close to the docks as possible. High volume does not necessarily mean high SKU count, it can also indicate high pallet load count. Further, highest use of cube comes when random storage is allowed.

The answer to cube utilization and finding goods which are randomly stored is a "stock-locater system." When a pallet load of material is put away, a record is made of the place it is stored and of the material on the pallet; thus, 24 cases #10 cans Beaumont peach halves in Zone 4, Area B, Row 23. A fairly simple system has the fork-truck operator enter on a log sheet where he puts each pallet handled, the name of the material, and the location number in the racks. (This method works best with simple racks.) Someone must tell him the product name or identifier if he doesn't know it. Later the sheet is turned over to a clerk who transcribes the data to a suitable filing system. Pallets can be widely scattered in the warehouse, but the information on a given type of item is on a single file sheet. When the materials are needed, the location numbers for the pallet loads needed are transcribed from the file, crossed off on the file, and the pick list is given to the fork-truck driver. He has no trouble in finding the pallet loads.

More sophisticated, and with less clerical effort, is a tag system. A sample tag is shown in Figure 5-1. The tags come in continuous prenumbered rolls and are printed

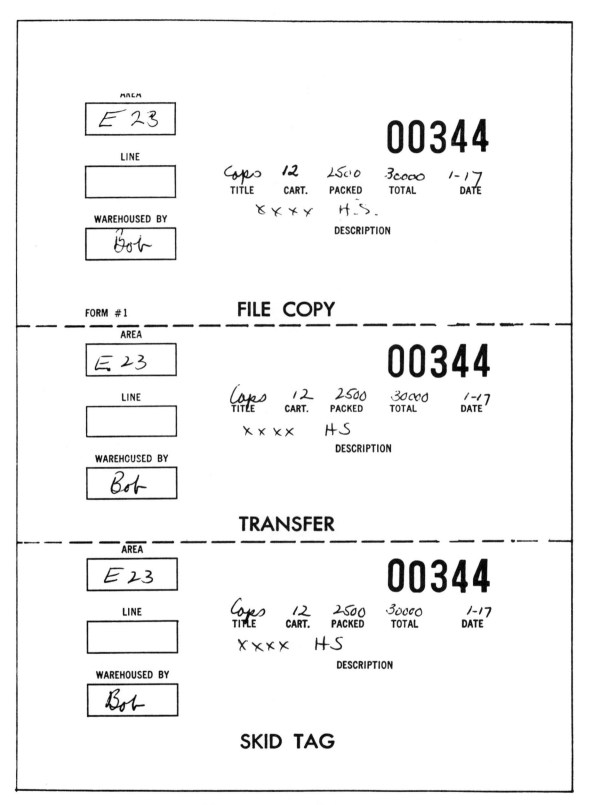

Figure 5-1. *Stock-locater tag.*

147

with variable data right at the unloading dock, on a suitable printer, or if only a few are needed, they may be handwritten. Machine printing is preferable when 15-20 sets of triple tags are needed. In use, one of the set of three tags is stapled to the end of side of a pallet stringer where it can be easily seen in the storage pile. The fork-truck driver writes the storage location in the proper spaces (in Figure 5-1, area line or area row). The two remaining tags are given to the stock clerk for filing by product description or code. When needed, the stock clerk gives the transfer portion to the stock picker who returns it after he has located the pallet. At the point of shipment (or use), the pallet tag is removed when the pallet is emptied and returned to the stock clerk. He matches up the stubs received with the file stub; the file stub is sent to accounting to relieve inventory records; the remaining two stubs may be thrown away. There are several variations of this kind of tag system. As with any kind of system, human error causes more difficulty than the system itself. If the driver is interrupted while putting goods away, he may forget to make an entry on the log sheet or on tags to be filed. The pallet is then "lost" or cannot be found when wanted. With reasonable attention, a locater system will work very well.

Auxiliary Equipment

Jack-lift trucks are available in various capacities up to about 4,000 pounds. Simply, these are a pair of broad forks fitted with a hydraulic lifting system which raises them a few inches to lift a pallet just off the floor. The unit rolls on a pair of small-diameter wheels at the end of the forks and a larger-diameter wheel at the yoke end of the forks. The hydraulic system lifts the forks, depresses the small wheels, and holds firmly so that the load is balanced on three rolling points and can be moved. The load is pushed or pulled manually. The hydraulic pump is operated by the steering handle. Power-operated models are available. Forks to 85 inches can be supplied. The longer forks are used to handle two pallets in a miscellaneous order-picking situation.

Hand trucks are made in such a variety of models that only the maker's catalog will give a full listing. Units are made of hardwood, steel or alloy, or combinations. Wheels may be malleable iron or steel, with solid rubber or plastic tires, or pneumatic tires. Units weigh from 20 to about 150 pounds, and have a load-carrying capacity of up to 1,000 pounds. Special units are made for handling barrels, drums, kegs, bales, etc.

Four-wheel platform trucks are moved manually with loads up to about 6,000 pounds and by tractor for larger units. Most units are made with steel frames and hardwood decks.

Six-wheel platform trucks have caster wheels at each corner while the larger main wheels are at the middle. Caster wheels are usually half the diameter of the main wheels which range in diameter from 8 to 18 inches. Frames and platforms may be of wood or steel, or combinations of both. Platforms are 2 to 3 feet wide and 3½ to 8 feet long, with load capacities up to about 5,000 pounds. These trucks are especially useful for order picking in crowded conditions and narrow aisles. They are very maneuverable and can be turned 180 degrees within their own length. These units are usually moved by manpower.

Pallets are made of many materials, including the common hardwood units, paper, particle board, plywood, expanded polystyrene, pressed steel, high-density polyethylene, and others. Pallets are made in almost any size the buyer specifies. The trucking industry has tried to standardize on 32" x 40," 40" x 40," and 48" x 48." A 42" x 54" pallet offers advantages in semi-trailer loading in that 20 four-way pallets can be placed in pinwheel pattern in a 40-foot unit by fork truck, giving a tight-stacked, full, uniform floor load.

Pallets are either two-way or four-way, which means that forks can enter a pallet on two sides only or on all four sides. In some cases, the top surface overhangs the stringers to give what is called a "wing" pallet. The overhang assures there will be enough room between adjacent pallets for the entry of the outriggers of a straddle fork truck. The wings may also be used to catch a "bar sling" when units are to be sling handled.

The common wood pallet is usually nailed together with cement-coated or drive-screw nails. Less often they are put together with wood screws or bolts. Use of common nails is unsatisfactory because they work loose too easily, causing damage to stored goods and providing a shorter pallet life. Under ideal conditions of storage and use, pallets should last a long time, but the ideal is seldom achieved. Idle pallets are often stacked out in the weather where they are subject to sun, rain, and frost. Stringers are split by being hit by fork points. Forks are not always entered parallel to surfaces, so that a plank at the entering side of the pallet picks up too much of the lifting load and is pulled loose. Tilting of piles in storage may result in great "racking" strains when forks are forced into the pallet in order to retrieve the unit.

Double-faced, bolted plywood pallets are claimed to withstand the rigors of poor handling practices very well. Although the first cost of these pallets is substantially higher than the common pallet, the overall cost is said to be less because of their long life. Pressed steel pallets have even higher first cost, but are almost indestructible, and over the very long term are competitive in cost with the common pallet. The cost penalty is severe if these pallets are shipped out and not returned.

Disposable Pallets

Disposable or single-trip pallets are made of scrap wood, cheap new woods with very light construction, expanded polystyrene, special configurations of corrugated board, and other similar constructions. Although called "single trip," they can some-times be reused before failing, but the life is not very great in most cases. Their use developed with customer demand for palletized shipments, a reluctance to pay deposits, cost of return freights, and vendors' reluctance to ship out good wood pallets and handle the paper work with returnable units. Where standard-grade pallets are shipped out and a deposit collected, the pallets may be a long time coming back and worn out to boot.

Slip sheets are made from semi-chemical hardwood pulps and supplementary long fibers, yielding a strong, hard, semi-rigid board which is only a fraction of an inch thick and of very modest cost. These are of two types. The first requires only full tapered forks on the truck, and these are driven under the pallet load by fork-truck power. The second type has a turned-up edge which is mechanically grasped, and the load is pulled up onto the forks with a push-pull device mounted on the fork-truck.

Skids

A single-faced pallet (not mentioned above) consists of three stringers and a top deck. Truly, this is a skid. The single-faced pallet can be used for stacking to a limited extent, but the loads are concentrated on the stringers. These pressure points may well cause damage to the goods on the lower pallet.

A skid platform typically has a steel-bound hardwood surface with steel legs at the corners (dead skid), or steel legs and lift socket at one end and fixed wheels at the other end (live skid). An eccentric-wheeled lift unit raises the steel legs from the floor so that the skid can be moved manually. Dead skids are moved with fork lifts. Skids normally are not used for stacking, except for those specially fitted with corner posts. This configuration is most often seen as skid boxes for loose items.

Dock Boards

Perhaps the most satisfactory portable dock board is the magnesium unit because of its light weight and good strength. The largest unit for truck loading has an axle load capacity of about 14,000 pounds at a 60-inch span and weighs in at 250 pounds. The unit for railroad cars is only slightly heavier.

In selecting a dock board, it should be recognized that rise should be kept low for rapid operations, but in any event should be held to 10 degrees with most fork trucks. A board 36 inches long will handle a height difference, dock to vehicle, of plus or minus 6 inches; a 48-inch board, plus or minus 8½ inches; and a 60-inch board, plus or minus 10 inches. The board should be at least a foot wider than the fork truck using it, and should have side rails to prevent accidentally running the fork truck off the edge of the board. There should be adequate detents to prevent the board from shifting to a position where it could drop under load.

For permanent installations, boards are usually made of steel, but the same rules on slopes apply. There are a variety of designs available, ranging from units shifted by hand, actuated by a truck backing into a trigger mechanism, to power-operated ones.

BIBLIOGRAPHY AND FURTHER READING

(1) Barnes, R.M., *Work Sampling*, New York, N.Y., John Wiley and Sons, Inc., 1958. A basic text on work sampling techniques.

(2) Bolz, H.A., and Hageman, G.E., editors, *Materials Handling Handbook*, New York, N.Y., Ronald Press, 1968.

(3) "Distribution Manager," published monthly by The Chilton Co., Bala-Cynwyd, Pa.

(4) *Distribution/Warehouse Cost Digest*, Washington, D.C., published by Marketing Publications, Inc., biweekly. Offers many practical suggestions for costing, standards, layouts, etc. in warehouses.

(5) Grillo, E.V., and Berg, C.J., Jr., *Work Measurement in the Office*, New York, N.Y., McGraw-Hill Book Co., Inc., 1959. A text on clerical work measurement.

(6) Heiland, R.E., and Richardson, W.J., *Work Sampling*, New York, N.Y., McGraw-Hill Book Co., Inc., 1957. The explanations are clear and there are a number of case studies.

(7) Jenkins, C.H., *Modern Warehouse Management*, New York, N.Y., McGraw-Hill Book Co., 1968. Complete coverage of warehouse operations.

(8) "Leasing in Industry," New York, N.Y., National Industrial Conference Board publication #127, 1968. An overview of the leasing industry and its practices.

(9) Maynard, H.B., Stegemerten, G.J., and Schwab, J.L., *Methods-Time-Measurement*, New York, N.Y., McGraw-Hill Book Co., Inc., 1948. The book offers a view of the predetermined time standard technique. Instruction is required to develop a working understanding.

(10) Nadler, G., *Motion and Time Study*, New York, N.Y., McGraw-Hill Book Co., Inc., 1955. A basic text on industrial engineering work measurement techniques.

(11) Vreeland, B., "Private Trucking from A to Z," New York, N.Y., Shippers Conference of Greater New York, Inc., 1969. As the title says, a thorough coverage.

(12) Zebrowski, E.R., "Use of a Computer in Development and Control of Warehousing," New York, N.Y., *Industrial Engineering*, published by American Institute of Industrial Engineers, January, 1968. Logic diagrams and discussion of a computerized system for storing and retrieving goods in a nonautomatic warehouse.

Chapter 6

C ost analysis in the distribution area is not new. Warehouse cost studies, analysis of delivery costs, material handling cost analysis, and many other types of studies have been made for years. The various functions that we now look at as a part of the materials management activity have been divided in the past into several areas of responsibility. Materials handling has been a part of manufacturing and field warehousing. Raw materials procurement has rested with purchasing. Selling is a marketing responsibility. All phases of transportation have been handled by the traffic group. Inventory management may have

DISTRIBUTION COST ANALYSIS
AS A MONEY-SAVING TOOL

153

been assigned to sales, to manufacturing, or to financial, or in part to all three. See Table 6-1 for a listing of factors in the distribution area.

TABLE 6-1
Materials Management Cost Factors

Raw Materials

Availability in proper quantity and quality.

Alternate sources of supply.

Means of transport to the factory.

Terms of transport to the factory; i.e., F.O.B. point.

Inventory control.

Cost of holding inventory.

Loss, damage, obsolescence costs.

Storage costs.

In-plant handling costs.

Conversion

Labor utilization.

Overhead absorption.

Depreciation methods.

In-process inventory.

Loss, damage, obsolescence costs to in-process inventory.

Setup costs.

Production planning.

Raw materials turnover.

Raw materials recovery or yield.

Finished goods inventory control.

Finished goods warehousing.

Finished goods inventory costs.

Packaging.

Finished goods shipping to customers.

Finished goods shipping to field warehouses.

TABLE 6-1 (Cont.)

Selling

Advertising and promotion.

Selling expense.

Credit terms.

Payment discounts.

Supply alternatives.

Product line proliferation.

Small orders.

Warranty costs.

Services to customers.

Distribution

Transportation

Private motor truck - owned or leased.

Private rail cars - owned or leased.

Common carriers - rail, water, air, motor, bus.

Shippers' cooperative.

Freight consolidators.

Warehousing Operation

Space utilization.

Labor use.

Inventory

Control.

Holding cost.

Turnover.

Dormant items.

Loss and damage.

Reorder practices.

TABLE 6-1 (Cont.)

Order Entry System

    Receipt of customer order.

    Order processing.

    Order transmission to shipping point.

    Invoicing and invoicing delays.

    Rates and routings.

    Credit investigations.

    Receipt of funds.

With this kind of divided responsibility, changes made in the name of cost improvement can have the results shown in the following. For a chemical process, a certain ore was purchased in parcels of 4-5,000 tons. This ore was partially processed at the mine and then delivered to the factory by ocean steamer. As received, the ore was dry and free flowing and at the factory was entirely stored in a covered bin from which it was recovered by gravity for use. The traffic department entered negotiations with the steamship company for a new charter to achieve lower freight rates. Agreement was reached to take full cargos of 11,000 tons of ore with freight reduced 25¢ per ton. Savings on an annual basis were about $30,000. So far the change looks good. However, look at what happened to other costs:

(1)   Average inventory increased from about 2,500 tons to about 6,000 tons. The value of the increased average industry was about $70,000; a foregone profit opportunity of $17,500 was incurred in the holding cost. This is, of course, a hidden cost.

(2)   Unloading of smaller parcels was handled very simply through mechanical equipment leading directly to the storage bin. The larger parcels required storage outdoors on the ground for the excess material. Additional unloading costs to move ore to the storage pile location, pile it up, cover it to protect against rain and wind loss, and subsequent reclaiming operations were incurred and amounted to 10¢ per ton on all the ore. This cost was spread through several accounts and was hardly noticeable, yet amounted to $12,000 per year.

(3)   With the smaller parcels, ore was available from the bins ready for use in a dry, free-flowing condition. With the larger parcels, the portion stored in the bin was in this condition, and only a portion of the material stored outdoors

was also free flowing. About 1,000 tons of the outside ore absorbed water from the ground and had to be redried at a cost of $1/ton. With 11 shipments received annually, the cost was $11,000 per year.

(4) The $30,000 "saved" in ocean transportation costs resulted in increases in other costs of $40,500. The new charter arrangement provided benefits only to the steamship company.

This is not an extreme example, but may occur at any time when due consideration is not given to all related costs. With raw materials, much the same inventory rules apply as with finished goods. The concepts of economic order quantity, order point, lead time, and safety stocks are equally applicable. As with finished goods, there are and must be managerial overrides. For instance, the possibility of war cutting off the normal source of a raw material because the supply is pre-empted for defense purposes leads prudent management to build inventories far above normal levels. It may be impractical to build inventories enough to last through a conflict, but time can be gained to develop alternate sources or alternate raw materials. Stocks are also increased to cover an anticipated lengthy strike. These moves are logical, as well as necessary to the maintenance of the operation.

Raw Material Cost Factors

Some of the factors to be considered in the raw materials area and evaluated in terms of overall costs include:

- Can raw materials be scheduled for delivery in economic delivery units at shortest practical intervals?

- Is source of supply sufficiently dependable that safety stocks can be held to a minimum?

- What are the total delivered, unloaded, and reclaimed costs associated with alternate sources of supply? Investment in safety stocks must be considered.

- Can arrangements be made to move finished goods in one direction and raw materials as a return load? Such round-robin arrangements may prove economical for private carriage if there is enough volume to keep the equipment busy. An economical arrangement may often be made with a common carrier on such moves, even where it might be attractive to move the goods by private carriage.

- Are volume levels high enough to warrant the use of inland barges or ocean transport?

- Can advantage be taken of a multi-car arrangement where a number of rail cars are moved under a single bill of lading as a single unit? The ultimate arrangement here is a leased train, which is being used today to move grain from midcontinent elevators to seaports and coal from mine to central power stations.

All of these concepts must be evaluated in terms of effect on safety stocks and total average inventory, penalties for running out of stock, added or variable unloading, storage or rehandling costs, and possible effects on factory costs. The penalties of running out of stock are related to customer service, although in many cases these are offset in time through the protection of inventories. Some businesses do not have an inventory shelter in finished goods — examples include power, transportation, and telephones. The political consequences of a power outage due to failure to manage fuel supplies effectively could be very costly. On the other hand, an interruption on an auto assembly line might be little noticed at the customer level when new car stocks are at their normal highs. Penalties here would be largely in failure to use manpower, piling up of supplies from vendors, loss of profit on units not produced, etc. Penalty costs run the gamut from little to much. There is no rule except that each business must examine its own operations and determine its own penalties.

Manufacturing

Conversion of raw materials to finished goods is not usually a responsibility of a materials management group. Decisions made in the materials management area necessarily have an impact upon manufacturing operations and costs. It is wise to consider what the effects may be. We have already examined some of the variables in the procurement and in-bound delivery area but we must also have a raw material supply adequate to assure the stability of the manufacturing operation. Economic run sizes are, or should be, related to the costs of changing over from one sequence of processing to another. Frequent changeovers may be a result of demands from the marketing group. These are difficult to combat other than by showing what happens to costs. However, improper demand forecasts, together with the explosion of the forecasted demand into raw material needs, has the same effect as does failure to establish proper order quantities and safety stocks.

Other factors to evaluate include the effect of materials management decisions on factory labor utilization and related overhead absorption, in-process inventory, storage costs due to loss-damage-obsolescence, production scheduling, raw material turnover, packaging costs, finished goods inventory control and inventory costs, warehousing costs, and costs of shipping finished goods.

Marketing

Marketing is not a materials management responsibility but analysis of marketing activity may help to improve profitability. To demonstrate: it is quite common with basic commodity type chemicals, such as soda ash and sulfuric acid, to arrange a "cross haul" agreement with another manufacturer, under which you supply a product of suitable quality to certain of his customers in an area close to your factory, while he, in turn, supplies an equivalent quality and tonnage to your customers in the area of his factory. This arrangement is very useful when the factories are in different parts of the country and where there are equivalent tonnages to be exchanged.

Distribution

It is in this area that major efforts in cost analysis occur. While it is possible to find costs in the distribution area which can be improved without recourse to a system cost analysis, the greatest economies will be developed in considering the system "transportation-warehousing-inventory-paper work-factory-marketing" as a whole.

The transportation network includes more than 200,000 miles of railroad trackage, 100,000 miles of airways, 30,000 miles of inland and coastal waterways, and several million miles of streets and highways. The equipment and services using this network is discussed in detail in Chapter 9. Analysis of the cost of moving goods can be very rewarding. First it is necessary to get a sample of the shipments moving from a warehouse for a period of at least a month. A listing is made of the weights moving to various customers, or alternately, destinations. Where a customer is found to be making many small demands, the sales group should be notified with the suggestion they contact the customer's buyers to point out the possibility of workload reductions in the customer's purchasing, receiving, accounts payable, and other departments when small purchases are consolidated to a weekly or semi-monthly basis. The benefits to the vendor will be fewer orders from the customer, perhaps fewer stockkeeping entries, lower freight bills if goods are sold on a delivered basis, and less invoicing and accounts receivable work.

With motor carriers, a "round-robin" arrangement can be made sometimes, where there is internal cross-haul traffic in sufficient volume. As an example, a factory in the Cleveland area may be serving a warehouse and major customers in the Philadelphia area, while a factory in the Philadelphia location may be serving a warehouse and customers in the Cleveland-Akron-Youngstown region. Where there are several loads a month each way, it may be possible to negotiate a rate for a full load each way (a round-robin load) that is appreciably better than the usual one-way rate. Such arrangements cannot always be made, but they should be looked for.

The Railway Express Agency offers a shipping-cage service for consolidation of small shipments from your shipping point to a common destination delivery area, where the wheel-mounted cage is loaded with miscellaneous shipments to a given destination and moves at the more economical rate for large shipments. Upon arrival, cages are emptied and individual shipments delivered at a local rate.

Warehousing Costs

Costs associated with running a warehouse include:

- Rent on land and buildings or depreciation on same.
- Depreciation on installed facilities.
- Repairs on buildings and equipment.
- Taxes on land, buildings, and equipment.
- Taxes on inventory.
- Utilities, heat, light, power, water, sewerage, telephone.
- Insurance on buildings and contents.
- Interest on the average inventory.
- In-bound freight.
- Out-bound freight.
- Obsolescence in stock.
- Stock losses and damage.
- Labor costs for picking, packing, shipping, paper work, truck drivers, janitors, workmen, supervision.
- Trash removal.
- Snow removal.
- Operating costs on owned trucks.

Costs such as rent or depreciation, taxes, insurance, supervision, and staff help and utilities are, for the most part, fixed costs. Freights, labor costs, and repairs are variable costs. There is some variation in some fixed costs; likewise, some of the variable costs will approach being fixed — especially where volume is stable. But when volume is unstable, it will be found that little can be done with the so-called fixed costs, while the variable costs will move up and down with volume.

It is possible to take the total cost and divide by the number of shipments and arrive at a cost per shipment. It is also possible to arrive, in a similar fashion, at a cost per case, or per barrel, or per hundred-weight, or whatever other measure you choose. The one thing these measures have in common is that they are misleading. For example, in a study made by the author, it was found that the labor cost to pick, pack, and ship a single small unit from shelf stock was 91¢, while the labor cost to pick and ship a full carton of the same item was only 27¢, and to pick and ship a pallet load of cartons hand-stacked in the carrier was 19¢ per carton. In the same study, it was found that cost of processing paper work for an order at the warehouse was $1.74. Thus the cost, exclusive of receiving and storing, for the single unit (1 pound net, 5 pounds gross) was $2.65. For the carton (12 x 1 pound net, 27 pounds gross) it was $2.01. The cost per carton when a pallet load was moved to a carrier and hand-stacked was about 26¢ each. If the single unit first mentioned was converted to an equivalent carton, the cost would be $31.80/per carton.

This highlights an area in which warehousing costs can best be attacked. Careful examination of costs and product mix will show typically that 20% of the SKU's account for about 70% of the volume moving through the warehouse. Inventory of these items may be turning ten to 20 times per year. Another 20% of the SKU's will account for perhaps 20% of the volume and may be turning five to ten times per year. The remaining 60% of the items will account for about 10% of annual volume and will be turning from zero (dormant stock) to five times per year. Fast-moving items are generally held with physically large stocks. Slow movers may occupy relatively little actual space because stocks are typically small, but the cost of storage per unit sold will be much higher for the slow mover than the fast mover because: (1) it is on hand so long; (2) it must be accessible, and utilization of floor space (or cube) is very low.

There are other factors besides cost to be considered in determining whether to continue stocking slow movers, but none of these should be considered dominant unless fully supported, and even then they should be periodically reviewed. Alternates should be sought, in any event. Some of the arguments advanced for maintaining stocks of slow movers are:

"We have plenty of space in the warehouse." If true, a smaller warehouse may serve better.

"We need a full line to serve the market." Would it be more economical (and practical) to supply these items from another warehouse, from the factory direct, or from the factory as a deferred shipment on next warehouse replenishment?

"Customer insists that we hold in stock for him." Does the volume of business justify this kind of support? If yes, hold the stock — if not, seek alternates.

"Stock is a safety stock to protect the customer in event of delivery failure from the factory." A valid reason, but an examination of delivery failures vs. the cost of holding stock is in order.

Case Study

Beta Corporation maintained field warehouses at Boston, Providence, Bridgeport, and in the New York metropolitan area, to service customers with commodity and specialty type chemicals. Some of the commodity type products were liquids and were delivered to the trade in owned tank trucks or were packaged for delivery to smaller customers. All other materials were packaged. With the development of the Connecticut Turnpike and the Interstate Highway system, it became apparent that the bulk chemicals could be delivered more economically into the Bridgeport area by new larger tank trucks from a New Jersey factory or from the Providence terminal, dependent upon location of customers. At the same time, other commodity-type packaged chemicals were simultaneously withdrawn from Bridgeport, leaving only the specialty chemicals. With the removal of the commodity volume from Bridgeport, there was a small reduction in labor, but most of the crew was retained. It was now found that the expense of running the warehouse was about equal to the profit in the goods still being sold out of Bridgeport. (This further illustrates the need for careful analysis of costs, as in the unit-carton-pallet example mentioned previously.) Analysis of the Bridgeport business showed a total of about 80 customers for the specialty chemicals, of whom 16 accounted for more than 75% of the volume. Further analysis of alternates showed the New York area warehouse could absorb the paper work and, with the addition of one laborer, all of the materials handling. A carrier was found who would and did give next-day delivery from the New York area, which was the same as was obtained from the Bridgeport warehouse. For the major customers, the prepaid freight costs from the New York area warehouse were about double the Bridgeport rate, but this was largely offset by a net reduction of in-bound freights to the New York area vs. Bridgeport. Small shipments were given to United Parcel Service for area delivery as a drop shipment by common carrier truck from the New York area, with about a one-day increase in delivery time. The net result was a reduction in cost; i.e., an increase in profitability almost equal to the cost of operating out of Bridgeport.

Summary

There is no easy way to analyze distribution costs, but the sure way is to follow the goods throughout the system and evaluate the costs connected with each phase of the handling, including paper work, freights, and overheads, and make similar evaluations for alternates.

BIBLIOGRAPHY AND FURTHER READING

(1) "Bibliography on Physical Distribution Management," Washington, D.C., National Council on Physical Distribution Management, 1967. A listing of published material on the subject, and, from examination, it appears to be comprehensive,

(2) Heskett, J.L., Ivie, R.M., and Glaskowsky, N.A., Jr., *Business Logistics*, New York, N.Y., The Ronald Press Co., 1964. This excellent book covers in much detail business logistical systems, or, as others have called it, physical distribution.

(3) Magee, J.F., *Industrial Logistics*, New York, N.Y., McGraw-Hill Book Co., Inc., 1968. This is another excellent book on the details of logistical (physical distribution) systems.

(4) Smykay, E.W., Bowersox, D.J., and Mossman, F.H., *Physical Distribution Management*, New York, N.Y., The Macmillan Co., 1961. Another solid coverage of the field with somewhat more emphasis on the theoretical aspects.

(5) Taff, C.A., *Management of Traffic and Physical Distribution, 4th Ed.*, Homewood, Ill., Richard D. Irwin, Inc., 1968. This book is traffic oriented and provides thorough coverage of that field.

Chapter 7

In attacking problems of materials management and physical distribution, we are often faced with a decision concerning the true scope of the problem. Before proceeding, it is worthwhile to take time to think through the steps to be followed in reaching a solution. The standard problem-solving technique is a good approach:

1. Define the problem.
2. Gather the data.
3. Construct a model.
4. Enter the data into the model.
5. Test the solution.
6. Implement the solution.
7. Review and follow up.

IMPLEMENTING QUANTITATIVE METHODS

Define the Problem

Definition of the problem is especially important in materials management because at times an action at one point will produce reactions at more than one other point, as we have seen in discussions above. Thus if we are considering ways to lower the unit cost of moving goods into a warehouse, we must not look only at transport costs, although this answer seems obvious. We must also consider the possibility of changes in the costs of warehousing, the availability of warehouse space, the effect of lower unit cost on labor costs, the effect on service to other warehouses, the effect on turnover rates, and other factors. This seems like overstressing the obvious, but the self-evident is commonly overlooked. Spend the time to think through the ramifications of the problem and the problem will be half solved.

Gather the Data

The first benefit in defining the problem lies here. With the problem well-defined, we readily can set up an organized plan for collecting the necessary data. If our problem definition is good, a single pass at the data may be all that is required. Recognize, however, that in gathering and using data, other channels of possible action may be uncovered and perhaps further data-gathering effort will be required.

Construct a Model

Model construction is discussed in detail later in this chapter. Briefly, a model is a graphic or mathematical representation of the problem or of a tentative solution.

Enter Data into the Model

It is at this point that we speak of "solving the problem." In truth, we are really solving the model. Any reader who has worked around computers knows that a program is a sort of model, and more often than not it doesn't work the first time. The program (model) is tinkered with until it does work. The program output may include a number of error messages or diagnostics which aid in clearing up the errors of omission, commission, and logic. With other types of models, our own insights and observations are required.

Test the Solution

Discretion says, "Try it on a small scale." Business managers are not too upset if a field trial in a small section of the problem area is unsuccessful. A small-scale failure is a small price to pay to try out a new idea. The small trial can point out weaknesses in the proposed solution as readily as a large-scale trial. With modifications made, if required, we would be ready to expand the solution to the whole system.

Implementation

This is the general application of the solution. Again a plan is very worthwhile. Implementation is itself a problem, so the whole problem-solving technique is invoked again at this point. The model in this case is a timetable for implementation. It would include such things as preliminary sessions in the field to inform, a written procedure, advance pretraining in the method, and installation of the method with on-the-job training, with day-to-day follow-up for a period of perhaps two to four weeks.

Follow-Up

The designer and developer of a solution often overlooks this step. It is assumed that once implementation is accomplished, all is well. Such confidence! This assumption overlooks the fact that field personnel have had only minimum exposure to the logic and reasoning that lead to the problem solution. Their basic understanding of the solution is necessarily thin. True enough, they may absorb the routine mechanics of the solution very quickly, but until sufficient time has passed to develop sound understanding, the implementation stands on shaky ground. Thus the need for continuing follow-up, which may continue for as long as a year, depending upon the complexity of the new method introduced.

Data Handling

Averages

When the man in the street speaks of something as being "average," he probably means an arithmetic average. This is obtained by adding up all of the items in the experienced sample and dividing by the number of items. In fact, this man's average is more likely to be an intuitive figure. But when data are added and then divided by the number of data items, the result is the "average" or "mean." Expressed symbolically, the mean is written $\bar{x}$ (pronounced "x bar") and the calculation is:

$$\bar{x} = (x_1 + x_2 + x_3 + \dots \dots x_n)/n = \frac{\Sigma x}{n} .$$

For many of the calculations we make, an arithmetic mean is entirely satisfactory, but not when speeds or prices are involved. For example, a man goes for a walk along a country road. He is in no hurry, so he walks at only 2 miles per hour; however, when he has gone a mile it starts to rain. He turns around and, hurrying now, walks at 4 miles an hour. What is his average pace? If we take the arithmetic average of 2 mph and 4 mph, the answer is 3 mph. But this is wrong because the man walked one-half hour at 2 mph and only one-quarter hour at 4 mph. The elapsed time was 45 minutes to cover the 2 miles walked. His average pace was then 2/.75 = 2.67 mph. This type of average is called a harmonic mean and the formula is:

$$H = \text{harmonic mean} = n/\Sigma\,(1/x),$$

where n = number of values and x = observed values. In our example, n = 2 and x = 2 and 4.

Another mean is the geometric mean or G. This is used to obtain averages for systems which are following a geometric or exponential growth pattern. Population growth often responds to a geometric pattern. The formula is

$$G = \sqrt[n]{x_1 + x_2 + x_3 + \ldots\ldots x_n}\ .$$

It should be noted that G will show a lower mean growth than $\bar{x}$, but in this situation $\bar{x}$ is the wrong calculation.

Distributions

The Normal Distribution

If the sample data from which an arithmetic average is calculated is plotted, in many instances, the data will be found to be "normally" distributed. For example, if we were to measure the height of 100,000 men in the United States, we would probably find the average height was about 5'6", but we would probably find one or two who were only 4 feet tall and possibly as many who were 7 feet tall. Men who were about 5'6" would be the most commonly observed. If we plotted this data, we would find the heights to be normally distributed. The curve thus generated can be represented

by the equation $y = \dfrac{1}{\sigma\sqrt{2\,\pi}}e^{-(x\,-\,\bar{x})^2/2\sigma^2}$. Figure 7-1 shows the ideal form of the curve.

Note that solution of the equation depends upon only two variables: the mean $\bar{x}$ and the standard deviation, plus the constants π = 3.1416 and e = 2.7183. The derived curve has a number of interesting properties:

a. The maximum ordinate occurs at the mean, $\bar{x}$.

b. As values of x depart either to the right or left of the mean, the curve drops rapidly to zero values of the ordinate.

c. The area under the curve can be demonstrated to be equal to unity. This leads to the next property.

d. The probability of a random number, x, occurring within given limits of x

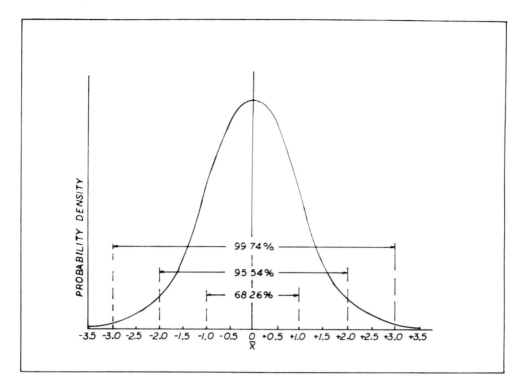

Figure 7-1. *Normal distribution.*

is equal to the area under the curve enclosed by lines drawn parallel to the ordinate at the limiting values.

e. About 68% of the values of x will fall within ±1 standard deviation of the mean.

f. About 95% of the values will fall within ±2 standard deviations, while about 99% are within ±3 standard deviations.

One use of the normal distribution was shown in Chapter 2, Managing Inventory Successfully. The texts in the Bibliography, #2, 6, 8, and 9, give further illustration of its use in quality control and statistical applications.

The Poisson Distribution

The name is that of the mathematician who first derived the relationship in the 1830's. The distribution is useful when the probability of occurrence of an event is low, as in the case of slow-moving inventory. Thus we would expect to have days when there was no demand and others when the demand was only for one or two units; there would be few days when demand was many more than two or three units. Other uses

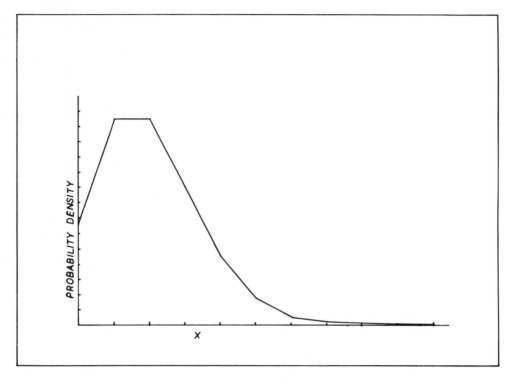

Figure 7-2. *Poisson distribution.*

for the Poisson distribution may be found in the same texts referred to previously. The equation for the Poisson distribution is written:

$$p\,(x) = e^{-\sigma}\,\bar{x}^{x}\,/x\;!$$

The mean value, $\bar{x}$, of a Poisson distribution is equal to the variance of that distribution from which the standard deviation, σ, is $\bar{x}$. The curve of the Poisson distribution is not smooth, in that it represents events in a given space. Thus with slow-moving items, the curve in Fig. 7-2 could represent the probability of demands from zero to 11 units on a given day. Since we do not deal usually with fractional units or fractional days, the curve becomes a point-to-point representation.

Sampling

In some situations, a huge number of individual transactions must be analyzed. As an example, a year's invoices must be examined to determine the dollar pattern of sales. Even a modest-sized business will issue anywhere from 100,000 to 500,000 invoices in a year. To look at each invoice would be a tremendous chore, but it really isn't necessary to study all these pieces of paper. A 2 or 3% sampling will provide statistically reliable information and will more easily supply the desired answers. Repeat checks can be made with the same small effort. However, before taking samples from invoice files, you must make certain that these files have not been stratified by some selection technique, such as filing by dollar value. If the invoices have been filed sequentially by invoice serial number, then selecting invoices with serial numbers ending with any pair of numbers between 00 and 99 will serve to give a random and satisfactory 2% sampling. The same principle applies to other kinds of populations to be sampled.

Regression

This method is also known as the "least-squares" method described in Chapter 1 and is used in determining the slope in scattered data, such as occurs in demand histories and in other sets of observed data. The mathematical solution will give a "best fit" straight line through the data. It is well to plot the data and get a scattergram to see by observation whether trend or seasonality may actually exist. Fortunately, it is possible to run through some fairly simple calculations and determine a correlation coefficient. The coefficients run from +1.0, through 0, to -1.0. A coefficient of +0.92 would indicate that the calculated "fit" very probably has a true positive slope, while a negative coefficient of the same numerical value would indicate just as strongly the opposite case. Values close to 0 indicate little probability of the existence of true slope or that data is highly scattered.

Models and Simulation

A model is a representation of real life, or of an idea or concept. It is developed to explain or illustrate a real or proposed situation. We have all constructed or used models without truly knowing we were doing it. City street maps and organization charts are models. So are algebraic equations.

There are three kinds of models: (1) the reduced or enlarged scale replica; (2) the analog; (3) the symbolic model. Industrial reduced scale models are constructed from engineering drawings to determine whether there will be construction conflicts, poor material flow, or other problems. Scale models of trains, airplanes, buildings, and the like may be used for toys, decoration, or promotional purposes. The analog uses a substitute for the real thing; an aerial photograph of ground areas may be a two-dimensional shaded representation of the ground. With different filters and color film, other characteristics can be represented. In an analog computer, it is often possible to substitute electrical currents for temperature, pressure, agitation, reaction conditions, and so on. By calibrating the currents used, a base representing the best knowledge of the system — say a chemical reactor — can be charted. Then by changing the currents, one at a time, representing temperature, pressure, agitation, and so on, the effect of varying the physical conditions can be estimated. The program put into the analog computer is a "model" — the variation of conditions is "simulation." This kind of experimentation is relatively easy and much quicker and cheaper than trial-and-error experimentation in a real reactor.

Symbolic models are just that — a concept expressed in symbols, which may be, and often are, mathematical. Thus the equation for a quadratic relation

$$a^2 + 2ab + b^2 = x$$

is a symbolic model. In Chapter 2, Managing Inventory Successfully, we used the economic order quantity formula

$$EOQ = \sqrt{\frac{2CD}{c_h}}$$

and explained that c_h was related to the cost of possession. If management were to ask how we could best reduce inventory with least jeopardy to service, we would look to reducing the EOQ. If we had been using 20% as the cost of possession, we could re-calculate new EOQ's using 25-30-35% and higher values to any desired level. With a computerized inventory model, we could hold safety stocks steady and derive new inventory levels for each of the selected costs of possession. This latter procedure is also simulation.

Systems Analysis

In the area of physical distribution, there are many opportunities to use systems analysis. By definition, systems analysis looks at administrative systems and procedures, staffing, data flow, and control, and prepares flow charts showing how the work moves, as in Figure 7-3.

Systems analysis is closely related to the methods and procedures analysis of the industrial engineer. In fact, these tools overlap very considerably. Combined with work simplification, the industrial engineering method covers analysis of existing processes and procedures, the flow of material and paper, the management of men in relation to their work, and the preparation of a flow chart, as in Figure 7-4. While the format and symbols are different, the approach is generally the same, for we then have a model of an existing or proposed system. Either technique is valuable in visualizing an intangible system.

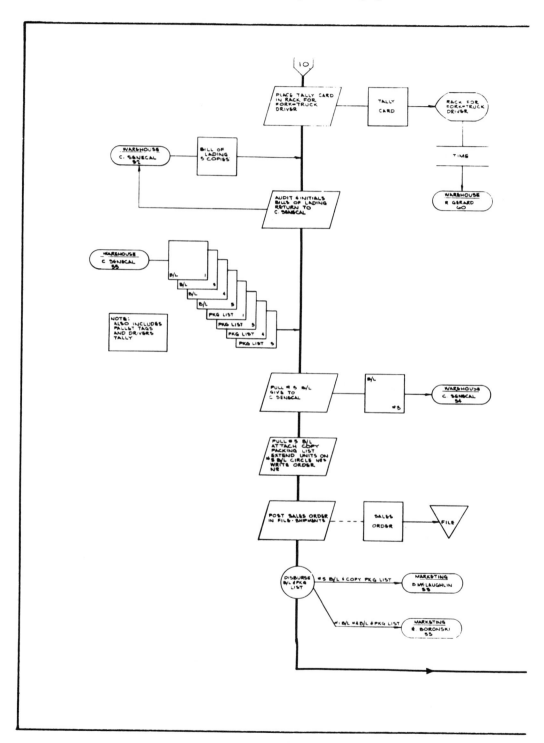

Figure 7-3. *Systems analysis flow chart.*

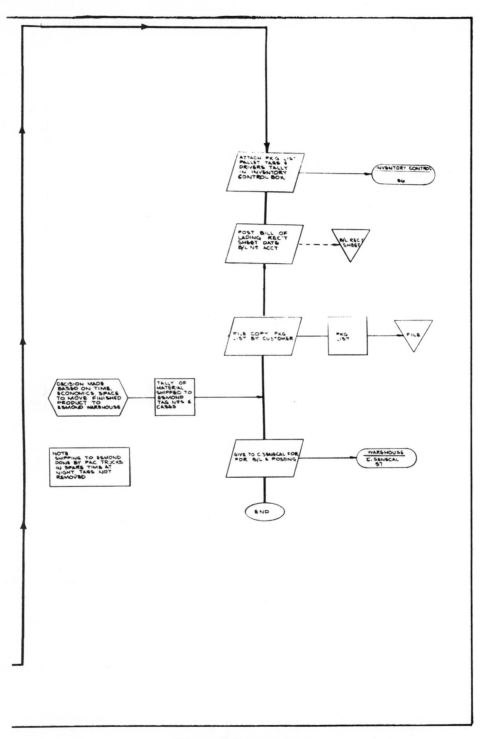

Figure 7-3. (Cont'd)

C806 AD5-63			

PROCESS CHART

SUMMARY			
METHOD	PRES.	PROP.	SAVE
OPERATION	3.09		
OPERATION INSPECTION	1.41		
INSPECTION	.14		
TRANSPORTATION	.27		
DELAY	.05		
STORAGE			
MAN HOURS	.0827		
DISTANCE TRAVELLED	25'		
TOTAL COST			

SUBJECT CHARTED W.T.T.

OPERATION Order entry

CHARTED BY W.A.B.

CHART NO. ____ SHEET NO. ____

DATE March 16,

PLANT Philadelphia

DEPT. Sales Office

OPERATION / OPER. INSP. / INSPECTION / TRANS. / DELAY / STORAGE	DIST.	TIME 1/100 min.	PRESENT METHOD DESCRIPTION
●□□⇨ᴅ▽	–	7	Pick up customer order.
○□■⇨ᴅ▽	–	14	Read customer order.
●□□⇨ᴅ▽	–	5	Tear page from order desk memo pad- Form 211C.
●□□⇨ᴅ▽	–	9	Attach customer order to 211C.
●□□⇨ᴅ▽	–	27	Retrieve Master Price Card for customer, adj. file.
○■□⇨ᴅ▽	–	16	Check MPC for special price quotation- yes.
○■□⇨ᴅ▽	–	122	Check bid book (on desk).
●□□⇨ᴅ▽	–	221	Apply special price to 211C, apply proper product code to 211C. (7 items).
○■□⇨ᴅ▽	–	3	Check credit reference OK - yes.
●□□⇨ᴅ▽	–	8	Paper-clip MPC to 211C.
○□□⇨ᴅ▽	–	5	Batched for flexo and checker. Each.
○□□⇨ᴅ▽	25'	27	To flexo.
○□□⇨ᴅ▽	–	–	Time lapse for flexo.
○□□⇨ᴅ▽	by others		Return from flexo.
●□□⇨ᴅ▽	–	32	File MPC.
○□□⇨ᴅ▽			
○□□⇨ᴅ▽			*Reference-Chart 27, Flexo.
○□□⇨ᴅ▽			Chart 28, MK-checker.
○□□⇨ᴅ▽			* Related Philadelphia studies.
○□□⇨ᴅ▽			
	25'	496	⬅— TOTAL

Figure 7-4. *Industrial engineering process chart.*

Linear Programming

Linear programming is probably the most widely used of the operations research techniques. Its value lies in its ability to select the one best solution from among a multitude of choices. Examples are:

(1) A company with several factories making essentially the same products has major and minor customers spread around the United States. In addition to supplying the trade directly from the factories, there are also many ware-housing points to be served. What would be the best combination of ware-houses, factories, and customers allocated to these factories and warehouses, to achieve maximum profit?

(2) Tar residues from about 50 coal-coking plants at various points in the northeastern quadrant of the United States are to be channeled into four processing centers for the recovery of contained solvents and organic chemicals. Each of the processing centers has different capabilities and cost structures. Each of the coal tars has a different average analysis. Which residues should be sent to which processing center and in what quantities, to have the best combination of freight, processing costs, and profits?

Timely manual solutions to these problems are impossible in a practical way. Preparing the required matrix of simultaneous equations with the necessary cost data will take the full time effort of five to ten skilled men for as long as two years. A manual solution could take many years to complete. So first off, an involved linear program model will require a computer, a large one, for a solution. Running time will be but an hour or so. With the model built, it is relatively easy to update cost and other variable elements and run the model through the computer again for an update.

Three Methods

There are three linear programming methods, but two are really special forms of the third. These are the assignment, transportation or stepping-stone, and Simplex methods. The first two are the simplified forms. The assignment method might typically be used to determine how five power plants could be supplied with coal from three mines at least transportation cost. Problems of this type have a set of needs which must be satisfied by a set of facilities. This set can be derived by matching on a whole-unit basis a unit of facility and a unit of requirement.

The transportation-stepping-stone method is not limited to the transportation of goods in spite of its name, but to the procedure which is used in the solution of the matrix. In terms of our interest, this method can be used to establish the best location for a factory, distribution center, sales office, or similar problems in other areas of interest. Method requires that a unit of any input yield one unit of any output; that cost or profit resulting from the conversion is a constant at any level, and inputs and outputs are equal and known.

The Simplex method is not in itself a simple one, but is so-called because it is so much more simple than any other method of solving the kinds of problems mentioned above. The Simplex will handle any linear programming type problem, but in some instances simpler techniques are used in preference. As already mentioned, setting up the Simplex matrix takes far more time than it takes the computer to process the program.

Linear programming procedures are beyond the scope of this book, and are more often than not the subject of a book themselves. For the reader who wants to delve into the theory and mechanics of the methods, he is referred to the Bibliography, especially #2, 3, and 10.

Queueing or Waiting Lines

Waiting line problems are seen every day. A service station has a certain number of pumps — if there are many automobiles waiting for service, you may either enter and wait or drive on to be served at a different service station. In one case you may estimate that you will not have long to wait, and in the other you have estimated the wait will be longer than you care for. When you drive off, the dealer has lost a sale. Supermarkets must process their customers through the checkout lanes, lest the customers decide they can be waited on with less delay elsewhere.

Telephone systems recognized this problem early. Parties did not want to wait very long, if at all, to get a line on which they could make their calls. How many circuits are required to provide this kind of service during the busy part of the day? A man named Erlang developed the initial mathematical solutions to the telephone problem in 1909. It was the midforties before the theory was extended to other areas, such as toll gates, supermarket checkout, gas stations, loading doors at warehouses, and many others. In any of these situations, we may find that at times there is more demand than the facility can handle, and at others there is slack time. If there is persistent excess demand, we first look at our methods to see if we can speed up the operation. Extra manning at gas pumps and checkout lanes are examples, as is the exact change booth at the toll gates. If this does not resolve the problem, then what extra facilities will we need? On the other hand, excess facilities may exist; the writer has seen at least one warehouse with loading doors which are not opened for months on end.

So we are faced with the task of finding a balance between facilities, size of staff, and the length of time customers will wait in line (where a customer is anyone waiting for service of some sort). It is easier to describe the problems than to solve them. The mathematics involved are complex and application requires a person trained in mathematical procedures. For the curious reader, texts listed in the Bibliography do a good job for the mathematically inclined. For the reader interested in determining the number of loading doors for his warehouse, there is fortunately a pamphlet available that has provided answers for many combinations between arrival of up to 60 trucks per hour and servicing rates varying from 0.1 vehicle per hour to 15 per hour. Desai and Yanouzas have reported that in a study of a service line in a Greek department store arrivals were close to Poisson in distribution, so that use of Poisson techniques gave solutions very comparable to queueing techniques. If this approach can be extended, solution of waiting line problems may be simplified.

Monte Carlo Methods

Mathematical analysis can give formulas by which precise answers may be obtained. In some cases, the mathematics of the solution is so involved that solution is burdensome; in other cases, an analytical solution cannot be reached at all. However, we know that we can approximate solution by experiment, sometimes called "trial and error." If we need a high degree of accuracy, we run the experiments over and over again.

"Monte Carlo" is the name given to an experimental paper simulation involving the use of sampling through the use of random numbers. Monte Carlo is used where taking of physical samples is either too costly or impractical. For example, we cannot experiment on the number of loading doors required in a warehouse. Again, we might find it too expensive and slow to determine by experiment the number of trucks needed to make 500 deliveries per day in the most economical manner.

Let us illustrate the above: On a given hour and day of the week, the management of a supermarket knows that 2.4 customers arrive at the checkout lanes each minute and that the standard deviation is 0.8. It is also known that the average time for a single clerk to process a customer (i.e., to ring up the items), make change, and bag purchases is 3.63 minutes, with a standard deviation of 0.9. To solve the problem of how many of the checkout lanes should be staffed during the selected period, we must realize that customers do not arrive at an "average rate" but at random rates. We can simulate this arrival rate if we construct a table similar to Table 7-1. We can simulate as many days as we wish, but we would probably do what is shown in the table — simulate five days with a given set of random numbers, and then repeat several times using different sets of random numbers. The table shows but one set of trials.

In the first column, we show the number of checkout stations operating and, in the second, a number to distinguish between the five days in the sample. The third column has a series of random numbers obtained from a random normal number table. (Bibliography #11 is one source of such a table). The probable number of customers arriving at the checkout lanes is simulated in the fourth column, by taking the average per minute arrival rate, 2.4, and adding to it the standard deviation multiplied by the random normal number in column three. Thus $80 = (2.4 \times 60) + (0.8 \times -1.329)(60)$. The sixth column shows another set of random normal numbers to be applied to service times which are calculated the same way as the arrival times. The seventh column is the available minutes for operating the checkout lanes. The eighth column shows the excess customer waiting time if the sign is + but idle checkout time if the sign is –.

TABLE 7-1
Monte Carlo Method Solution

Number of Stations	Day	Table Value	Arrival Rate/ Hour	Table Value	Service Time/ Hour	Available Checkout Time-Min.	Excess Time	Waiting
	1	-1.329	80	-1.381	191	540	-349	Checker
	2	1.284	206	-0.574	630	540	+90	Customer
9	3	0.619	174	0.096	616	540	+76	Customer
	4	0.699	178	1.389	869	540	+329	Customer
	5	0.101	149	1.249	708	540	+168	Customer
	1	-1.329	80	-1.381	191	600	-409	Checker
	2	1.284	206	-0.574	630	600	+30	Customer
10	3	0.619	174	0.096	616	600	+16	Customer
	4	0.699	178	1.389	869	600	+269	Customer
	5	0.101	149	1.249	708	600	+108	Customer
	1	-1.329	80	-1.381	191	660	-469	Checker
	2	1.284	206	-0.574	630	660	-30	Checker
11	3	0.619	174	0.096	616	660	-44	Checker
	4	0.699	178	1.389	869	660	+209	Customer
	5	0.101	149	1.249	708	660	+48	Customer
	1	-1.329	80	-1.381	191	720	-529	Checker
	2	1.284	206	-0.574	630	720	-90	Checker
12	3	0.619	174	0.096	616	720	-104	Checker
	4	0.699	178	1.389	869	720	+149	Customer
	5	0.101	149	1.249	708	720	-12	Checker

Would the store manager actually staff up with 12 checkers? It is more likely that he would pull stock handlers to bag up groceries, leaving the checker to ring up sales and make change only. This will greatly reduce processing time. When the lanes clear, the handlers would go back to their regular jobs until the lines backed up again.

Calculations would be required for other hours and other days to finally arrive at proper staffing levels, but the calculations and observation of arrival and servicing rates are easily done. Thus Monte Carlo methods can be used to reach solutions to problems where a normally distributed range of factors exists.

BIBLIOGRAPHY AND FURTHER READING

(1) Drake, Sheehan, Sweeny, and Hupp, Consultants, "Shipper-Motor Carrier Dock Planning Manual," 1916 P Street NW, Washington, D.C., American Trucking Associations, Inc., 1969. A practical application of queueing theory with clear explanation of use of the tables given.

(2) Enrick, N.L., *Management Operations Research*, New York, N.Y., Holt, Rinehart and Winston, 1965. Linear programming methods, queues, inventory management, sampling, and statistical analysis are clearly discussed.

(3) Ferguson, R.O. and Sargent, L.F., *Linear Programming, Fundamentals and Applications*, New York, N.Y., McGraw-Hill Book Co., 1958. A thorough coverage not beyond the ability of the average reader. Contains many examples to illustrate the method.

(4) Maynard, H.B., *Handbook of Business Administration*, New York, N.Y., McGraw-Hill Book Co., 1967. Especially good are section 6, "Materials Management," and parts 8 and 9 on Industrial Engineering and methods improvement.

(5) Maynard, H.B., *Industrial Engineering Handbook*, New York, N.Y., McGraw-Hill Book Co., Inc., 1963.

(6) Moroney, M.J., *Facts from Figures*, Baltimore, Md., Penguin Books, Inc., 1958. An entertaining and clear explanation of the basics of statistical methods.

(7) Morse, P.M., *Queues, Inventories and Maintenance*, New York, N.Y., John Wiley and Sons, Inc., 1958. A book for the professional. Strong mathematical approach.

(8) Sasieni, M., Yaspan, A., and Friedman, L., *Operations Research*, New York, N.Y., John Wiley and Sons, Inc., 1959. A sophisticated presentation.

(9) Thiel, H., Boot, J.C.G., and Kloek, T., *Operations Research and Quantitative Economics*, New York, N.Y., McGraw-Hill Book Co., 1965. A broad introduction to O.R. methods and procedures.

(10) Vandegrift, J.B., "Simplified Linear Programming," 75 York Road, Willow Grove, Pa., J. Benton Vandegrift Associates, 1958. A detailed explanation of the various L.P. methods together with many examples.

(11) Weast, R.C., *Handbook of Tables for Probability and Statistics*, Cleveland, Ohio, The Chemical Rubber Co., 1968.

Chapter 8

Much has been written on the advantages and disadvantages of going into, or being in, the trucking business as an adjunct to a primary business. In this chapter, we will explore them and look into the methods of evaluating a proposed or existing operation.

Private Carriage as a Business

When trucking is conducted as a lesser part of a manufacturing business or a distribution business, as an example, the trucking operation is called "private motor carriage" or, in short, "private

THE PROS AND CONS
OF PRIVATE MOTOR CARRIAGE

181

carriage." Should your company be engaged in private carriage? The answer to this is both yes and no. Whether you expect to, or do, operate one or two trucks or a fleet of several hundred, you must preplan and continue to organize the scope of activities, types of equipment to use, and the extent to which you will deliver (or pick up) your own freight. Once operations are started, they must be carefully and intelligently managed. Trucking is not a simple business — there are complications and ramifications that are not thought of by the neophyte. These problems will be covered as the chapter develops. Successful operation depends upon close control of all phases of the trucking business. In this respect, it is no different than the primary part of your business. So, if you are willing to do the detailed planning required, if you are willing to expend the effort to manage trucking on a day-to-day basis, and if you will set up and utilize the same type of close controls used in other phases of your business, go to it. The answer is yes; you should earn a satisfactory return on your investments in fixed and working capital and in managerial and supervisory talent.

If, on the other hand, you do not see the need for detailed effort, management, and controls, the answer is no. Stay away from private carriage, lest you lose money on the operation. As an example of only one of the problems in private trucking, studies of large samples have shown that less than 10% of those in private carriage have adequate to good cost control systems. The remainder have inadequate ones or no cost system at all! Return on investment can equal 15% or more, but only where close attention and careful management are expended.

Advantages of Private Carriage

What are the reasons for being in private carriage? First and foremost is the opportunity to reduce delivery costs. This reason is cited by those already in private carriage as being either first or second in importance. Matching it is the opportunity to provide better delivery service to customers. There is the possibility of obtaining a better return on investment than in investing the same amount of money and attention in other phases of the business. There is better control over loss and damage to goods in transit. Private carriage also provides a measure of real delivery costs and this information is used in negotiating improved rates with common carriers. Marginal benefits include drivers being a source of intelligence on what customers are buying from competitors; possibly lower inventories (but with good delivery, customers may let you hold stocks for them) and perhaps extension of marketing area.

Disadvantages of Private Carriage

There are two sides to every coin — there are disadvantages to private carriage. Perhaps the greatest disadvantage is the need to have a balanced operation. Balanced operation means having the tonnage leaving the factory or warehouse on private carriage balanced with tonnage coming in on private carriage, with only a small amount of empty mileage on each round trip. This concept of balance is extremely important to profitability, especially when loads move out much more than 150 miles. At the 150-mile mark without return loads, the operation approaches break-even; at 200 miles or more, trips generally result in a loss. Since profit on a trip is measured by the cost of in-house operation vs. common carrier, it is apparent common carriers must have a good level of balance between loads flowing in opposite directions, with their rates set to reflect this balance. In the case of local small deliveries, the common carrier generally runs his trucks on a daily or alternate-day route, scheduling deliveries and pickups for many customers, while with private carriage there is sales pressure to make small deliveries regardless of trucking efficiency.

Other disadvantages include the requirement for skilled and knowledgeable management which may not be available; administrative attention in the areas of state and federal regulation of carriers; liability problems; bargaining with a separate union or a group within a plant union having a different set of problems; costing and cost distribution problems; leasing or investment problems; etc.

Regulations and Laws

There are millions of motor trucks on U.S. highways and some 90% of these are entirely or partially freed of federal regulation. Among the exemptions are those which do not cross state lines, farm trucks, agricultural cooperative trucks, and newspaper trucks. There are substantial lists of nonmanufactured agricultural products which are exempt from regulation, but all specific exemptions are closely spelled out. It is beyond the scope of this book to discuss these. There is one federal regulation which all trucks face when engaged in interstate commerce and that is the Federal Highway Administration safety regulations. Each state has its own set of motor vehicle laws. Operation across state lines offers no problems for the small pickup and panel trucks, but for the large straight trucks, or semi- and full-trailer units, there are almost as many different rules as there are states. For the large units, attention must be paid to such things as height, width and length of units, gross loaded weight, axle weights, axle spacing, permissible and unpermissible combinations, frost laws, etc. It will be found that a regular haul across several states will be limited by the requirements of the state crossed which has the most rigid restrictions.

In addition to the regulations spelled out by the ICC for safe operation, which cover mechanical conditions, signal and head lamps, etc., there are also rules covering drivers' hours of work (briefly, ten hours maximum driving, 12 hours on duty in any 24-hour period, maximum six days out of seven) and measures controlling the carriage of hazardous materials, such as certain chemicals, flammables, compressed gases, explosives, and the like (see Bibliography #3, 6, 9). Details are beyond the scope of this book.

Costing

Costing is not simple and, unfortunately, not exact. Use of figures gives the impression of precision, but judgment enters strongly in arriving at distribution of costs. For example, the size of loads can vary and the cost of running the truck at say three-quarters load is the same as at full load for a single-stop delivery. The cost of delivering multi-stops in urban areas is more expensive than intercity single stops. Where cost per ton-mile delivered may be a good measure for intercity operation, cost per day or cost per hour operated may be more significant for urban operation. With urban delivery, it may be more meaningful to break down the cost of delivery to cost per unit weight delivered. If the deliveries range from 25 pounds to several hundred pounds, with 15 deliveries made daily, the average cost per delivery will show a prohibitive unit cost on the small order. On intercity deliveries, cost of delivery must be assessed on the basis of a round-trip mileage if the truck returns empty, but on a one-way mileage if there is a full return load. Other complications include the possibility of less than full return load — does the weight hauled cover full allocated and out-of-pocket expenses? With less than full loads, there may have been a management decision to "do it anyway" in order to satisfy a customer, but how do you allocate costs? Effective management of a private carriage fleet will require constant attention to costs to prevent the operation from being a drain on corporate profits.

Typical expenses in truck operation will show driver costs to be almost half of the total cost, followed in descending order by fuel and oil, maintenance, depreciation or lease costs, insurance-licenses-taxes, tires, and miscellaneous items. Difficulty comes in allocating these costs to trips, deliveries, package, etc., but cost can be readily calculated as cost per ton-mile. Ton-mile unit costs can be reduced by running more miles (with owned trucks); i.e., fixed costs are spread thinner and this accounts for the common practice of allowing drivers to work in excess of eight hours per day but still within federal restrictions. For control of costs on a fleet, it is most practical to divide the fleet into two or more parts; i.e., intercity and urban hauls, and further into regions if operating nationally. On intercity hauls, the cost per mile operated can be as low as 35-40¢ per mile in the southern states to 50-65¢ per mile in the high-density traffic or mountainous states. On urban deliveries, per-mile costs are almost meaningless. Hourly costs may run as low as $6-7 per hour to as much as $15-20 per hour, depending upon wage scales and many other factors. As a starting point, you could do worse than to follow the uniform accounting systems prescribed by federal regulations for common carriers.

Cost Variation

Delivery of 40,000 pounds of goods from Philadelphia to Pittsburgh to one customer will be cheaper than delivering 40,000 pounds to 40-50 customers in Philadelphia. More equipment is needed in the latter case, and with receiving restrictions on hours of delivery, a driver will do very well to make 15-20 deliveries per day. If 40,000 pounds were to be delivered to 50 customers, the average delivery would be 800 pounds, with actual deliveries possibly being in the range 100-3,000 pounds. Taking into consideration the waiting time in getting to the unloading dock, backing in, unloading, taking care of any special handling for the customer, paper work at each customer stop, and travel to the next customer, with such low weight an elapsed time of 30 minutes per customer would not be excessive. It would not take much longer to deliver 5-10,000 pounds at a stop. On the other hand if the stop is for only 40-50 pounds, the driver may well hand-carry the delivery in from the street and soon be on his way. As opposed to these local "peddler" loads, long- and short-haul, full-load deliveries are relatively simple. The product is stacked in the trucks, sometimes by night loaders; the driver runs to his destination for complete unloading at only one point; and then either returns home empty or goes to a nearby point to pick up a return load. Small local deliveries involve establishing an economical route for the deliveries, loading of goods in the truck in the proper sequence for delivery, preparation of many delivery tickets, and once on the road all of the little incidents repeated over and over, as described above. Preanalysis of variable costs for small local deliveries is complicated; it should not be undertaken by persons lacking experience in the small-order delivery area or a thorough knowledge of the delivery area and its problems.

When private carriage is available, sales personnel assume sometimes that small orders can be delivered the same day, or at worst on the next day. While this can usually be worked out to everyone's satisfaction on full loads, it can be an economic nightmare on small-order deliveries. Examination of customers' small-order patterns over a period of several months will provide an insight as to whether you should consider zoning the area to be serviced with deliveries scheduled appropriately to the volume moving, whether you should route randomly through the territory on a daily basis, or whether you should be in this type of delivery at all. Control over this kind of operation involves industrial engineering work measurement and standard-setting concepts. Both of these areas are beyond the scope of this book but additional reading in these areas is listed in the Bibliography.

Vreeland (Bibliography #11) cites the method of W. L. Fayle of the Burlington Mills Corporation for costing truck runs in intercity transport. This method not only shows how to cost the run but also indicates how it can be used as a planning tool to establish multipoint runs which will earn the desired net revenues, and how runs might be adjusted to meet desired net if original net is too low.

Entry into Private Carriage

At some point in time, carriage of goods will be scrutinized for its profit potential, either through pressures to improve profitability of the basic business or because of curiosity about why the competition is trucking its own goods. The decision to enter private carriage is as weighty a problem as expansion of facilities for manufacturing, establishing a new warehouse, or any other capital investment. It should be studied just as carefully. If a knowledge of private carriage is lacking in the organization, it must be obtained from outside. The Private Truck Council of America and The

Private Carrier Conference, both of Washington, D.C., can provide a wealth of information. Through business contacts, it should be possible to review the problem with companies already in the field. It is also possible to buy the services of a consultant. Care should be taken to get a person who is truly knowledgeable in the field.

With all the information gathered from these sources, the next step would be to make an analysis of the shipments currently being made. Several consecutive months will usually suffice unless your business is very erratic or seasonal, then it would be better to look at a year's activity. First, all shipments should be tabulated by customer and destination. From this data, the variation in size and frequency of shipments can be established. Were all shipments substantial or were they a mixture of large and small? Establish the over-the-road distance from your location to the customer's, both ways, by the shortest and quickest routes. Consider what traffic conditions will be. For example, cross-town traffic in New York City may move at only 2 or 3 miles per hour while freeway traffic may average over 50 miles per hour. City truck driving seldom averages as high as 10 miles per hour. Cross-country (nonfreeway) trucking will generally average around 35 miles per hour.

Next examine all receipts of goods from vendors during the same period, using the same criteria as on shipments. With this data, tabulate, or plot on a map, the top 15% of volume for both the customer's and in-bound goods. Compare frequencies to see if round-trip loads are available.

Annual Cost of Operation

The following factors are included in the estimate of annual cost of operation, which is the next step:

- Depreciation or lease costs — for first estimates use depreciation rather than lease costs. Light delivery trucks will have a useful mileage life similar to a passenger car, while heavy-duty equipment may run 500,000 miles or more before wearing out. Be conservative in estimating life for depreciation.

- Fuel usage may be as low as 1½-2 miles per gallon for the heavy-duty equipment and up to 12-14 miles per gallon for the light unit. Manufacturers can give you some guidance on this.

- Tires — life depends upon many factors and may range from 20,000 miles or so on small trucks to 100,000 miles for the heavy-duty tires used on the larger units. Additional miles can be obtained through recapping the tires used on large trucks, with two or more recappings possible.

- Insurance is required for liability, property damage, fire, and theft.

- Licenses will cover state and city requirements. If involved in interstate commerce, a federal tag will also be needed. It is necessary to register in other states for fuel and/or ton-mile taxes.

- Taxes include excise taxes where these are assessed, fuel taxes, ton-mile taxes, personal property taxes, and the like. On a light delivery truck these taxes may be only a couple hundred dollars, while the largest possible carriers may be paying more than $4,000 per year.

- Tolls are a special kind of use tax found on roads and bridges.

- Repairs — without experience, the best source of information is the manufacturer, or perhaps a leasing company will help out. This is a very tough cost to estimate because the way the truck is used or abused is a major factor in costs. Another problem develops from getting equipment too light for the service, especially undersized engines and transmissions. Profits are made by having equipment that runs with a minimum of lost time, not by saving a few dollars on the first cost.

- Garage costs — for storage, minor repairs, lubrication, etc.

- Driver costs — make realistic estimates of the time the driver will actually work and allow for overtime. For example, you may want your driver to be at his first stop at the beginning of the customer's receiving day and make deliveries until the end of the receiving day. This implies leaving early and getting back late. Remember to include vacation coverage and fringe benefits.

- Supervisory and administrative costs.

From the analysis of customers served and vendor locations, pick out the trips which account for 65-75% of the volume moving out-bound and ignore the rest. It will be found that 15-20% of the customers will account for the major part of the volume. Then, starting with the largest customer, begin matching up cost of private carriage vs. common carriage cost, simultaneously keeping track of the hours or days required to accomplish the deliveries. When the delivery time reaches a year's utilization of the equipment, compare common carrier costs with estimated cost of private carriage. The sum of the estimated costs for the various trips during the year should not be less than the total estimated annual cost of operation. If there is a substantial difference, recheck the calculations. Assuming that the calculations are all correct, and that the cost of private carriage is lower than common carrier cost, you have a measure of the profitability of private carriage. You may decide to go ahead.

Selection of Equipment

The Romans used to say "Caveat emptor" — "Let the buyer beware." Today we are more apt to say, "You get what you pay for." Before trying to decide what equipment will cost, it is first necessary to determine what kind of apparatus will best meet your needs. If your deliveries are going to be essentially parcel delivery with many stops, a standard panel truck might be best. If deliveries are in the 100-1,000 pounds range, with a number of stops, a 5-ton straight truck may be most suitable. If route weights are in the vicinity of 35,000 pounds with only a few deliveries made from each load, a tractor-semi-trailer unit is indicated. The same kind of unit would probably be best for high-speed intercity movement, though a more substantial tractor might be required to assure reliable service on the road.

Where maximum payload is important, attention must be given to weight-saving construction — Fiberglas fenders and cab, aluminum chassis and trailer frames, magnesium wheels, etc. Every pound that is taken from vehicle weight can be translated into revenue payload. Considering all these factors, you should establish your own specifications and have all vendors quote against these. This should be done whether buying or leasing. It is wise to establish these specifications before asking for any quotations or you may innocently include elements which can be supplied by only one source and then find it difficult to make price comparisons. Such comparisons are handled in much the same way as with fork trucks. (See Chapter 5.)

Photo courtesy of Allied Chemical Corp., Morristown, N.J.

Photo 8-1. *Semi-trailer acid unit.*

Equipment Types

Photo courtesy of Allied Chemical Corp., Morristown, N.J.

Photo 8-2. *Fluorocarbon dispersant gas semi-trailer.*

The reader has probably seen many types of trucks, but in brief the following sums up the range of equipment, although there are a great many variations:

- Light- and heavy-duty panel trucks, up to about 10,000 pounds GVW.
- Straight trucks with box, up to about 10,000 pounds GVW.
- Single drive-axle tractor with single-axle semi-trailer, up to about 40,000 pounds GVW. May also use tandem-axle semi-trailer.
- With the tandem trailer, GVW will be about 50,000 pounds.
- Tandem drive-axle tractor plus tandem semi-trailer, up to about 70,000 pounds GVW.
- Tandem drive-axle straight truck plus full trailer, up to about 80,000 pounds GVW.
- Single-axle trailer, plus single-axle semi-trailer, plus full trailer, up to about 80,000 pounds GVW.

Photo 8-3. *Double-bottom acid unit.*

State laws vary widely on permissible axle loads and must be taken into consideration when selecting equipment. There are further restrictions on width, length, and height of trailers. Many states do not permit the use of double trailers at all, or may limit use to certain highways, or require special permits to operate. Since these laws are constantly changing, it is pointless to include them here. However, The National Highway Users Conference periodically publishes a summary of these restrictions, as well as other pertinent detailed information. (See Bibliography #8.)

Use of Leased Equipment

The details of leasing were discussed at some length in Chapter 5 and will not be repeated here. However, there are some problems concerning leased trucks which do not arise with other types of equipment. When operating owned trucks, you may have drivers on your own payroll or you may obtain them under some kind of agreement from a firm specializing in supplying skilled drivers to those who need them. In either case, there is no conflict with federal regulations. When you operate leased trucks, you must be aware that it is an illegal practice to lease trucks from a company and obtain the drivers from the same or a closely affiliated one. The key criteria are: (1) can the leased equipment and the drivers be arranged for by means of a single contact?; (2) are the drivers under the full control and direction of the user?

Common carriers are closely regulated by the federal government, but as a benefit of this regulation they are awarded operating rights between certain points and to some contiguous spots along the routes between these points. If a leasing company supplies equipment and drivers (other than for certain types of contract haulage) either openly or by subterfuge, there is an implied offering of common carriage, usually at less than common carrier rates. This is unfair competition and a violation of the operating rights of one or more common carriers. Knowingly or unknowingly, utilization of equipment and drivers from a common source, or sources which are closely affiliated, renders the user subject to heavy penalties. The use of drivers from a hiring service is not forbidden as such. In fact, drivers may be legally obtained from any agency which is in no way connected with the leasing company. The employment agency's responsibility must be only to pay the men for the time worked and bill the user at the agreed-upon rates.

The responsibility for the day-to-day direction of these men, for control over their observation of the federal safety and working regulations, and of any state regulations, must rest with the company hiring these "rented" drivers. The responsibilities for control are precisely the same as if the men were on the company payroll. If these conditions are met there is no conflict with the law, but if, in fact, these responsibilities rest with the employment agency — watch out! There may be difficulties ahead.

Summary

There are both advantages and disadvantages to private trucking. With careful preparation, continued good management and control, and a proper respect for the many rules and regulations, it is possible to run trucks profitably. Equipment should be carefully selected to meet the specific needs of your own business and, once in hand, should be carefully maintained. A good cost system, one similar to the common-carrier uniform accounting system, is a necessity. Without an adequate cost control system, expenses cannot be regulated properly. Knowledge about profits or losses will be lacking. If you are willing to spend the management and supervisory time required; if you are willing to learn the ins and outs of the trucking business; if you are willing to limit the operation to the areas where you can effectively operate — then private carriage may be the area in which to improve the profitability of your business.

BIBLIOGRAPHY AND FURTHER READING

(1) Barnes, R.M., *Motion and Time Study*, New York, N.Y., John Wiley and Sons, Inc., 1949. A basic industrial engineering text.

(2) Barnes, R.M., *Work Sampling*, New York, N.Y., John Wiley and Sons, Inc., 1958.

(3) "Drivers Handbook and Digest of ICC Driver Regulations," Washington, D.C., Private Truck Council of America, Inc., 1966. Covers the area of responsibility of drivers. Written for driver use.

(4) Editorial article, "Private Carriage — All We Want Are the Facts," Cleveland, O., *Handling and Shipping*, published by Industrial Publishing Co., October, 1967. An analysis of the pros and cons of private carriage.

(5) "Keep it Legal," Washington, D.C., Private Carriers Conference, American Trucking Association, 1969. A discussion of private carriage practices which are definite or borderline law violations.

(6) "Motor Carrier Safety Regulation, Parts 390 through 397," Washington, D.C., Bureau of Motor Carrier Safety of the Federal Highway Administration, 1969. The safety bible of the motor carrier industry.

(7) "Questions and Answers for A.S.T.T. Examination," Washington, D.C., Traffic Service Corp., 1968.

(8) "State Size and Weight Limits," Washington, D.C., National Highway Users Conference, annual. Comparative statement of the laws covering dimensions, gross weights, etc. in all states.

(9) "Transportation of Explosives Act," U.S. Code Title 49, Parts 171-190.

(10) *Truck Rental Guide*, Chicago, Ill., Midwest Publishing Co., 1968. The hows and whys of truck renting.

(11) Vreeland, B., *Private Trucking from A to Z*, New York, N.Y., Shippers Conference of Greater New York, Inc., 1969. Complete coverage.

Chapter 9

Private motor carriage was discussed in the previous chapter, and in this chapter we will take a short look at the operation and management of privately owned or leased railroad equipment. Before doing this, we will first examine the various kinds of transportation services available for the movement of private property.

Parcel Post

Parcel post is widely used for handling small packages and in most cases the cost is less than that of other services. Parcel post can be sent anywhere in the United States,

CHOOSING THE BEST ALTERNATIVE MODES OF TRANSPORTATION

with delivery time comparable to other modes of transportation handling individual small shipments. There are length plus girth restrictions of 100 inches on package dimensions; there is a weight minimum of 1 ounce and a maximum of 70 pounds. There are also limitations on the type of goods carried, with corrosives, flammables, poisons, and others prohibited. Rates vary with weight; i.e., the rate per pound decreases with increasing weight of package and with the distance carried — it costs more to ship further.

Parcel Service

Parcel service was developed from a delivery service for department stores with limited service area to a service that covers many parts of the country. Delivery times are about the same as with parcel post and with comparable costs. Individual packages are limited to 50 pounds and there are restrictions on the type of goods carried, especially dangerous commodities.

Package Express

Package service is offered by many of the intercity bus operators, and with some of the nationwide systems, packages can be moved to any place the buses run. Maximum weight for packages in this service is 100 pounds. Packages must not exceed 85 inches in maximum dimension nor may the sum of height, width, and length exceed 141 inches. Commodity restrictions include corrosives, flammables, poisons, liquids, explosives, firearms, odorous materials, live animals, and extremely fragile items. There is usually no pickup and delivery service; i.e., goods must be taken to and picked up at the bus terminals. A shipment weighing 25 pounds and moving 200 miles will cost about $3, while 100 pounds moving the same distance will cost about $6.

Freight Forwarders

Forwarders operate no equipment but utilize the equipment of railroads, motor carriers, or airlines just as any other shipper would. Their function is to consolidate small shipments from many shippers into single large loads to be handled as a single shipment. The advantage to the shipper or receiver is that goods move more expeditiously than if sent via the same carrier as a single small shipment. The forwarder bills the shipper at the small-package freight rate but pays the carrier at the lower-volume rate. It is within this spread on freight rates that the forwarder performs the consolidation and other services and makes a profit. Best service is obtained when origin and destination both lie on the carrier's route. Off-route deliveries can be arranged, but the goods then move as small shipments.

Rail Express

REA Express provides pickup and delivery service in urban areas throughout the United States. Originally, all express goods moved on cars that were part of passenger trains. Today, some express cars are included in freight trains, while other intercity movements are being handled in REA over-the-road trucks. Service is supplied both for small-package shipments and for full-carload movements. REA handles many items which other small-package carriers will not touch, such as valuables, money, and firearms. Cost of the service is higher than the cost of similar services offered by common-carrier motor trucks.

Air Express

Air express service is a division of REA Express, directly serving all cities having air service. In addition, many other cities are also served where the final delivery is made by rail and/or truck. Shipped property moves via passenger plane with the usual restrictions on size and handled commodities. Air express is a premium service, with goods moving on passenger planes that have a high priority. Transportation costs on long hauls will run about double the cost of surface express for small shipments (up to 25 pounds) but may run four to five times more costly on shipments in the 100-pound range. These ratios do not necessarily hold on shorter hauls because of the impact of terminal and delivery costs.

Air Freight

Air freight is another premium service with property moving in individual shipments, size and weight limited only by the capacity of available aircraft. Shipments generally move out to destination on first available space. Transportation costs are about half as much as for air express, for long shipments of 100 pounds. For small shipments, air freight and air express rates are comparable. Again, these cost comparisons do not necessarily hold on shorter hauls.

Deferred air freight moves out on the basis of a minimum delay of two days on delivery. The cost of this service is somewhat lower than regular air freight, and thus may be advantageous on long moves.

Comment on Premium Services

The economics of air express or air freight obviously cannot lie in transportation costs, as the rates are considerably higher than for other modes of transport. The economy of air transport is measured by looking at the total cost of the service plus related costs. These related costs include the cost of holding inventory, receiving and warehousing costs, ordering and expediting costs, packaging costs, and other lesser cost items. A decrease in the replenishment lead time will lead to reductions in cycle and safety stocks (which means inventory reduction), in ordering and expediting costs, in less expensive overpacking, etc. These savings will often offset the higher cost of air transport and yield a more economic laid-down cost at the destination. This is especially true when costly materials are involved. If the calculations do not show a lower cost, you cannot afford to use air transport for routine shipments.

There are other reasons for using air transport. There is the emergency requirement for repair parts for shutdown equipment; there is the daily shipment of perishables, such as live lobsters and flowers, that cannot be delivered in saleable condition by slower transport; there are items with time value, such as style goods and promotional materials; there are items needed to keep an assembly line running; etc. Here the economics are related to premium prices on perishables, to the value of having certain things at a given place at a certain time, to down-time expenses, or to similar situations.

Piggyback Service

Piggyback service is transportation of over-the-road trailers on a railroad flatcar. This is called "trailer on flatcar" by the railroads, or TOFC service. The most commonly used piggyback plans are plans #1 and #2. Plan 1 covers the movement of motor carrier trailers on a railroad-owned flatcar between railroad terminals, or ramps, with the movement to and from the ramps being the motor carrier's responsibility. Under plan 2, the railroad provides door-to-door service using only its own equipment. About two-thirds of all piggyback service is handled under these two plans.

Of the other plans, under plan 2½ the shipper provides the trailer and the railroad provides the terminal service; in plan 3 the railroad provides ramp-to-ramp service for two trailers on one flatcar, but the shipper makes the arrangements for the delivery of the trailers to the shipping ramp and for removal from the receiving ramp. Under plan 3½, we have the same service as in plan 3; only a single trailer is handled, but at higher cost. Plan 4 covers the movement of a privately owned, loaded or empty TOFC flatcar, while plan 5 is a coordinated service offered jointly by a motor carrier and a railroad.

There is no particular cost advantage to the shipper when goods move in a common carrier trailer via piggyback. There is improved delivery in that piggyback trains move on regular schedules, especially between the larger centers. Only the very worst weather will delay the trains. Another advantage lies in the maximum load limitations. The railroads expect 40,000-pound loads, and this service provides the means of getting around any load limitations that may exist in intervening states.

Railroads

Railroads are almost entirely in the long-haul carload hauling business. Only a small per cent of rail freight is LCL, which is defined as any shipment which is not a carload, and doesn't necessarily mean small-package operations. A carload itself has no fixed weight, only the weight specified in the tariffs covering the commodity hauled. About three-quarters of all rail freight moves from origin to destination with no rehandling enroute, even though passing over several railroads. This occurs because of the interchange of cars between the railroads.

Compared to motor trucks, railroads are at some disadvantage on short-haul movements of up to about 100 miles because trucks can make a pickup in the morning and deliver the same day. With a rail car, loading may well be completed in the morning but switching of the shipper's yard occurs only once a day. The car is then moved to the railroad yard for sorting into a train headed toward its delivery point. During the night the train may move to the destination, where it undergoes another sorting operation before it is turned over to a switching crew for delivery to the receiving factory. This might be accomplished on the second day, with the car ready for unloading on the third morning. If the car were to be interchanged twice enroute, delivery could be delayed another two days.

As the delivery distances stretch out, the advantage begins to swing to the railroads. When distance reaches about 350 miles, freight rates begin to favor rail movement because of the lessened impact of terminal costs.

The rails have moved toward the use of new concepts in handling high-volume shipments. The integrated train containing specialized equipment is utilized to handle certain kinds of commodities in great tonnage. The unit train and the leased train are variations of the idea of moving solid trainloads of materials between two points on a single bill of lading, with stops only to change train crews.

Recently, cars with load capacities in the 70-100 tons range have been placed in service. The advantage to the shipper lies in an improved freight rate if he can ship the larger quantity. There is a minor advantage in being able to use a single loading door and have only a single car to prepare for shipment, compared to the use of two 40-ton cars. Other designs which are replacing the older cars include the damage-free or DF car and the bulkhead car. The DF car is equipped with suitable cross-braces and panels which permit cross-bracing the car at any desired short interval, thus preventing or minimizing the shifting of lading during switching operations. The bulkhead car is fitted with two sets of internal steel doors, mounted on internal tracks along the sides of the car. Freight is stacked in one end of the car; one pair of doors is then moved into a tight position against the face of the piled freight and locked in place. The process is repeated at the other end, and if desired, the space between the doors at the center of the car may also be loaded. This is a great economy to the shipper because at present-day wage and material costs, bulkheads and restraints fabricated at the time of loading may cost several hundred dollars. The DF and bulkhead cars obviate this expense and hold in-transit damage to levels comparable with those experienced in motor trucks.

Besides boxcars of various dimensions, railroads offer a wide variety of other cars, including open and covered hopper cars, gondola cars, cattle cars, rack cars for pulp wood, automobile carriers, and a great variety of other special, limited-application equipment.

Motor Trucks

Motor trucks come in almost as many varieties as railroad cars. There are straight trucks which may have platform, stake, dump, van box, or other body styles. There are full-trailer and semi-trailer units which may have low-bed, tank, box, pole, van, dump, or other special trailer construction. There are the so-called "double bottom" units which consist of a tractor, semi-trailer, and full trailer. Depending upon the state, some of these latter units may be as much as 110 feet long. Common carriers are not limited to the type truck they use, but it appears that the usual unit is a tractor plus a semi-trailer in most states. The newest trailers are generally 40 feet long and 9 feet wide (outside dimensions). Agitation is developing for the states to authorize longer and wider units with corresponding higher load limits.

Photo courtesy of McLean Trucking Co., Winston-Salem, N.C.

Photo 9-1. *Forty-foot semi-trailer box unit.*

A motor common carrier is one offering to transport private property for the general public within certain specified areas, either in interstate or intrastate commerce, or both. All common carriers do not handle all kinds of private property. Some specialize in hauling furniture, liquids, automobiles, general freight, and other materials.

There are more than 10,000 common carriers in the United States. Some of these serve very small areas while others operate from coast to coast.

Contract common carriers have only a single, or at most a few affiliated customers. Contracts are generally long term. There are about 20% as many contract carriers as common carriers. Exempt carriers operate on a "for hire" basis and haul only (for the most part) exempt agricultural products: fish, livestock, newspapers, and other similar items. It is said the typical exempt carrier operates three or four units with possibly 50,000 in this type of carriage.

Photo courtesy of McLean Trucking Co., Winston-Salem, N.C.

Photo 9-2. *Local-delivery pickup trucks.*

Other Types of Carriage

There are thousands of miles of coastal and inland waterways that are plied by towboats and barges. Commodities are handled in quantity, usually in parcels of not less than about 500 tons and more frequently of 1,000 or more tons. Cost of transportation is very low but the speed of travel is very slow.

Ocean transport is by ship, with a high proportion of the cargoes carried in bulk form, such as oil, ores, and the like. Other commodities, such as natural fibers, spices, tea, cocoa, and manufactured goods, move in boxes, crates, bales, bundles, and similar containers. There is a growing trend for packaged materials to move in special containers, similar to the box trailers used by motor common carriers, and to be handled aboard ships specially designed to store containers. There are also lighter-aboard-ship, or LASH ships. With these, lighters are preloaded, floated to the ship, lifted aboard, carried to the destination port, and floated under tow to shore. With this type of ship, goods may be delivered to ports without docks or deep-water piers, and at the same time the ship can unload and be on its way much quicker than it would if cargo had to be unloaded piece-by-piece onto a local lighter.

Privately Operated Rail Equipment

The introduction of privately owned railroad stock, as distinguished from railroad-owned, is said to date back to the early oil fields of Pennsylvania. In the beginning, crude oil was moved from the wells to the point of processing in barrels. The railroads were reluctant to build special cars for handling bulk oil but agreed to handle the cars if the shipper supplied the equipment. Since the railroads normally supplied all equipment to the shipper, an agreement was reached that the railroad would pay the owner of the equipment a mileage allowance to help amortize the cost of the cars. At the same time, any demurrage incurred by customers of the owners would be payable to the railroads.

Once established, the pattern was set for industry to build all kinds of special cars to meet its requirements for the shipment of bulk liquids or gases and various kinds of dry bulk products. Today, the shipper doesn't necessarily have to own any specialized equipment. Many types are available from companies specializing in the leasing of railroad cars. Still, some companies do own all, or almost all, of the cars they use. The advantages and disadvantages of leasing have already been discussed in Chapter 5.

Tank cars for liquid products are made up of many types of materials, including plain steel, alloys, and specially chosen metals. Cars may be heated; that is, the lading is hot when loaded and may be reheated by means of internal steam coils at the destination, with steam from customer mains. Some cars are bare, others are insulated. Some operate at atmospheric pressure, others at elevated pressure. All of these variations are as requirements dictate. Cylinder cars are available for carriage of compressed gases. Cars for handling dry products may also be owned or leased, but usually only in the event of some special characteristic of the goods shipped. But whether handling few or many cars, the cost of operating them is an expense which must be controlled, as are other costs in the business.

Cost Controls

The following illustrates one type of cost control:

(a) The average daily cost of owning (depreciation plus maintenance) or leasing is $6 per day.

(b) The mileage credit per loaded mile is 13¢.

These two figures are fixed. If you lease, the lease costs are a contracted uniform expense, although the mileage credit may be applied to offset the monthly charges up to the amount of the monthly charge; any excess credits belong to the lessor. If you own the equipment, the cost may vary from month to month with variation in maintenance, but over the long period, or over many similar cars, will vary only slightly. The loaded mileage credit has been fixed by agreement between users, carriers, and the government and is readjusted at rather long intervals.

The variable elements in the cost calculations are:

(c) The time the car is out of service for repairs.

(d) The time the car is at the factory for loading.

(e) The time the car is stored at the factory, either empty or loaded.

(f) The time the car is in transit from factory to customer, and vice versa.

(g) The distance from factory to customer location.

(h) The time the car is held by the customer.

Out of Service

Painting, preventive maintenance, tank car lining or heating coil repairs, and in-transit shopping to repair elements which affect train-operating safety are the commonly experienced repair outages. With new equipment, lost time for repairs should be very low. For a group of cars of varying age, a 5 to 7% rate of repair outage can be expected. When service demands are high, some types of repair may be deferred; i.e., painting, but work will be done in time, when the demand slackens.

At Factory

The time the car is at the factory for loading is affected by variation in sales demand, between-trip reconditioning (i.e., cleaning which may be required), and possible use as temporary in-plant storage capacity. If time in plant is very low, say around one day per trip, it may indicate insufficient cars in the service. This can lead to interrupted deliveries to customers. On the other hand, long average stays at the factory indicate too many cars in the fleet or a heavy cutback in product demand.

In-Transit Time

Transit time is a function of the distance travelled and of the number of classification or interchange points through which a car must move. Occasionally, extreme bad weather or in-transit repair to brakes, journal boxes, etc., add to in-transit time. It will be found that running times are reasonably consistent with perhaps a plus or minus variation of 10% around the mean.

Time at Customer Plant

Time at customer plant may run from a single day upwards. The longer delays usually occur when the vendor has provided the customer with a trip lease for his convenience.

Customer Service Costs

Looking only at the time the car is used to service a customer, let us consider a customer located 200 miles from the factory and with a minimum of interchange-classification requirements, so that round-trip in-transit time averages five days. We can then look at the effect on the cost of delivery for various holding times at customer location. Table 9-1 depicts the cost per delivered ton, with the various days of delay at

TABLE 9-1
Effect of Customer-Unloading Delay

Net weight shipped	=	40 tons.	
Loaded mileage	=	200.	
Mileage allowance	=	$0.13 or $26.00 per trip.	
Car cost per day	=	$6.00.	
Transit time	=	5 days, average.	

Days at Customer	Days Away from Factory	Total Car Cost $	Earned Mileage $	Net Car Cost per Trip $	Cost per Delivered Ton $
1	6	36.00	26.00	10.00	0.25
3	8	48.00	26.00	22.00	0.55
5	10	60.00	26.00	34.00	0.85
7	12	72.00	26.00	46.00	1.15
10	15	90.00	26.00	64.00	1.60
15	20	120.00	26.00	94.00	2.35
20	25	150.00	26.00	124.00	3.10
25	30	180.00	26.00	154.00	3.85
50	55	330.00	26.00	304.00	7.60

TABLE 9-1 (Cont'd)
Effect of Customer-Unloading Delay

At one day at customer, 12 days in transit for 600 miles:

1	13	78.00	78.00	0.00	0.00

At one day at customer, 22 days in transit for 1,500 miles:

1	23	138.00	195.00	–57.00	–1.43

At one day at customer, 30 days in transit for 2,500 miles:

1	31	186.00	325.00	–139.00	–3.47

At one day at customer, 2 days in transit for 10 miles switching:

1	3	18.00	1.30	16.70	0.42

the customer, and also shows the effect on costs for variation in the distance the car moves. It is seen that the longer the customer holds the car, the higher the delivery costs will be. Further, looking at the 10-mile delivery with a cost of 42¢ per ton, consider that a semi-trailer truck unit will deliver this same tonnage in one day and at less than half the cost. Thus, there is a range of delivery by motor truck which will be more economical than rail. The exact range will depend upon the variation in rail transit time and customer holding time, with the assumption that semi-trailer is not left at the customer location. You may be unable to switch the customer from rail to truck because of his own more apparent advantages.

Cost Allocation

In-plant car costs might be considered as rail fleet overhead, and these expenses pro-rated over the trip costs. The principal in-plant outlay is the per diem cost of owning or leasing the equipment. Other expenses include the straight-time, overtime, and fringe costs for loading and any required cleaning costs, the record-keeping costs, a portion of the costs of operating and maintaining the factory rail system, and possibly a factory overhead allocation.

Bulk-loading techniques are usually quite speedy, or may only involve the shunting of production by the operator into a car rather than running it into a storage tank or bin. The labor requirement may well be less than an hour, or possibly $3-$4 per car. Clerical costs are usually nominal and overhead allocations only a fraction of the direct costs. Thus the cost per load for a one-day stay at the factory might show:

Per Diem Car Cost	=	$6.00
Loading Cost	=	3.00
Clerical Cost	=	0.35
In-Plant RR Operation	=	2.00
Overhead	=	1.00
Total	=	$12.35

These costs might well be allocated to the customer service cost on a "per trip" basis, while the per diem costs for stays longer than one day could be allocated on a "per day out of the plant" basis. The foregoing is offered to illustrate the method of analyzing freight car costs rather than to suggest a specific method for the reallocation of cost accounts, since reallocation falls within the bailiwick of accounting philosophy. However, efforts should be directed to keeping the cars on the road delivering the goods. In this way, delivery costs are kept low and so are in-plant car costs.

Private Operations Profit

Keeping in mind that the mileage allowance from the railroads is based on the concept of amortizing the shipper's investment and repair costs for the equipment, a "profit" in operating rail cars should not be expected. The goal should be to break even. If cars are to be used for temporary storage at the customer location, at the factory, or at a company warehouse, the per diem costs of owning or leasing should be so allocated, and not considered as a part of the cost of delivering goods. If this is done, and the supply of cars is in balance with the shipping needs with fairly steady business, breakeven costs can be achieved.

BIBLIOGRAPHY AND FURTHER READING

(1) "How Air Freight Can Increase Profits by Reducing the Total Cost of Physical Distribution," New York, N.Y., Emery Air Freight Corp., 1965. Covers the economics of air freight.

(2) Taff, C.A., "Management of Traffic and Physical Distribution," Homewood, Ill., Richard D. Irwin, Inc., 1968. Thorough coverage of the traffic function.

Chapter 10

T his chapter deals with the relationships between purchasing, packaging, traffic, and computers and the Materials Management Department.

Purchasing

It is not the purpose of this section to discuss the structure and functions of a purchasing department. There is ample coverage in the literature on these points. There is, however, a strong interface between purchasing and the inventory manager in the materials management group. In Chapter 2, Managing Inventory Successfully, we discussed economic order quantities as one of the factors leading to optimum

INTERFACING THE MATERIALS MANAGEMENT OPERATION

inventory levels. From the purchasing point of view, the annual cost of ordering must be balanced against the annual cost of holding. This is the precise objective of the inventory manager. Now it sometimes happens that many inventory items are secured from the same vendor and there may be volume discount possibilities plus some freight advantages. Thus the buyer and the inventory manager should get their heads together to find out whether a little violation of the strict EOQ rules might not lead to an economic gain. As an illustration, 13 chemicals used in processing and re-

TABLE 10-1
Group Buying

Product	O.Q. lb.	O.P. lb.	Cycle Stock on Hand	St'd. Pkg. lb.	Ave. Weekly Usage	Week's Supply on Hand	Needed	Order
A	12,000	4,500	8,000	200	1,500	5+	0	9,600
B	1,000	120	300	100	40	7.5	0	0
C	500	30	320	100	10	30	0	0
D	8,000	1,800	4,200	300	600	7	0	0
E	2,250	270	1,775	250	90	20	0	0
F	750	45	0	50	15	0	750	750
G	24,000	18,000	19,100	400	6,000	3+	0	24,000
H	4,200	480	1,720	700	160	11	0	0
I	3,100	360	2,110	100	120	17+	0	0
J	15,000	5,700	9,560	500	1,900	5	0	3,000
K	600	36	480	100	12	40+	0	0
L	1,400	81	1,295	100	27	48	0	0
M	100	6	72	25	2	37	0	0

L.T. = 3 weeks

Monthly sales	EOQ
20 M up	1 month's sales
10-20 M	2 month's sales
5-10 M	3 month's sales
2-5 M	6 month's sales
under 2 M	12 month's sales

N.B. No price breaks because quantities to be ordered are within annual requirement and order quantity limits.

packaging operations are purchased from one vendor. Average usage of these items ranges from 2 pounds to 6,000 pounds per week. Order points range from 6 pounds to 18,000 pounds. Item F has gone below the order point and has annual requirements of only 750 pounds. Rather than pay LTL freight rates, is it possible to buy some of the other chemicals at the same time and thus reach a more attractive freight rate? In Table 10-1, the data on all 13 items are given. Items besides Item F which might be ordered are those with cycle stocks closest to their order points. Item F is down to the safety stock level and must be reordered. Item G is almost at the order point and Items J and A are a couple of weeks further away. An order should be entered for the needed 750 pounds of Item F, 24,000 pounds of Item G, 9,600 pounds of Item A, and 3,000 pounds of Item J. For the last two items, quantity is less than the usual order quantity. The total quantity has a gross weight of slightly less than 40,000 pounds.

Price Breaks

Another problem arising from time to time does relate to price breaks. With the increased quantity at a price break, there may also be a lower freight rate. With the lower price and possibly lower freight rate, there are also cost increases. As an example, Product Q is being used at an average rate of 600 pounds per week. The economic lot size for purchasing is 8,000 pounds. Lots of this size are priced at 35¢ per pound. The vendor suggests a price of 33¢ per pound in lots of 20,000 pounds. Is there a true savings in this? A few calculations will illustrate:

8,000 pounds of Product Q is a 13-week supply while 20,000 pounds is a 33-week supply. The average inventory over 13 weeks is 4,000 pounds, and at 25% per year, the cost of holding the average inventory is 4,000 pounds x $0.35 x .25/52 x 13 = $87.50. With the proposed increased purchase quantity, the cost is 10,000 pounds x $0.33 x .25/52 x 33 = $522.72. To put the two situations on the same basis, the $87.50 must be multiplied by 33/13 = $222.25. Because of the increased average inventory, our cost of holding over a 33-week period has increased by $522.72 - $222.25 = $300.47. But there is a freight benefit. At 8,000 pounds the freight rate is $2.40 per cwt., while at 20,000 pounds it is only $1.80. Over a 33-week period, freight on 8,000-pound lots would be 80 cwt. x $2.40 x 33/13 = $487.58, while for 20,000 pounds the freight would be 200 cwt. x $1.80 = $360. Freight savings would be $127.58. Further, with chemicals, there is an analytical cost for checking the quality of the item. At a cost of $50 per analysis, the 8,000-pound lot requires 33/13 analyses or a period cost of $127. In addition there is the cost of purchasing of $15 per order, or $38.10 for the 8,000-pound lots. Summarizing:

Cost of goods savings	=	–$400.00
Cost of holding, increase	=	+300.47
Freight, savings	=	–127.58
Analysis, savings	=	–77.00
Purchasing, savings	=	–23.10
Total	=	–$327.21 per order cycle @ 20,000 pounds

In this case, there is an advantage in the proffered price break amounting to about $500 per year. If there is room in the warehouse, and if the risk of spoilage is low, and if management is willing to invest in the added inventory rather than elsewhere, then the offer at the lower price would be acceptable. After all, the return on the average additional investment is about 26%.

Computerized Purchasing

In Chapter 11 a computerized materials management system will be described. As a part of the described system, requirements for raw materials, packaging components, and other items are generated for several months ahead. With this information, purchasing has the ability to approach vendors to arrange blanket orders, annual requirement orders, and consolidated orders against which the computer could issue releases subject to manual review. A generalized flow pattern is shown in Figure 10-1. Although not shown therein, other features such as expediting notice, vendor performance analysis, and various exception reports can easily be generated. This illustrates the growing trend towards the use of computers in the purchasing-materials-management area.

Packaging

Whatever the item sold to the ultimate consumer, it is almost always delivered to him in some kind of a package. The package may be a vial, tube, envelope, bag, ampoule, jar, bottle, box, cylinder, pail, drum, tote bin, or, by a little exaggeration, in a tank car, barge, or ship. In the main, it is the contents the customer is interested in. The package should not damage the contents by scratching or abrading them, nor should it impart undesirable odors or taste. It should protect the contents from contamination, pilferage, or damage.

Hazardous Items

A package should be strong enough. Hazardous materials such as flammable liquids and solids, oxidizers, corrosives, flammable and nonflammable compressed

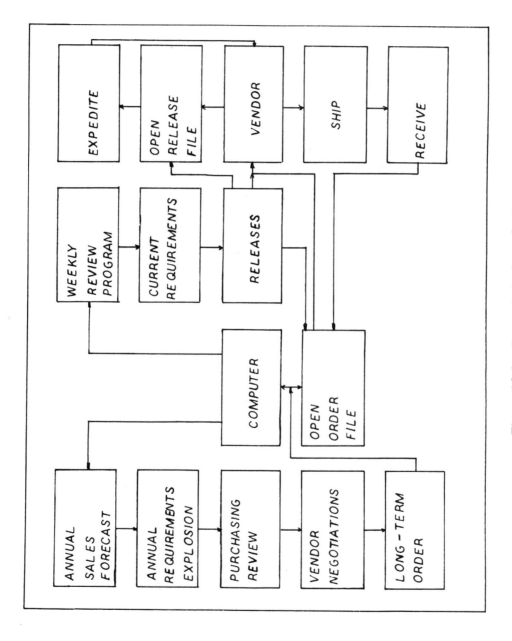

Figure 10-1. *Computerized purchasing.*

gases, poisons, tear gas, radioactives, and explosives are under D.O.T. regulation. These regulations are spelled out together with rules on shipping containers in Agent T.C. George's "Tariff No. 23" (Bibliography, #4). This tariff covers a listing of all hazardous and explosive articles by name, including some 1,100 items; regulations applying to shippers; regulations applying to rail carriers; regulations applying to common, contract, and private motor carriers by public highway; shipping container specifications; and tank car specifications. If a shipper wants to move an item he knows to be hazardous but which is not included in George's "Tariff" or supplements thereto, or if he desires to ship a new type of package not covered in the container specifications, he must make application to the Hazardous Materials Regulation Board of the D.O.T. for a special permit. At the time of application, he must supply all necessary information needed to show hazards and describe how it is proposed to protect against these hazards.

The packages specified in George's "Tariff" offer a very high degree of protection to the goods being transported, but this is secondary to the protection afforded against injury to those who must handle the containers at any point. When we move away from regulated commodities, we find the same degree of protection being offered to the packaged materials when the items are very valuable, but now the emphasis is strictly on protection of the package contents.

Packaging Other Items

As we move away from hazardous and high-cost items, packaging tends to become something less than 100% protection of the goods shipped. There are, however, forces at work to keep the containers from becoming too skimpy, and both are economic in nature. While every shipper recognizes the outside container to be a means of affording some degree of protection to the goods, he also knows the package is ultimately thrown away, recycled, or otherwise destroyed. It is to the shipper's advantage to use the cheapest package he can, without generating excessive loss of goods and customer complaints. Putting a price tag on customer complaints is not easy, but perhaps a measure is the loss of potential profits. The value of lost or damaged goods may (and I say this advisedly) be recovered from the carrier. In any event, there is a balance point between money saved on the package and other expenses.

Transit losses may be recovered from carriers, but they are looking out for their own economic interests also. Broken containers result in too many claims and added handling costs; therefore, the carriers prescribe minimum specifications for containers in their freight classifications, in order to minimize any damage to goods while they are in their possession. The specifications are very detailed, so that for most shipping containers it may well be taken that the carrier's specifications are minima. The shipper can and should move up from this point, so that his higher package cost is in balance with his lower loss experience for the package he ultimately uses.

Storage Problems

In warehousing products packaged in corrugated paper boxes or fiberboard containers, there is a problem with high humidity conditions. The paper fibers absorb moisture which lowers the rigidity of the structure. The container, whether carton or drum, will then deform more rapidly under load than it would under low humidity conditions. If the product within the container is a canned item, and the carbon fits snugly to the contents, the cans themselves will offer all the support needed for quite high stacking. We do have situations where items such as screw caps for bottles are, in effect, bulk-packed in a carton, or a granular material is packaged in a fiber drum but does not quite fill it. When this occurs, it will be found that handling causes the contents to settle, leaving air space at the top of the container. Under humid conditions, the side walls will deform. When such containers are in pallet stacks under these conditions, the stacks develop dangerous tilts, and even tumble over. To avoid falling pallet stacks, it may be necessary to limit stack heights, seek heavier container constructions, or resort to pallet racks.

Package Testing

To develop an outside package that will stand up in common carriage, we need a more speedy feedback than we can get from trial and error. In fact, we cannot afford to develop container information this way. A container testing facility is the answer to this problem. One of the key test measures in such a laboratory is a 4-foot drop test. Why 4 feet? This is typically the height of the floor of a railroad car or truck body above ground. Goods are sometimes unloaded by dropping them from the doorway or tailgate to the ground, and a container should stand this kind of handling. In the laboratory, a container would be tested in a drop-tester by dropping a filled unit on a corner, an end, a side, top, or bottom, with a different unit being used for each test. The object is to see whether the contents are protected, whether the seals hold, and whether there is container failure. A filled drum would be dropped on a top and bottom chine, on the side, and on both ends. Again, a different drum is used for each test.

A controlled-temperature humidity chamber is used to check the degree of protection offered by barrier board to the container contents, the effect of moisture on adhesives, warping, and decomposition of the container. A dry-heat or dry-cold chamber offers similar checks. A tumbler box simulates handling through chutes with sudden stops or changes in direction. A jolter simulates a rough-riding vehicle. A swing-tester is used to check the strength of glass carboys under loaded and empty conditions, simulating the shocks that might be experienced in carriage. Other machines are available for testing bursting strength of corrugated board or fiberboard and paper, and for testing puncture resistance. The use of this equipment is not limited to developing new containers, but is also used for periodically checking the quality of containers and components purchased for routine use.

Traffic

It has been well said that the basic objective of traffic managers is to purchase transportation services, to do this in an optimum way, and to satisfy the requirements of speed, cost, and various departmental plans and objectives. (See Bibliography #2.) In some ways, the traffic function is similar to that of a purchasing department, but with a difference. Whereas a purchasing department has considerable latitude to negotiate purchases under the usual limitations of commercial law, the traffic department buys in an area which is fenced in by strict federal and state regulations and in which the price paid is usually fixed for any given move. However, the price paid, that is the freight rate, is not quite that simple either, because there are class rates, commodity rates, exception rates, and various extra or special charges, such as stop-off, detention, switching, and so on. There are literally millions of freight rates because not only are there the rates already mentioned, but these are also spelled out for the movement of goods between each pair of thousands of origin-destination couples in the carrier's system.

Rates are not the only concern of traffic. There are also routings to be examined. To a neophyte, it might seem that the shortest, or the least expensive, way to route a shipment would be the best way to ship. The cheapest way to ship might be by water. If quantities are great enough and if slow movement is no problem, this might well be the way to go. Style goods, perishables, expensive articles, low-volume items, and many others would not be moved this way. The fastest way may be equally unsatisfactory, depending upon what is being shipped. About the only time that tonnage of coal was moved by air was during the Berlin crisis. The criteria for this particular move were not economically based. The point of all this is that there are no simple answers in arriving at a "best rate" or a "best routing." There is a combination of different types of carriage, diverse routes, variable speeds of movement, dissimilar levels of service available, and varied costs. It is through the multiple choices available that the path best suited to the business and its customers must be found.

Traffic Interfaces

Traffic has a concern for how goods are packaged and loaded for shipment, so that in-transit damage or loss is held down and customer satisfaction may be achieved in this respect. Traffic also has strong capabilities of assisting in locating new facilities, both for warehousing and manufacturing. Through experience in the field and knowledge of the different modes of transportation, traffic can give guidance on site selection and thus lead to the best combination of expeditious shipments and flexibility in the choice of carriers. Their advice can also have a desirable effect on the levels of inventory which would have to be carried in a warehouse.

Materials management must work closely with traffic if, in fact, it is not already included in the materials management area of responsibility. The movement of goods is a major factor in physical distribution, and the need to arrive at the best overall costs for servicing customers requires a balancing of warehousing, transportation, inventory, and other costs to which both groups must make their contribution.

Computers

Today, all major corporations have one or more computer installations. A substantial proportion, but by no means all, of the middle-sized corporations also have installations, but very few of the small companies have made the step. In spite of the widespread use of computers there is an astonishing amount of ignorance about them, perhaps a feeling that these esoteric machines respond only to those who are privy to their secrets. There can be no question; a computer is a complicated piece of electronic gear. So are the new electronic desk calculators. The older rotary electric desk calculators are marvels of mechanical ingenuity. What is the point? A desk calculator is also a computer. It is doubtful whether many readers have never operated a desk calculator at some time or another. You say, "But you do not have to program a desk calculator!" Not true, programming of a desk calculator is a simple manual operation. Keys are punched in a certain sequence, then the activator button is pressed, and the machine adds, or subtracts, or multiplies, or divides just as you wished. There are features on some of the rotary calculators that are similar to memory in the machines we call computers, such as holding a constant multiplier. A very rudimentary memory indeed! The new electronic calculators may have as many as 40 memory steps, which permit repetitive solution of complex problems with the entry of only a few pieces of variable information. Programming of these machines is also done with the fingers, as with the older machines.

Since all is fair in love and argumentation, I will make the flat statement that a computer is a very large desk calculator. It adds and subtracts, it multiplies and divides, it compares and decides, but only after you have told it what to do through a program. Unfortunately, these kinds of programs cannot be entered by punching keys on the side of the computer. Instead, it is done outside the computer by working out the logic of the solution. In reality, this is done for the desk calculator also. The next step is different — a program must be "written." In this program, you prepare a set of instructions telling the computer the various steps to be followed to arrive at an answer, The instructions are completely detailed — and must be — for the machine is just that, a machine, and it cannot fill in gaps in the instructions. After a program is written it is tested, either by using real data or by entering made-up data called test data, which will give an indication of how well the program functions. It will frequently be found that the results obtained are not what was expected, and it becomes necessary to scrutinize the program to see what was done wrong that caused improper answers. This phase of the work is called debugging. When all of the bugs are out, the program will turn out the expected answers.

Computer Languages

Unfortunately, a computer does not "understand" English or any other spoken language. It comprehends instructions only when they are prepared in machine language. A few programmers can write programs directly in machine language, but it is very tedious and time consuming, and the programmer may have trouble remembering all the involved detail. When mistakes are made, debugging can be very difficult. This problem was recognized very early in the computer era, and secondary languages were developed which were then translated into machine language within the computer itself by means of a device called a compiler. There are a great many programming languages, such as Autocoder, COBOL, FORTRAN, in several varieties, PL-1, and many others. Some of the language names originate from the purpose for which they were designed, thus *com*mon *b*usiness-*o*riented *l*anguage or COBOL, and *for*mula *tran*slation for FORTRAN.

Programming

Who can write programs? Is programming difficult to learn? Many people have little difficulty learning how to program. In fact, some persons can learn to use the *b*eginner's *a*ll-purpose *s*ymbolic *i*nstruction *c*ode or BASIC language in a few hours, writing programs that run. One of the writer's engineers taught himself BASIC over a weekend, including writing a program, debugging, and getting the results back. This is not thought to be unusual. Most time-sharing systems use BASIC or a language of similar simplicity and ease of comprehension. From a simple language such as BASIC, it is a matter of application and growth of understanding to move on to FORTRAN or one of the business languages.

Shared-Time Systems

It is not necessary to write programs for every problem to be solved. Companies offering shared-time computer services also proffer an extensive library of prepared programs. In our area of interest, these cover such topics as:

Analysis of variance.	Forecasting.
Differential equations.	Least-squares method.
Evaluation of complex functions.	Linear programming.
After-tax return.	Plant expansion.
Business analysis.	Random-number generators.
Calculations in distribution.	Regression analysis.

Capital investment.	Sample mean and standard deviation.
Cash-flow analysis.	Sample size determination.
Critical path method.	Statistical analysis of data.
Engineering problems.	Transportation analysis.
Financial analysis.	Distribution analysis.
Many others.	

Shared-time service includes a hands-on manual for each desired program, showing how to call out the program, enter data, and the format of the results. Costs of these services are quite small compared to those of an in-house computer. As an example, one service company looks for a $100 initiation fee and $100 per month minimum billing. Operating costs are $11 per hour terminal connect time, 5¢ per second for central processor time, 3¢ per second for read-write time, and similar charges for other services. It has been found that billing will average about $20-30 per hour for all services while connected to the terminal. In addition to these costs, there will be a rental cost of less than $100 per month for a manual, tape-reading, acoustic-coupled teletypewriter, plus telephone charges from your location to the central computer being used. You may have in-house programs to handle all of these miscellaneous tasks, and if so by all means use them in your own computer. However, if the programs are not available, or if you do not have a computer, the shared-time concept is an inexpensive way to get computer service and develop some computer know-how.

Shared-Time Example

Figure 10-2 shows an actual program prepared by the user in FORTRAN IV. The first eight lines describe the program in English, while the remainder is the computer program for an ABC analysis of labor usage on 324 maintenance jobs, including the format for the report. Line 95, "PCNTL = 5.0," is the instruction to print out the largest job and the jobs falling at 5% cumulative increments through all the data; it is used in line 1082 to calculate K. By suitable manipulation of statements 95 and 1082, the program will print out all of the data in proper sequence. Figure 10-3 shows the manner in which the labor usage was entered in round dollars, while Figure 10-4 shows the report printed out by the computer. The whole thing was run in about ten minutes.

Do not hesitate to use a computer. If you do not want to go through the bother of writing out programs and you have a computer group, have someone in that section do it for you. If you do not mind doing your own programming, you can readily learn.

```
:L
1C              SAMPLE PRØGRAM FØR ABC ANALYSIS
2C              *********************************
3C DATA IS FED INTØ THE PROGRAM FROM CARDS,TAPE,ØR A SYSTEM FILE. IN
4C
5C FILE.THE PRØGRAM WILL PRINT ØUT A CØMPLETE LISTING ØF VALUES IN ABC
6C ØRDER ØRLIST ØNLY STATED VALUES WHICH APPRØXIMATE  STATED PERCENT=
7C ILE LIMITS. PCNTI=5,WILL PRINT A(I)THRU A(N) IN INCREMENTS OF
8C 5 PERCENTILES.
70 DIMENSIØN DATA(500)
80   CALL ØPENF(1,"VALUES")
90 N=330
95 PCNTL=5.0
100   READ(1,4)(DATA(I),I=1,N)
110  4 FØRMAT(10F7.1)
120   PRINT 6
130  6 FØRMAT(10X,"VALUES",5X,"CUM.%ØF",5X,"CUM. % ØF",/,21X,"ITEMS",
140&7X,"SUM ØF VALUES",/,"--------",4X,"---------",4X,
150&"--------",/)
160 CALL ABC(N,DATA,PCNTL)
212-421090 PRINT 12,(I,A(I),PN(I),PA(I)
400 END
810 SUBRØUTINE ABC(N,A,PCNTL)
820   DIMENSION A(500),PN(500),PA(500)
830   NM1=N-1
840   DØ8 I=1,NM1
850   L=I
860   IP1=I+1
870   DØ7 J=IP1,N
880   IF (A(L)-A(J))6,7,7
890   6L=J
900   7CØNTINUE
910   ATEMP=A(I)
920   A(I)=A(L)
930  8 A(L)=ATEMP
940   DØ 9 I=1,N
950  9 SUMA=A(I)+SUMA
960   ABAR=SUMA/N
1060  DØ10 I=1,N
1070   PN(I)=FLØAT(I)/FLØAT(N)
1072 ASUM=ASUM+A(I)
1080   10PA(I)=ASUM/SUMA
1082 K=(FLØAT(N)*PCNTL/100.0+.5)
1090   PRINT 12,(I,A(I),PN(I),PA(I),I=1,N,K)
1092 PRINT 14 ,SUMA,ABAR
1100  12FØRMAT(3X,I3,F10.1,F11.4,F13.4)
1102  14FØRMAT("-------------------------------------------"/F16.1,/,
1103&F16.1
1104&,//)
1110   RETURN
1120   END
```

Figure 10-2. *Program for ABC analysis.*

```
VALUES
 70.0   140.0    18.0    17.0    52.0    35.0    18.0     0.0    86.0    34.0
 57.0    26.0    43.0    52.0    69.0     9.0    52.0    26.0    22.0    56.0
 39.0    60.0    30.0    34.0    34.0    34.0    34.0    34.0   103.0    17.0
 64.0    35.0    13.0    52.0    43.0    34.0    52.0    56.0    36.0    72.0
 35.0    35.0   107.0    18.0    53.0    88.0    79.0    83.0    35.0    18.0
  0.0    44.0    62.0    35.0    31.0    35.0    48.0    15.0     0.0     0.0
 88.0    62.0    97.0    27.0    44.0    36.0     9.0    70.0    92.0    53.0
 35.0     9.0    35.0    44.0    35.0    70.0    53.0   112.0     0.0    44.0
192.0    95.0    77.0    69.0    72.0   185.0   158.0    70.0   104.0    70.0
 34.0    53.0    86.0   103.0    47.0    26.0   103.0    44.0   112.0
 34.0    26.0   116.0    56.0   262.0   106.0   129.0    18.0
116.0     0.0    67.0   138.0    80.0    77.0   172.
281.0   185.0    53.0    69.0    52.0    47                              .0    53.0
  0.0    73.0    34.0    95.0    17                             .0   174.0    49.0
 26.0   129.0    43.0    6                            .0   128.0    42.0    40.0
383.0    22.0    3              .40.0    18.0    70.0    88.0    26.0
176.0                           18.0    76.0    62.0    36.0    58.0     0.0
                         26.0    66.0   246.0   146.0    35.0    18.0    18.0
                 93.0   176.0   340.0    70.0    22.0    79.0   105.0    26.0
        115.0    89.0    53.0    44.0   193.0   132.0    72.0    31.0    89.0
435.0    35.0    18.0    53.0   105.0   169.0    95.0     0.0    36.0    61.0
 66.0   154.0    86.0    71.0    67.0   320.0   320.0    35.0    35.0    40.0
 88.0   141.0   123.0    22.0     0.0    44.0    80.0    45.0    71.0    70.0
 75.0   175.0    36.0    23.0     9.0    77.0   568.0    70.0   201.0   177.0
 79.0     0.0   105.0    18.0    44.0    18.0     0.0    26.0   687.0    53.0
417.0   499.0   755.0   649.0    27.0   511.0   188.0   140.0   649.0   325.0
 70.0   120.0   828.0     0.0   649.0     0.0   993.0   869.0     0.0   528.0
```

Figure 10-3. *Data for ABC program.*

	VALUES	CUM.%OF ITEMS	CUM. % OF SUM OF VALUES
1	993.0	0.0030	0.0276
18	377.0	0.0545	0.3027
35	228.0	0.1061	0.4368
52	177.0	0.1576	0.5284
69	140.0	0.2091	0.6039
86	116.0	0.2606	0.6637
103	100.0	0.3121	0.7139
120	88.0	0.3636	0.7570
137	75.0	0.4152	0.7952
154	70.0	0.4667	0.8287
171	65.0	0.5182	0.8610
188	53.0	0.5697	0.8882
205	48.0	0.6212	0.9128
222	43.0	0.6727	0.9338
239	35.0	0.7242	0.9513
256	34.0	0.7758	0.9676
273	26.0	0.8273	0.9814
290	18.0	0.8788	0.9911
307	9.0	0.9303	0.9986
324	0.0	0.9818	1.0000
SUM	35990.0		
AVE.	109.1		

Figure 10-4. *Results of ABC program.*

BIBLIOGRAPHY AND FURTHER READING

(1) Ammer, D.S., "Purchasing for Profits," Boston, Mass., *Harvard Business Review*, May-June 1961, pages 135-143.

(2) Colton, R.C. and Ward, E.S., *A Practical Handbook of Industrial Traffic Management*, Washington, D.C., The Traffic Service Corporation, 1965. Covers a great many areas in the purchase and use of freight transportation services.

(3) Crowther, J.F., "Rationale for Quantity Discounts," Boston, Mass., *Harvard Business Review*, March-April, 1964, pages 121-127.

(4) George, T.C., "Tariff No. 23: Publishing Hazardous Materials Regulations of the Department of Transportation, Including Specifications for Shipping Containers," New York, N.Y., Bureau of Explosives, Association of American Railroads, August 3, 1969. Complete regulations for shipment and packaging of hazardous materials.

(5) Higgins, C.C., "Make or Buy Re-examined," Boston, Mass., *Harvard Business Review*, March-April, 1955, pages 109-119.

(6) Lewis, H.T., "Evaluation for Forward Buying," Boston, Mass., *Harvard Business Review*, March-April, 1951, pages 37-44.

(7) Maynard, H.B., Editor-in-Chief, Grunwald, E.A., Farmer, S.C., and Johnson, F.L., *Handbook of Business Administration*, Section 6, Chapters 3, 4, and 5, New York, N.Y., McGraw-Hill Book Co., Inc., 1967. The three chapters briefly outline the management of a purchasing department, effective purchasing, and value engineering. Cushman, F.M., Section 6, Chapter 6 covers transportation cost control.

(8) McCormick, E.M., *Digital Computer Primer*, New York, N.Y., McGraw-Hill Book Co., Inc., 1959. Although not new, the author has written a readily understood presentation on computers. He has covered elementary coding, number systems, computer logic and control, arithmetic and logic units, storage, and input and output. Well-suited to the reader who wants to know something, but not everything, about computers.

(9) Perry, J.H., Editor-in-Chief, *Chemical Business Handbook*, New York, N.Y., McGraw-Hill Book Co., Inc., 1954. Section 9 is a 72-page description of the organization, function, and operation of a traffic and transportation department.

(10) Stelzer, W.R., Jr., *Materials Management*, Englewood Cliffs, N.J., Prentice-Hall, Inc., 1970. A strong coverage of materials management from the purchasing point of view. Good chapters on production planning, purchasing policy and strategy, contract law, and value analysis.

(11) Taff, C.A., *Management of Traffic and Physical Distribution*, 4th Edn., Homewood, Ill., Richard D. Irwin, Inc., 1968. A comprehensive presentation of the traffic activity.

(12) Widing, J.W., Jr., and Diamond, C.G., "Buy by Computer," Boston, Mass., *Harvard Business Review*, March-April, 1964.

Chapter 11

Prodco Manufacturing Company* is engaged in the manufacture and distribution of industrial, fine, and laboratory chemicals, both organic and inorganic. Business volume has increased annually for many years. At the time this study began, customers could select from a catalog of several thousand different chemicals. These were offered in packages ranging from 1 gram to a tank car. The chemicals are manufactured at eight different factories located in various parts of the country. A minor part of the annual volume consists of rehandled goods.

Two types of forecasting were in use.

CREATING AN EFFECTIVE COMPUTERIZED SYSTEM

---

*A fictitious company. The situation described has been set in the chemical field but is actually a composite of several types of businesses observed, as is the approach to the solution described herein.

The first was a sales department projection of the annual dollar volume. The second was a computerized month-to-month projection of demand using exponentially smoothed invoice data, but because of the manner in which records were processed, this forecast was limited to a statement of the total weight of a chemical rather than a breakdown into the several package sizes. Inventory was managed manually by categorizing the chemicals according to average monthly dollar volume. Reorder points, replenishment quantities, and safety stocks had been set for each of the categories on the basis of number of months of supply to fill the average demand. This procedure was modestly sophisticated and had worked reasonably well over the years. Inventory records of the perpetual type were manually maintained. Adjustment of products between inventory categories as sales levels changed, and the subsequent adjustment of reorder points, safety stocks, and replenishment quantities, were not always kept up-to-date.

Major field inventories were maintained in about 15 market areas, together with minor stocks at other locations. These stocks were held both in owned and public warehouses. Stock control rested with field sales management.

Factory production and packaging planning reacted to replenishment orders issued daily by stock control as reorder points were reached. The new replenishment orders were fitted into the work schedules at the first available open date, or were expedited if demand had pulled stocks down into the safety stock level.

Inventories tended to climb persistently and were then forced back down by management edict. At times of cutback, replenishments were delayed or quantities were cut back, or both. Fast- and slow-moving items were treated alike. As might be anticipated, increased demand sometimes coincided with the inventory cutbacks, with predictable effect on customer service.

A System Study

Following recovery from one of these episodes, it was suggested that existing practices and procedures for managing the business left much to be desired. There had to be a better way. In order to find this better procedure, a three-man team was assigned to explore the system. They were responsible for determining the nature and scope of system problems as seen from various points of view within the organization. It was seen that recognized problems would also be the symptoms of the underlying weaknesses in the current management practices.

As a first step, the team visited the factories and interviewed all persons who might be in a position to be aware of system problems. Interviews were carried down to levels where the study team was finding no new thoughts, or were reaching people who were insufficiently exposed to the overall scope of the operations to have any idea that anything was wrong. The same procedure was followed at the central offices where the manufacturing, purchasing, sales, and accounting departments were covered. Visits were then made to a number of the sales offices and warehouses. By this time, the team was running into heavy redundancy on problems, but this reinforced earlier findings and placed emphasis on critical areas. Points not visited were asked by mail to comment from their vantage point. There was heavy response, but little new information. Three months elapsed in the data gathering stage.

Analysis of Data

One member of the team was assigned to take the mass of responses and gathered information and analyze it, and then define the scope of the problem to be faced together with an action plan. Among the problems cited were:

- The total demand forecast; i.e., demand for the total weight of a chemical was inadequate to the needs of the manufacturing group. They needed to know the forecasted unit demand so they could turn out the required quantities of SKU's. The dollar forecast was useless to both manufacturing and distribution.

- Inventory replenishment actions at the factories did not always reflect actions being taken in the several sales offices, or did not reflect field needs sufficiently far in advance.

- There was no means of forecasting demand for more than one month ahead, and this forecast was usually late in reaching the factories. Thus there was no lead time within which planners could work.

- With a forecast that was only a month ahead at best, there was no means of accurately forecasting workloads or men and equipment. A forecast to infinity was required to provide a basis for a master plan from which labor requirements, equipment loadings, raw material requirements, etc. could be established months ahead on a reasonably firm basis for the near future and on a tentative basis for the longer periods.

- Inventories at most field warehouses were out of balance with market demands, largely because review of order points and order quantities was done manually from records which were insufficiently detailed for the purpose. A thorough review was very time consuming. As a result, sales personnel neglected to make the reviews or limited action to those items they knew showed frequent stock-outs in the recent past. In many cases the stock-outs were due to transient problems at the factories, but adjustments were not reversed when the factory problem was corrected.

- There was no ready means of identifying where alternate stocks of goods were located which might be used to meet a demand at a point where stocks were depleted. There was a further lack of central control to permit systematic identification of dormant and excess stocks at the various locations. Transfer of these items to other locations where they might be sold or other corrective measures taken seldom occurred.

- Lead times, difficult to establish in any event, were unrealistically long because of the "play safe" syndrome. This, of course, resulted in excessive safety stock protection in raw materials and finished product.

- A general complaint: lack of enough specific information about the activities within the system to permit managers at various levels to make enlightened decisions for effective control. Particularly desired was a means of determining where pinch points were developing.

Findings

As the analysis proceeded, it became apparent that a computerized information system was required to serve as a base for a manufacturing and distribution action program. There was just too much detailed data in the system to be handled quickly by hand. It was also seen that an SKU demand forecast was a must in any new system developed. In turn, the forecast had to be married to an inventory system. Once these two were available, the door would be open to a series of data manipulations which would yield the various detail and action reports needed in an improved system. To accomplish the SKU demand forecast, it would be necessary to abandon the overly simple product coding system which was in use because it could not be computerized. A digital coding system was required which would uniquely define product group, product, SKU, and other germane information. The available sales history would have to be converted from the simplistic format to digital coding. Several years' billing history was available on magnetic tape. It was known that billing always trailed demand, sometimes severely; it was the only data available and under the circumstances would have to serve as demand history. All inventory records would have to be converted to the new coding structure. Thus when SKU forecasts were matched to SKU stock records, probable run-out dates could be established.

If the business had been consumer oriented, the effect of promotional efforts would have been buried in the data. However, the tapes had a wealth of information on sales to various industries, demand by state and county, and other data, all of which proved useful in certain analyses made.

Rough Outline of System

With this data, and suitable files, labor requirements in the various costs centers could be projected on a "range" basis for months ahead. This would be the tool for planning factory manpower and factory equipment loadings. There would then be ample time for making change in manpower and examining various alternates. On the same basis, projections of raw material requirements, container needs, analytical workloads, and various miscellaneous related labor loads could all be projected.

The conclusion was reached that a system such as this would be hampered if it were to operate on the basis of billing data and its inherent time lag. A means to capture demand when it occurred was also required.

These and other closely related factors were reviewed with the systems and data-processing department. S&DP prepared estimates of the time required to make detailed analyses of the existing system, work out the logic charts for the new system, and write and de-bug the necessary computer programs. It was seen that a team varying from three to 12 persons at different times would require about four years to complete the job, including field training and implementation. The price tag read "up to $400,000."

Benefits

With this kind of expenditure, it was also necessary to look at the potential gains other than at the intangible "better way." What would it cost to operate such a system once it was placed in operation? Through parallel studies, it was found that major reductions in inventory at better balance could be achieved through use of the computer. Further, it was seen that once data was entered in the computerized system with all of its files, all subsequent data handling would be done electronically with a savings in clerical effort throughout the system. Electronic auditing of input data would improve the overall accuracy of the record keeping. There would be reductions in required warehouse space and more economical movement of goods throughout the system. By amortizing the cost of building the new system over a period of years and using the yearly amortization charge, together with the routine cost of operating the new system, it was found that savings greatly exceeded costs and the project was financially attractive.

The foregoing was summarized into presentation format, and reviewed and tailored by the original three-man team to a final form. The report was submitted and a short while later a verbal presentation was made to the top management group, where the decision to proceed was made.

First Steps

A member of the study team was appointed project leader. As representative of the interested line and staff groups, he provided liaison with the S&DP section and gave the required guidance and direction to that group. The first step was to flow-chart all of the existing paper-work procedures in the existing system and identify the decision and other action points. It took two men six months to complete this work. As a measure of the complications of the business, the flow charts and supporting documentation filled a file drawer. While this work was going on, a start was made in educating the systems analysts, who were to design the details of the new system based on the scope of the problems to be solved. A beginning was made in analyzing the information on the billing tapes.

This latter task was known to be a rough source for information, and it was expected that there would be difficulties in converting the magnetic tape data into the new coding formats. Also, it was not appreciated how many inconsistencies can be handled readily in a manual system, and that there can be no inconsistencies with a computer. As an example, a quarter-pound may be written ¼ #, ¼ lb., or 4 oz. There were many other anomalies which were eventually resolved by creating a dictionary of terms for the computer. About five years of billing data were converted into a reasonable replica of the demand for the time span. The requirements for an initial forecast were finally in hand.

Model Building

With operations research personnel, work got underway in developing the models for establishing the type of demand the various SKU's were responding to. It was found in this particular system that demands were horizontal, trend, seasonal, and trend-seasonal, and these, in turn, were either "well-behaved" or "lumpy" in character. A model was constructed for making an initial forecast, and another was utilized for making monthly updates of the demand projections. Parameters were established for automatically signalling item forecasts that were out of control for manual review and adjustment. Provision was also made for automatically reinitializing an item forecast if the inventory manager failed to make any corrections for several months. Further provision was made for manual overrides of the computer forecasts to reflect changes in levels of activity reported from marketing. Changes, such as gain or loss of customers, were used to modify forecasts, and thus were promptly reflected in desired inventory levels.

Inventory analyses were provided which yielded information about stocks:

(a) The dollar value of the midpoint inventory called for by the system. This value is reached by summing the safety stocks plus one-half of the order quantity for all of the SKU's.

(b) Dollar value of the actual inventory.

(c) A count of the number of items more than 10% above OP + OQ, together with the value of the excess stock and the actual value of the items in this group.

(d) A count of the items between (c) and the safety stock, together with midpoint and actual values.

(e) A count of the items in the safety stock range, together with midpoint and actual values.

(f) A count of the items with no stock, together with midpoint value.

(g) A count of the number of open replenishment orders for each of (c), (d), (e), and (f).

(h) A listing of every SKU showing a change in actual inventory value of plus or minus $3,000 from the previous month to the current month.

Inventory models were developed which would provide the selected degree of product availability at the factories. In effect, the chosen policy provided the greatest degree of availability for the high-volume products and accepted the greatest risk of stock-outs with the very slow-moving items. Within this model, two types of replenishment rules were established: (1) the economic order quantity rule for the well-behaved products; (2) a cost penalty rule for poorly behaved or "lumpy" products. There were also a number of exception type rules; e.g., one which established a method of allocating a limited supply of bulk material between competing SKU's to provide, under the circumstances, the best use of limited bulk and optimum response to customer demand.

Capture of Demand

In the meantime, a method was devised for capturing the demand at the time it occurred. This involved setting up a stock record in an on-line computer and input terminals located in the sales offices. Historically, inventories and their replenishment had been the responsibility of the sales office in whose territory the stocks were located. All record keeping was done manually. Factory stocks were the responsibility of the factories. With the new system, demands against stocks anywhere in the system were entered against the appropriate stock record with a response indicating availability. This entry captured the demand at the same time it was "committing" the goods for the specific order. Later another entry would relieve the committed inventory when the goods were actually shipped. Other features of the program would provide the means for making other normal inventory entries, as well as generating stock status reports, dormant and excess stock reports, and automatic stock replenishment documentation.

Initial Implementation

At this point, the system was sufficiently developed; it had the capacity to capture a great deal of data and manipulate it to determine stocking levels, replenishment quantities, safety stocks, demand trends, etc. It took about 20 months from the project's start to reach this point of development. In anticipation of arriving at this point, a team spent four months in the field visiting every sales office and manufacturing location, training personnel in the theory and practice of the new system. Thus, when the programming was completed, implementation was started at the main factory and at nearby sales offices. At three- to four-week intervals, the remaining sales territories were to be added to the system. That was the plan, but Murphy's law works to the second power with computer systems, so that implementation took longer than the first plan. Nevertheless, this work was completed in four and one-half months. This was followed by a six-month effort of revisiting the offices and factories to re-enforce the training, trouble-shooting and improving and tightening the computer programs. When this work was done, the project was 30 months old.

A complete annual inventory had long been a yearly activity. With the next one due in about three months, it was decided to forego a physical check prior to implementation, although some locations did make a verification for their own peace of mind. Initial order points and order quantities were accepted as stated by the field, but the overall plan called for an automated adjustment of these values as soon as a six-month demand was captured in the computer.

Excess stocks had been identified and located; order points and order quantities were refined to reflect actual demand against the system. Inventory levels began to drop as anticipated. An unexpected benefit was the generation of ABC analyses for every stocking point. These led the way to a more realistic structuring of the product line, and to an evaluation of the performance and need for the warehouses. A number of warehouses were closed as a result and stock levels were drastically reduced in all the others.

Final Phases

While all the implementation fieldwork was going on, the systems and programming work continued. Weekly and monthly review procedures were completed and the master files were expanded to final size and checked out. From the inventory records within the new system and the new forecasts, explosion techniques generated the most probable loads on manufacturing and packaging cost centers, the probable demands against warehouses, and through secondary explosions the probable manpower requirements in manufacturing, packaging, order picking and packing, shipping, analytical labs, etc. Implementation of these programs moved along smoothly and were soon routine. Programs to prepare a production plan then were completed, as were programs to spell out monthly requirements for raw materials, packaging components, and various other items used in the business. Purchasing took this information and used it to further refine the application of blanket orders. This, in turn, led to computer-generated releases against these orders. At this point, 44 months had elapsed, and the assignment as originally defined was complete.

The assignment was complete, but in one sense this type of project is never consummated since it is an interface with a dynamic activity. Competition alone would force change from the outside, but more desirably change comes from the inside as a result of the growing awareness of the computer as a tool.

Problems

What were the main problems? The obvious ones were: (1) developing the correct logic for the system; (2) writing the programs to generate the desired information; (3) the start-up problems in going so deeply onto a computer. Beyond these, is the difficulty of getting the attention and real participation of the various line and staff persons who will be affected by the changes generated by a new, highly sophisticated system. During first contacts, interest is stirred. However, the question is soon asked, "How soon will all this come about?" When the truthful reply has to be "Two or three years," there is an unspoken reaction of "Dreamer," "Pie-in-the-sky," or "Why should I worry? I'll be promoted from this job before then." So the answers given to questions are honest enough, but later it is found that you didn't ask the right questions, or enough questions, or that replies were not really comprehensive. This leads to program errors and the "sunk" feeling that you should have thought to ask a few more questions, or "Why didn't I think of that?"

Outright hostility was rare. Due to the long period of gestation of a major project, those outside the project develop the previously indicated reactions or get the feeling the team will not bring the project to fruition. "They'll never get it to fly" might sum up the feeling of those not on the team. This leads to a covert lessening of cooperation. This is annoying more than anything else.

The toughest problem is to get to a majority of people and spend enough time with them to develop true understanding and feeling for the dozens of new procedures which are coming. With the mobility that exists in a large organization, you almost never get through to enough people to cover the staff changes that are always occurring. Every effort must be made to advance training and indoctrination by every means possible. Forwarding of detailed written procedures, follow-up explanations in person, group discussions of the new procedures, repeat sessions, initialization with training demonstrators over a period of weeks, are all required. This must then be followed by a period of time on their own for staff members to uncover the areas where understanding is lacking. After that, the follow-up begins in earnest; refresher training is given. It is also necessary at this time to reach out to inform persons in areas beyond the immediate day-to-day operations, yet who are to some degree affected by them.

As with the old-time country preacher: You tell them what you are going to tell them, you tell them, then you tell them what you told them. It is very good advice, but it falls short — because you tell them yet again, and again, and again; hopefully, at longer and longer intervals as the new routines are learned and become habitual.

This problem of getting people to understand and habitually follow the new routine is really the biggest and most time-consuming one of all. Problems with logic, programs, and computers are simple in comparison.

INDEX